Studying
the Novel

Jeremy Hawthorn

Sixth edition

BLOOMSBURY ACADEMIC

First published in Great Britain by Edward Arnold in 1985
Second edition published in 1992
Third edition published in 1997
Fourth edition published in 2001
Fifth edition published in 2005
Sixth edition published in 2010 by:

Bloomsbury Academic

An imprint of Bloomsbury Publishing Plc
50 Bedford Square, London WC1B 3DP, UK
and
175 Fifth Avenue, New York, NY 10010, USA

CIP records for this book are available from the British Library and the Library of
Congress

ISBN: 978-0-34098-513-7
e-ISBN: 978-1-84966-046-4

This book is produced using paper that is made from wood grown in managed,
sustainable forests. It is natural, renewable and recyclable. The logging and
manufacturing processes conform to the environmental regulations of the country
of origin.

Printed and bound in Great Britain

www.bloomsburyacademic.com

£14.99

Studying the Novel

Also in the *Studying* series

Contents

Introduction to the sixth edition

It is now a quarter of a century since the first edition of this book appeared, and successive editions have expanded the treatments of some topics while introducing a number of quite new ones. The first edition included two pages discussing the differences between the novel, the novella, and the short story. These two pages have grown into a separate chapter over the course of time, which is how it is that a book whose title mentions the novel also includes an extended discussion of shorter fiction. It has seemed to both author and publisher unwise to alter the title of a known textbook; although this might have the effect of better matching title to present content, it might confuse those familiar with earlier editions. Moreover, as the chapter has been found useful by readers, omitting it in order to render the title more accurate does bring the saying about the baby and the bathwater to mind. On this matter I crave the reader's indulgence.

This sixth edition includes a more detailed and focussed discussion of narratology, covering both structuralist and rhetorical approaches. This will be found in Chapter 9. Chapter 3, on shorter fiction, has been (again) expanded to include an extended discussion of the 'anecdotal' and the 'epiphanic' short story and of the novella. Chapter 4 now includes an extended discussion of an exemplary postmodernist novel – Jeanette Winterson's *Lighthousekeeping*. This same chapter now concludes with a new section on the use of works of fiction to explore extreme historical events such as the Nazi Holocaust.

On page 219 of this edition readers will find a new feature – a Timeline of the Novel that records significant births, deaths, and publications. It does not of course aim at any sort of comprehensiveness, but is there to enable readers to build up a general sense of 'what was happening' and 'who was active' from year to year.

In the academic year of 2005–2006 I had the privilege of working as a member of the 'Narrative Theory and Analysis' team led by Professor Jakob Lothe at the Centre for Advanced Studies in Oslo. My discussions with team members during this year were both inspiring and productive, and I would like to thank Professor Lothe, my fellow team members, the staff at the Centre, and the Centre's leader Professor Willy Østreng, for a most enjoyable and valuable year. This sixth edition includes a number of late-ripening fruits from debates and discussions that took place at this time.

I am grateful to other friends and colleagues with whom I have been able to discuss ideas and issues while I have been writing this new edition – especially Paul Goring, Domhnall Mitchell and Csizmadia Balázs. They are not responsible for any errors or inadequacies in the final result.

Jeremy Hawthorn
Trondheim, Norway, January 2010

Chapter 2
Fiction and the novel

Preview

This chapter deals with:

- ↬ some preliminary definitions: novel, fiction, narrative
- ↬ the universality of fiction and the distinctiveness of literary fiction
- ↬ imaginary characters and real life
- ↬ prose and narrative
- ↬ showing and telling
- ↬ characters, action, plot
- ↬ novel, short story, novella: some preliminary comments

According to the *Oxford English Dictionary*, a novel is 'a fictitious prose narrative or tale of considerable length (now usually one long enough to fill one or more volumes) in which characters and actions representative of the real life of past or present times are portrayed in a plot of more or less complexity'. This may sound a bit like stating the obvious, but there are some important points contained in this very concise definition. Let us consider some of its component parts.

The universality and the distinctiveness of fiction

Gregory Currie has commented that fiction 'is one of those concepts like goodness, color, number, and cause that we have little difficulty in applying

1

but great difficulty in explaining' (Currie, 1990, 1). 'Telling stories' is an activity that is so central to our culture that we pay it little analytical attention. From a very early age we learn to distinguish not just between true and untrue reports, but also between different sorts of untrue reports – 'lies' and 'stories' for example. Fiction is much wider than the novel or, indeed, than prose fiction: jokes, imitations and parodies, songs and narrative poems can all be described as fictions – and wider, non-literary usages include such things as legal fictions and (perhaps) folk tales and urban myths (fictions do not have to take the form of a story or a narrative). Fiction has its historical and cultural dimensions; if fiction seems to be universally present in the lives of all human beings, it nevertheless assumes different forms in different ages and different societies. Not all fictions are novels, then, but the specific tradition or set of traditions which we refer to as 'the novel' is made possible by a far more widespread and fundamental reliance upon fiction in human society.

We can start with a number of seeming paradoxes: fictions are not true, but they are not lies; they typically describe that which is not real (in the sense that it has not happened or does not exist) but which is nonetheless not totally unreal; they can include references to existing people and events without jeopardizing their fictional status; they are designed to get readers or listeners to respond 'as if', but not (normally) to deceive them; even though readers are aware that fictions describe people who do not exist or events which have not happened, they nonetheless can produce real emotions, important reflections and even altered behaviour in the real world.

In their book *Truth, Fiction, and Literature: A Philosophical Perspective*, Peter Lamarque and Stein Haugom Olsen distinguish between fictional content and fictional mode, illustrating the difference by reference to Konrad Kujau's forgery which was presented to the world as Hitler's (genuine) diaries. As they remark, while it would be reasonable to refer to the content of this forgery as fictional, 'we should surely hesitate to call the finished product a "work of fiction" given the mode of its presentation' (17). These distinctions allow them to focus not on the structural or semantic properties of sentences 'but on the conditions under which they are uttered, the attitudes they invoke, and the role that they play in social interactions' (32). Such an approach leads to an emphasis on fictional storytelling as a convention with institutional resources or, to put it another way, as a more or less universally understood custom or family of customs within a culture.

If fiction is in one sense universal, those fictions that we call novels and short stories are arguably possessed of certain unique features. In her book *The Distinction of Fiction* (1999), Dorrit Cohn approaches the definition of fiction from a narratological perspective, and makes an impressively energetic case for the distinctiveness of *literary* fiction. Cohn suggests that literary fictions can be distinguished from other non-fictional narratives in three ways. First, the distinction between *story* and *plot* (in her terminology story and discourse) does not have the same validity for 'texts that refer to events that have occurred prior to their narrative embodiment'. You will find this point easier to understand after having read the discussion of story and plot on p. 140. Second, only in fictional narratives can narrators enter the consciousness of persons apart from themselves. (This argument is not necessarily refuted by pointing out that certain postmodernist historians also enter the consciousnesses of the historical figures about which they write, as it can be – and has been – claimed that so soon as they do this they stop writing history and start writing fiction.) Third, in non-fictional narratives the distinction between author and narrator does not make the same sort of sense as it does when applied to fictional texts (1999, 130). I take up some of the issues raised by fictional accounts of actual events in Chapter 4 in a discussion of stories written by survivors of the Nazi Holocaust (see p. 85).

In the 1950s the London *Evening Standard* ran a regular feature entitled 'Did it Happen?' The newspaper would publish an account of a striking experience, then ask readers to decide whether the experience really did happen, with the truth being revealed the following day. The authors ranged from Stevie Smith and Angus Wilson to Gerard Hoffnung and Benny Hill, and their contributions were gathered together and published as a book in 1956 (*Did It Happen?: Stories*). Reading through the contributions it is interesting to see what a writer has to do to leave the reader in doubt as to whether he or she is reading fact or fiction. All of the accounts are in the first person, and in no case does the narrator enter the consciousness of another person. No account suggests a distinction between author and narrator. Once we know whether the account is fact or fiction we can indeed recognize as Cohn suggests that the distinction between author and narrator, and that between story and plot, make a different sort of sense for the two types of account. But these are retrospective judgements. It is the entering of the consciousness of a person other than the narrator that seems to suggest most strongly that a narrative is fictional, and the authors of the 'fictional' accounts seem instinctively to have recognized this and to have avoided doing so.

Fiction, play, fantasy

Anyone who has watched a child grow and mature will know that he or she attempts to understand and master the world and his or her relation to it through modelled performances that we call play. However much we may like to think of play as sharply distinguished from the real, workaday world, relegated to 'free time' or 'relaxation', there seems little doubt that the rules of games can function as a model of the social and material restraints which we meet with in the world, and that play can help us to internalize these aspects of the world and of our operating within it. A number of recent theorists have developed this analogy in discussing the role that fiction plays in ordinary people's lives. In her book *Why we Read Fiction: Theory of Mind and the Novel* (2006), Lisa Zunshine writes:

> The cognitive rewards of reading fiction might thus be aligned with the cognitive rewards of pretend play through a shared capacity to stimulate and develop the imagination. It may mean that our enjoyment of fiction is predicated – at least in part – upon our *awareness* of our 'trying on' mental states *potentially available* to us but at a given moment *differing* from our own. (Zunshine, 2006, 17)

In his book *The Rhetoric of Fictionality: Narrative Theory and the Idea of Fiction*, Richard Walsh introduces another helpful analogy – that between fiction and 'exercise'. As he notes: 'When you go for a jog, you may not be trying to get anywhere in particular, but you are certainly not pretending to run' (Walsh, 2007, 45). The comment is clearly aimed at those who believe that when, for example, Charles Dickens wrote *David Copperfield* as a first-person narrative, he was pretending to be David Copperfield, and he wanted the reader to pretend that his novel really was written by the character. Both Zunshine and Walsh agree that the reader of fiction does not have to abandon a sense of who he or she is, or of who the real-life author is. Indeed they suggest that retaining such a sense is crucial to the reading of fiction.

Fictional stories present us with models of (especially) the social world with which we can empathize, but which we can observe because we are not constrained to act. According to Lamarque and Olsen (1994), readers 'often fantasize with fictive content, "filling in" as the whim takes them, and no doubt some genres of fantasy actively encourage this kind of whimsical response'. This is rather stern, and it becomes more so as the two authors then insist upon the need to distinguish between authorized and non-authorized responses – with 'the content itself and its presentation' as the source of this authority (89).

I call this a rather stern pronouncement in spite of the fact that as a university teacher I spend a lot of time telling my students that they need to be able to justify their responses and interpretations by reference to textual and other non-whimsical evidence. I do this because although the academic discussion of literature has to insist upon such standards in order to establish ground rules for discussion and debate, I do not think that readers (as against students or critics) of novels are – or ever have been – obliged to remain within the boundaries of the academically authorized. Indeed, were it possible to render 'whimsical responses' impossible, then I suspect that novel reading would be a lot less popular than it is today. This is not to argue that works of fiction impose no constraints on what we imagine while we are reading them. Indeed, it is precisely because our responses, our imaginings, have to confront and negotiate with what cannot be changed in a novel that the reading of fiction is able to model what it is like to live in the social and material world, and I expand upon this point in comments on computer games in Chapter 5.

Remember, however, that 'response' is not the same as 'interpretation'; my response may be different from yours, but we can try to reach agreement about our interpretation of a given work. Now this book is called *Studying the Novel*, not *Responding to the Novel*, and my emphasis throughout it is on those institutionally approved ways of categorizing, analysing and interpreting novels and short stories. I am concerned, in other words, with the ways in which those private, individual and utterly varied reading responses people have can be made public and discussed with others. If our talk to others about novels is to be more than a semi-comprehensible outpouring of our highly idiosyncratic reading experiences, then we have to anchor it to things that we can all share: textual details, scholarly procedures and so on. We should, however, be very careful to avoid the assumption that such public and 'objective' information represents all that happens when we read a novel.

Imaginary characters and real life

The novel depicts imaginary characters and situations. A novel may include reference to real-world places, people and events, but it cannot contain *only* such references and remain a novel. Even though its characters and actions are imaginary they are in some sense 'representative of real life', as the dictionary definition has it; although fictional they bear an important resemblance to what exists outside its pages. What exactly this resemblance is has been a matter of much discussion and dispute among literary critics, and it is arguable that it varies in kind from novel to novel. Even so, this resemblance to *real* life is one of the features that distinguishes the novel from other forms such as the epic and the romance (see the Glossary and also the discussion on p. 14), however much we recognize that 'real life' is a problematic concept. Later on in Chapter 4 we will see that the term 'realism' is one that, although arguably indispensable to discussion of the novel, requires careful definition and use.

It is common knowledge that people can 'lose themselves' in a novel. Even if the novel generally presents us with a recognizable, 'non-fantastic' world, we exercise our fantasy and our imagination to live within this world for short periods of time. But although readers can and do lose themselves while reading a novel, this does not mean that they are unable to mull over and learn from their reading experiences once they return to their everyday reality after finishing a novel.

The world of the novel is so familiar to us that we can on occasions recognize its distinctive qualities only by contrasting it to other genres. The Russian critic Mikhail Bakhtin points out, for example, that '[t]he world of the epic is the national heroic past', it is based upon a 'national tradition (not personal experience and the free thought that grows out of it)' and 'an absolute epic distance separates the epic world from contemporary reality'. The novel, 'by contrast, is determined by experience, knowledge and practice (the future)' (Bakhtin, 1981, 13, 15). The novel presents us with stories, experiences that are new; whereas those who experienced the epic knew what was to occur, when we pick up a novel we hope that our curiosity will be aroused by our wanting to know 'what happens'. As I will argue in Chapter 2, this difference has a lot to do with the different sorts of society from which these two genres emerge.

Prose

The novel is in prose rather than verse, although the language of novels may often strike us as very 'poetic' on occasions. It would nonetheless be a serious mistake to assume that the language of a novel is identical to that of ordinary speech or of most non-literary writing. Even so, the fact that the novel is in prose helps to establish that sense of 'real life' – of recognizable, everyday, 'prosaic' existence – that is the preserve of the genre. Generalization is dangerous, but prose has the potentiality of being a more transparent medium than, for example, verse. Reading a novel, our attention is not naturally drawn to considering the language as language. The tendency is more for us to 'look through' the language of the novel at what it describes and evokes than to 'look at' it – although novelists can write prose that arrests our attention as language, and many novelists are known for the manner in which they draw the reader's attention to their use of language. In the course of studying novels we must learn to pay more overt attention to their language than does the average casual reader.

Narrative

Novels and shorter works of literary fiction are *narratives*: in other words they all in some sense present readers with a 'telling' rather than an 'enacting', and this distinguishes them in an important sense from the drama. One useful way to define narrative involves reference to what Seymour Chatman has called 'double chronology' (1990, 114): the things that happen in a novel happen in a particular order, and the telling of what happens also takes place in a particular order. Importantly, these two 'orders' or chronologies are not necessarily the same, and the interaction between them constitutes a defining characteristic of the novel and of shorter fiction. Double chronology entails that built into the very fact of narrative is an act of looking back, of *re*counting. As the first-person narrator of Javier Marías's novel *Tomorrow in the Battle Think on Me* remarks: 'in fact, the person telling the story always tells it later on, which allows him to add things if he wants, to distance himself: "I have turned away my former self, I am not the thing I was nor the person I was, I neither know nor recognize myself. I did not seek it, I did not want it" (Marías, 1997, 308).

You will find more about narrative's double chronology in the discussion of story and plot on p. 140. Double chronology is a necessary but not a sufficient condition of a narrative, as it may apply also to plays and films. (*Citizen Kane* opens with the depiction of events which take place after the events that are recounted in the bulk of the film have taken place: the order-in-which-things-take-place is not the same as the order-in-which-we-witness-what-takes-place.) What is, I would argue, central to narration is the element of telling: events in a piece of prose fiction come to us mediated through a retailing and organizing consciousness that puts them into words.

Here I should note that not all narrative theorists would agree with my exclusion of film and drama from the category of narrative. In the previous paragraph, for example, I quote from Seymour Chatman, and the book from which his comment is drawn is entitled *Story and Discourse: Narrative Structure in Fiction and Film*. Those who argue that a film is as much a narrative as a novel generally base their view on the fact that the events and actions depicted in a film are (at least metaphorically) 'told' to us through the organizing work of a director. It is certainly the case that many of the analytical terms and concepts developed in the study of narratives in my narrow sense can also be used in the analysis of film and drama. For the student, the important thing to remember is that 'narrative' can be defined in both a narrow and in a more inclusive manner.

Moreover, although it is easy to make a distinction between prose fiction and drama or film, we often feel that novels contain very dramatic scenes, scenes that grip us with their immediacy. Reading such scenes, we may forget that what we learn of character and event is not experienced directly through a presentation or an enactment (as in the theatre or the cinema) but mediated through a particular telling, a narrative source. Take the opening of Henry James's short story 'The Lesson of the Master' (1888):

> He had been told the ladies were at church, but this was corrected
> by what he saw from the top of the steps – they descended from a
> great height in two arms, with a circular sweep of the most charming
> effect – at the threshold of the door which, from the long bright gallery,
> overlooked the immense lawn.

If our first impression is that we are witnessing a scene directly, a second glance will confirm that we are actually being *told about* the scene, which is presented as one character experiences it. The telling is such that we can visualize what is described – that is often the mark of an accomplished narrative – but we see what is first selected and then pointed out to us by a narrator or a narrative voice or source. Of course, this selection and presentation are fictional: the author is actually *creating* rather than selecting what we see. Nevertheless, as we read we are given the sense that the scene's potentially infinite complexity is reduced, ordered and explained to us through the organizing and filtering consciousnesses of a character and a narrator. Could any filmed version of the above scene lead us to think of the ladies as forming 'two arms'? Would we find the effect of the 'circular sweep' 'most charming' unless a character used these words? Would we know that we were experiencing the scene as a given character was seeing it? I will say more about the difference between film and prose narrative in Chapter 8.

An additional word of caution is needed at this point. You should be aware that there is a further way in which the term 'narrative' can be used both with a narrow and specific meaning and also with a rather wider one. This sense has nothing to do with such questions as whether films are narratives, but with the issues raised by calling a long novel a narrative when it contains long passages that are not strictly speaking narratives but may be lyric interludes or philosophical discussions. From a more restrictive perspective only parts of such a long novel would, then, qualify as examples of narrative: those involving the telling of events, the recounting of things that happen. (Clearly events can just as well be mental as physical: a sudden dawning of insight is as much an event as is the outbreak of the First World War.)

The words 'tell' and 'recount' are both related to the action of counting, or enumerating (think of a bank teller, who counts money). As 'tell' is etymologically related to 'tale' we can say that behind the act of narrative itself lies the idea of communicating things that can be counted. (Compare the French *conte*, for which a brief definition is provided in the Glossary.) If we limit ourselves to a restrictive definition of narrative, therefore, we must remember that neither *description* (of a beautiful scene) nor *argument* (about, say, the existence of God) are examples of narrative in this strict sense; they do not involve the telling or enumerating of discrete events or countable entities. However, the term 'narrative' is also conventionally used in a less restrictive sense to include everything that comes within the purview of a particular telling or recounting. From this perspective a novel is a narrative even though it contains passages of description and argument. If you think about it, much the same is true of our use of the word 'fiction'. After all, many statements in novels are literally true, yet we do not restrict use of the word 'fiction' to only those parts of novels that are untrue.

In Chapter 9 I will say more about *narratology* – a body of theory that has emerged in the past four decades out of attempts to generalize about different types of narrative, and to develop concepts and methods that can be used to classify and analyse narratives.

Characters, action, plot

The novel has *characters*, *action(s)* and a *plot*: it presents the reader with individuals who do things in a defining context or 'secondary world' (see p. 19) ruled over by some sort of connective logic: chronology, cause and effect, or whatever. In most novels we also find a connection between these three elements such that they form some sort of unity. A poem does not have to contain characters or a plot – or, indeed, any action – but it is only very rare novels which dispense with one of these elements, and in such unusual cases it is often a matter of dispute as to whether the net result is recognizable as a novel. Some recent narrative theorists have preferred to talk of 'actors' rather than characters, pointing out that a work of science fiction might be based on roles filled by non-human participants. I discuss the relationship between literary characterizations and the emergence of ideas of human individuality on p. 27.

We have of course to give the term 'action' a relatively broad meaning in the present context. Much recent fiction involves significant concentration upon what has been termed 'inner action': events taking place in a character's consciousness rather than in the social and physical worlds outside. It is nevertheless revealing that there are few novels that consist only, or mainly, of inner action. It is as if our view of the novel requires that it contain a significant amount of action more traditionally defined.

In Chapter 6, I will be talking about the important distinction between 'story' and 'plot' (see p. 140); at this stage I will limit myself to stating that the concept of plot involves some sense that the actions depicted in a telling represent a whole rather than merely a succession of unconnected events. Here again care is needed, for, as my comments on the picaresque novel in the Glossary make clear, certain novels are characterized by a very *episodic* structure. Jerome J. McGann makes the interesting comment that '[Charles Dickens's] early work is far more episodic than the later, so much so that many would be reluctant to call *Pickwick Papers* [1836–7] a novel at all' (McGann, 1991, 82). It seems that nowadays readers tend to like their novels to have plots that unfold to reveal some principle of unity rather than episodes that merely succeed one another in an order that is without significance.

Ian Watt has argued that the novel is distinguished by the fact that unlike the works of the great English and Classical poets and dramatists, its plots are generally not taken from traditional sources (Watt, 1963, 14). If we compare the modern novel with the prose fictions of antiquity, or the medieval romance, Watt's point is certainly justifiable. On the other hand, even the modern novel has recourse to certain recurrent plots and storylines (see the more extended discussion of plot on p. 140). As a result, many modern novels manifest an important and productive *tension* between their fidelity to the random and unpredictable nature of everyday life, and their patterning according to the demands of certain predetermined but widely different structures, from 'tragedy' to 'repetition' or 'the journey'. Novels can be written within traditions that are highly *formulaic* – that is, written to conform with a particular, pre-existing pattern. The popular romance of today with its shy blonde heroine who is finally appreciated by the good-looking hero after he has seen through the strikingly attractive but treacherous dark anti-heroine is but one in a long line of formulaic sub-genres that can be traced back to the folk tales of oral cultures.

Novel, short story, novella

Finally, the novel is of a certain length. A poem can be anything from a couplet to a thousand pages or more, but we feel unhappy about bestowing the term 'novel' on a tale of some forty or fifty pages. Of course it is not just a question of length: we feel that a novel should involve an investigation of an issue of human significance in such a manner as allows for complexity of treatment, and by common consent a certain length is necessary to allow for such complexity. In practice, therefore, we now usually refer to a prose narrative of some twenty or thirty pages or fewer as a short story, while a work that seems to hover on the awkward boundary between 'short story' and 'novel', having a length of between forty or fifty and a 100 pages, is conventionally described as a novella (plural: novelle or novellas). I say 'now', because some of these conventional categorizations are relatively recent, particularly so far as the short story and the novella are concerned, and some of the issues raised by dividing prose fiction into three main categories in this way are discussed more fully in Chapter 3.

Topics for discussion

- ↪ What elements must a novel contain to be a novel? Does the answer change as the novel changes?
- ↪ Is literary fiction different from other fictions? If so, in what ways?
- ↪ Do you read novels to escape from 'the real world', or to learn more about it? Or both?
- ↪ Can reading a novel change your life?
- ↪ Why do we classify novels and short stories as narratives?

Chapter 2

History, genre, culture

Preview

This chapter deals with:

↪ the problem of deciding when (and if) the novel was born
↪ the relationship between the novel and the romance
↪ the contribution of literacy, printing, a market economy and individualism to the novel
↪ the novel, secularism and urban experience
↪ the novel as a force for cultural centralization
↪ the novel: an imperialist and masculine genre?

When was the novel born?

In the first two editions of this book I referred to the 'running debate' between those who see prose fiction as 'a universal and ancient form with a continuous history' (Novak, 1991, 8), and those who prefer to emphasize the distinctiveness of the prose fiction which emerged in the early eighteenth century, and who speak of the novel as a new form which had its birth then. Even so, my account implied that although 'the novel' as category might be fuzzy round the edges, and might be in a state of permanent development and self-reconstruction, nevertheless this new literary genre emerged in the Europe of the late seventeenth and early eighteenth centuries and was clearly different from earlier forms such as that of the romance.

This, it has to be said, remains the consensus view. It is not without its opponents though, and recently the 'running debate' has heated up somewhat, especially following the publication of *The True Story of the Novel* (1996), a weighty study written by Margaret Anne Doody. Doody reminds her readers that the distinction between novel and romance is one that is not reflected in all languages in the way that it is in English, and she proposes that it 'has outworn its usefulness, and that at its most useful it created limitations and encouraged blind spots' (1996, xvii). For her, the novel 'as a form of literature in the West has a continuous history of about two thousand years', a fact which recent scholarship has denied or obscured (1996, 1). In order to press her case she advances a rather wider and more all-embracing definition of the novel from that which I quoted from the *OED* at the start of my first chapter; for her, a work is a novel if 'it is fictional, if it is in prose, and if it is of a certain length' (1996, 16).

A less comprehensive attack on the view that the novel emerges with Defoe, Richardson and Fielding is provided by J.A. Downie, who draws attention to the fact that 'writings calling themselves novels had been appearing in print in English for about a hundred and fifty years before the publication of *Robinson Crusoe* [in 1719]', and that while Richardson's *Pamela* did indeed lead to a sustained increase in the demand for fiction, Defoe's work did not (Downie, 2000, 311, 325).

There is no doubt that, if one defines the novel as Doody recommends, then it is quite correct to see it as a literary form with a continuous history of 2000 years, and it is certainly the case that the term 'novel' did not emerge for the first time in the eighteenth century. It is also the case that we should avoid falling into the trap of believing that the works on modern literature syllabuses were the only ones read by and exerting influence on readers and writers, and that (as I have already suggested) we need to be aware that there are continuities and lines of tradition that cut across the sharp dividing lines posited by talk of 'the birth of the novel'.

Critics other than Margaret Doody have also engaged in debate about the extent to which those 'novel' works produced by writers such as Defoe, Richardson and Fielding in the first half of the eighteenth century were or were not in direct line of descent from the chapbooks and the French fiction of the late seventeenth century, hundreds of which were translated into English and published in England at this time (Novak, 1991, 8). Moreover, even those who concur with the view that the modern novel emerges as a new literary genre in the eighteenth century concede that it still owes much to traditions and works, literary and non-literary, from earlier times. No serious student of the novel would deny, for example, that its development in the eighteenth century was profoundly influenced by works such as François Rabelais's *Pantagruel* and *Gargantua* (1532 and 1534) and Miguel de Cervantes's *Don Quixote* (1605–15) – whether or not one agrees to describe these works as novels.

My own view is that what happened to prose fiction in the course of the eighteenth century in Europe represents such a radical change that what, to sidestep debate, we can call 'the modern novel' merits and repays separate study. As Michael McKeon points out, it was the first modern 'novelists' themselves who affirmed that 'a distinct new form' had emerged: Richardson believed he had introduced a new 'species' of writing while Fielding claimed a new 'kind' or 'province' (McKeon, 1987, 410). (See too Samuel Johnson's comments on '[t]he works of fiction, with which the present generation seems more particularly delighted', on p. 16 later in this chapter.)

Ancestors and close relations

Claims concerning parentage are often controversial. One of the things that sets the novel apart from many other literary genres is its ability to incorporate the most disparate elements from human life and experience. It would be a serious mistake to assume that to trace the novel's descent we need to examine only a sequence of written forms, or of oral and written narratives. We should rather picture a family tree in which certain lines of descent involve various written forms, certain involve a succession of oral narrative forms, but others involve a wide range of very different elements. I have already suggested that fiction has an analogue in play, but other relatives are equally important: introspective self-analyses, both in diary and in unrecorded form; joke-telling; sermons; travel accounts; letters. What distinguishes the novel is, among other things, the heterogeneity of its ancestry, a heterogeneity that Mikhail Bakhtin has argued is mirrored in the variety of different 'voices' to be found in any single novel. He claims (and this is by no means uncontroversial) that, however many contradictions and conflicts are developed in a poem, the world of poetry is always illuminated by 'one unitary and indisputable discourse'. The novel, in contrast, is he argues characterized by that 'variety of individualized voices' that is 'the prerequisite for authentic novelistic prose' (Bakhtin, 1981, 286). It should be noted that the term 'voice' has more than a physical reference for Bakhtin, and includes ideological and existential elements too.

One of the impulses that often moves those who compile family trees is a desire to prove that all the discovered ancestors were respectable and legitimate. In the case of the novel, we have to be prepared to accept that many of its ancestors were neither. As J. Paul Hunter has put it:

> I join the debate here by arguing that the emerging novel must be placed in a broader context of cultural history, insisting that popular thought and materials of everyday print – journalism, didactic materials with all kinds of religious and ideological directions, and private papers and histories – need to be seen as contributors to the social and intellectual world in which the novel emerged. (Hunter, 1990, 5)

Even though it be true that fictional narratives can be found almost as far back as we have written records, those produced before the emergence of the modern novel lack many of the characteristics that today we associate with the novel. First, they are often in verse rather than prose. Second, they do not concern themselves with 'the real life of past or present times' but portray the experiences of those whose existences can only be said to resemble 'real life', however it is defined, in extremely convention-governed and indirect ways (gods or mythical heroes, for example). Third, their characters tend not to be individualized – to the extent that even the use of our familiar term 'character' is problematic. (We do not feel too comfortable calling a purely stereotyped or conventionally portrayed individual a character precisely because today the term 'character' is associated with *distinctive* traits, with some particularity or individuality.)

The etymology of 'character' is very revealing: the word comes from a Greek word for an instrument used for marking or engraving, just as 'style' is etymologically related to the word stylus and is also associated with a cutting instrument. As a result, the word's literal meanings – as the *OED* will confirm – are related to marks that distinguish and represent individuality (think of the obsolescent use of the word 'character' to mean a person's handwriting). From this we get the familiar *OED* definition: 'A personality invested with distinctive attributes and qualities, by a novelist or dramatist.' Our sense of human individuality, this etymology suggests, is closely related to making marks – to *writing*. Writing allows human beings to develop individualities, to be and to know themselves to be different, particular, unique.

Novel and romance

There is no better example of the problems attendant upon generic classification than those connected with the romance, universally agreed to represent one of the most important traditions contributing to the emergence of the modern novel. (The term 'roman', as Margaret Anne Doody reminds us [see p. 12], is the equivalent of 'novel' in many modern European languages. Etymologically the two terms tell different stories; while the word 'novel' comes from the Italian 'novella' – 'small new thing' – the word 'romance' evolves from a word denoting a concern with the Romans. Even in modern usage this sense of the novel looking forward to the new and the romance looking back to the old can be detected.)

The traditional chivalric romance which developed in twelfth-century France depicted not epic heroes but a highly stylized and idealized courtly life founded upon rigid but sophisticated conventions of behaviour. Like the epic (which it displaced) it often involved supernatural elements – another factor which in general terms distinguishes it from the modern novel. The distinction with which we are familiar is first commented upon in the eighteenth century, the century in which, I have argued, the novel appears in its recognizable modern form in Britain. Geoffrey Day quotes the following from a review of Frances Burney's novel *Camilla*, which appeared in *The British Critic* of November 1796:

> To the old romance, which exhibited exalted personages, and displayed their sentiments in improbable or impossible situations, has succeeded the more reasonable, modern novel; which delineates characters drawn from actual observation, and, when ably executed, presents an accurate and captivating view of real life. (Day, 1987, 6)

As Day notes, 'throughout the eighteenth century "romance" was seen by many as a term suggesting excessive flights of fancy' (1987, 6), and he quotes a number of examples of such a usage. He goes on to point out that this neat definition, one which served to distinguish the romance from the novel, was not universally accepted: many writers tended to lump the two terms together relatively uncritically. He comments:

> [T]hough there is a tradition of clarity of definition, there is vastly more evidence to show that those works now commonly referred to as 'eighteenth-century novels' were not perceived as such by the readers or indeed by the major writers of the period, and that, far from being ready to accept the various works as 'novels', they do not appear to have arrived at a consensus that works such as *Robinson Crusoe*, *Pamela*, *Joseph Andrews*, *Clarissa*, *Tom Jones*, *Peregrine Pickle* and *Tristram Shandy* were even all of the same species. (1987, 7)

(In case we should be tempted to feel superior to these dull individuals who were incapable of recognizing the birth of a new genre, it is salutary to stop and think about the enormous formal variety that this short list of works represents.)

In an extract from a letter written by the eighteenth-century man of politics Lord Chesterfield to his son, we can detect both the familiar novel–romance distinction and also a sense that the two categories overlap to a considerable extent.

> I am in doubt whether you know what a Novel is: it is a little gallant history, which must contain a great deal of love, and not exceed one or two small volumes. The subject must be a love affair; the lovers are to meet with many difficulties and obstacles, to oppose the accomplishment of their wishes, but at last overcome them all; and the conclusion or catastrophe must leave them happy. A Novel is a kind of abbreviation of a Romance; for a Romance generally consists of twelve volumes, all filled with insipid love nonsense, and most incredible adventures.
>
> ...
>
> In short, the reading of Romances is a most frivolous occupation, and time merely thrown away. The old Romances, written two or three

hundred years ago, such as *Amadis of Gaul, Orlando the Furious*, and others, were stuffed with enchantments, magicians, giants, and such sort of impossibilities, whereas the more modern Romances keep within the bounds of possibility, but not of probability. (Carey, 1912, 90; the original letter is in French, and is probably written in 1740–1)

Geoffrey Day points out that in his *Dictionary* (1755), Samuel Johnson also insisted on the importance of length, defining a novel as 'A small tale, generally of love'. Today Samuel Richardson's *Clarissa* (1747–8) is uncontroversially defined as a novel, but it is certainly not a 'small tale'; while Johnson's own small tale *Rasselas* (1759) cannot comfortably be assimilated into what we now think of as a novel. It is arguably only in the early years of the nineteenth century that our present understanding of what a novel is starts to emerge as a consensus view.

Although the development of the English novel is generally associated with a concern with the everyday and a rejection of the supernatural, those aspects of the romance that were repressed as the novel defined itself did not disappear from fiction altogether. Freudians claim that the repressed always returns, and the history of prose fiction would seem to confirm this: the fantastic, the supernatural, the other-worldly (whether defined in religious or in astronomical terms) constitute the novel's dogged shadow. Sometimes this family of repressed elements emerges within what we can call mainstream fiction in hints and suggestions (madness, dreams and fevered hallucinations are a favoured way of introducing the supernatural into fiction without directly challenging a realistic framework). At the same time this family of excluded romance components also survives in what we can call sub-genres such as the modern romance or the ghost story. As I will argue later on, it is noticeable how some of the elements excluded from what I have termed mainstream fiction suddenly reappear in forms associated with the electronic media. There are clear and, I think, undeniable lines of descent from the medieval romance through the gothic novel to fantasy games such as 'Dungeons and Dragons' and computer games such as *Tomb Raider* (for more discussion of this, see Chapter 5).

However, even if fantastic and romance elements survive in the novel, there is no doubt that an emphasis upon the this-worldly is fundamental to the novel's emergence as a major genre, and at the time of the birth of the modern novel in the early and mid-eighteenth century this emphasis was widely believed by contemporary readers to distinguish the novel from the romance. Geoffrey Day cites another useful contemporary definition that again defines the novel by contrasting it to the romance, from Samuel Johnson's fourth *Rambler* essay (1750). Johnson clearly has in mind what we now call the novel in these comments, but by labelling what we would now call the novel 'the comedy of romance', he defines it in relation to the traditional romance.

The works of fiction, with which the present generation seems more particularly delighted, are such as exhibit life in its true state, diversified only by accidents that daily happen in the world, and influenced by passions and qualities which are really to be found in conversing with mankind.

This kind of writing may be termed not improperly the comedy of romance, and is to be conducted nearly by the rules of comic poetry. Its province is to bring about natural events by easy means, and to keep up curiosity without the help of wonder: it is therefore precluded from the machines and expedients of the heroic romance, and can neither employ giants to snatch away a lady from the nuptial rites, nor knights to bring her back from captivity; it can neither bewilder its personages in desarts, nor lodge them in imaginary castles.

...

The task of our present writers is very different; it requires, together with that learning which is to be gained from books, that experience which can never be attained by solitary diligence, but must arise from general converse, and accurate observation of the living world.

This is what was seen to be new about the fictional narratives written by Defoe, Richardson and Fielding, whether or not these works were called novels. 'Life in its true state', 'accurate observation of the living world': these narratives have a relationship with *ordinary* life, with the *detail* of *contemporary experience*, both social and individual, which sets them apart from the romance. Michael Seidel sums up these characteristics as follows: 'a concentration on daily life in particularized settings; a sense of information and immediacy; conventions of behaviour that would appear, at least to a reading audience, as part of its recognizable world' (Seidel, 2000, 194). It is worth noting that Johnson thought that this characteristic of the emerging genre carried with it specific *dangers*. He noted that novels were

> written chiefly to the young, the ignorant, and the idle, to whom
> they serve as lectures of conduct, and introductions into life.
> They are the entertainment of minds unfurnished with ideas, and
> therefore easily susceptible of impressions; not fixed by principles,
> and therefore easily following the current of fancy; not informed
> by experience, and consequently open to every false suggestion and
> partial account.

These new and vulnerable readers would not have been tempted to model their behaviour on the old romances because these depicted transactions and sentiments 'remote from all that passes among men', but, fears Johnson, they may be so tempted by depictions of a world similar to their own.

> [W]hen an adventurer is levelled with the rest of the world, and acts
> in such scenes of the universal drama, as may be the lot of any other

man; young spectators fix their eyes upon him with closer attention, and hope, by observing his behaviour and success, to regulate their own practices, when they shall be engaged in the like part.

Thus whereas nowadays our cultural guardians are most worried that fantastic or unrealistic fiction or film may corrupt readers (think of the worries about the Harry Potter books!), for Johnson it is fiction that depicts our own familiar world that is most likely to pervert its impressionable readers.

Michael McKeon points out that 'even though Defoe, Richardson, and Fielding explicitly subvert the idea and ethos of romance, they nonetheless draw upon many of its stock situations and conventions', and he suggests that the 'general problem of romance in all three novelists is related to the particular problem of spirituality, equally antithetical to the secularizing premises of formal realism, in Defoe'. In addition, McKeon draws attention to the fact that the romance exhibits certain characteristics of formal realism, and that it continues to co-exist with the novel during the period of the latter's emergence (McKeon, 1987, 2–3). J. Paul Hunter too warns against drawing too absolute a distinction between the novel and the romance.

> We do the novel – and not only the early novel – a disservice if we fail to notice, once we have defined the different world from romance that novels represent, how fully it engages the unusual, the uncertain, and the unexplainable. When we admit such concerns as part of the novel's territory, it also allows us to see more clearly where the novel came from, for the novel is only the most successful of a series of attempts to satisfy, in a context of scientific order, the itch for news and new things that are strange and surprising.
>
> A closely related feature involves the novel's engagement with taboos. Operating from a position of semi-respectability from the start, the novel has always been self-conscious about appearing to be pornographic, erotic, or obscene. (Hunter, 1990, 35)

That contrast and tension between 'semi-respectability' and the 'pornographic, erotic, [and] obscene' is, if not a standard feature of the novel, certainly one of its recurrent features: the novel typically presents us not just with the ordinary but also with the extraordinary, the hidden and the repressed, which are to be found concealed in, or behind, the ordinary, the conventional and the everyday. Michael Seidel again has a useful comment, noting that while it is true that paradigms of romance such as victimage, forbearance and rescue remain entrenched in the realist fiction that emerges in the form of the modern novel, 'what is removed are those generic parts of romance that define causality and circumstance by forces inapplicable to the world of conventional experience' (Seidel, 2000, 196).

Before passing on, I would like to draw your attention to a couple of terms used by Hunter: 'different world' and 'territory'. In the course of a discussion of fiction and the electronic media later on in this book I will consider the concepts of 'textual world' and 'simulated world' provided by two commentators on 'electronic fiction' (see pp. 99–100). What readers seem always to require of a work of fiction is that it provide such a 'world', a distinct *space* within which characters can move that is governed by a clear, coherent and consistent set of rules and conventions. In realistic fiction the world concerned is very much like the reader's, even though it may be removed in time, space or culture from his or hers. In works of fantasy, the ghost story, science fiction or cyberfiction, the world we encounter is very different from that of the reader – although the two may share certain important common elements. But however different, it must offer the reader some sense of inner consistency. Neil Cornwell provides a useful comment taken from T.E. Little's *The Fantasts*:

> All writers of creative fiction are subcreators of Secondary Worlds. The secondary world of a non-fantastic writer will be as close to the Primary World as his talents and the needs of his art will allow. … A licence is granted to writers of 'normal' creative fiction to change the Primary World for the purpose of their art. Fantasy begins when an author's Secondary World goes beyond that license and becomes 'other'. … Such a creation should be called a *Tertiary World*. (Cornwell, 1990, 16, quoting from Little, 1984, 9–10)

Cornwell himself notes that Mary Shelley's *Frankenstein* (1818) can be seen as a key text, because in it religion has been replaced by science as the basis of a reality different from the everyday, a suggestion worth thinking about when you read my later comments on the novel and secularism (p. 30). Cornwell also suggests that we should see fiction in terms of a continuum that can be split into two. The first half-continuum is 'mimesis dominated'. It moves from *non-fiction* to *faction* to realism to *uncanny realism* to the *fantastic-uncanny* and ends in the *pure fantastic*. The second half-continuum takes up from the *pure fantastic* and moves through the *fantastic-marvellous* to the *marvellous* and ends up in *mythology* (Cornwell, 1990, 39). (You will find many of these terms defined in the Glossary. The term *mimesis* means 'imitation' or 'copying', but it is associated with theories of realism that see the job of the artist as that of accurately copying nature and human beings.)

Cornwell's proposed continuum is thought-provoking, but we should remember that many novels mix realistic and – say – supernatural elements. Think for example how many suggestions of the supernatural there are in Emily Brontë's *Wuthering Heights*, a novel that is also full of very specific references to a world of concrete objects and social realities. The supernatural in Brontë's novel is often associated with dreams (Lockwood's and Cathy's) and superstition (the belief of the locals that Heathcliff 'walks' after his death, reported by Lockwood in the novel's closing pages). What is I think important is that nowhere in Brontë's text is there unambiguous evidence of the existence of the supernatural or the ghostly.

At this point I am conscious of the voice of an imaginary reader of this book, a student of literature who makes the following complaint. 'During my study of the novel and shorter fiction I have read Horace Walpole's *The Castle of Otranto* (1765), in which a key role is played by a ghost; Feodor Dostoyevsky's "The Double" (1846), in which the hero Golyadkin encounters his double, who takes over his life bit by bit and is treated as the "real" Golyadkin; Robert Louis Stevenson's *Dr Jekyll and Mr Hyde* (1886), in which the hero alternates between a good and a bad identity; Oscar Wilde's *The Picture of Dorian Gray* (1891), in which a man escapes the ageing process while his picture depicts a representation of an older and older man; Henry James's *The Turn of the Screw* (1898), in which the ghosts of two dead servants (may) seduce two young children; Franz Kafka's "Metamorphosis" (1912), which opens with the hero discovering that he has turned into a giant insect; C.S. Lewis's *The Lion, The Witch and the Wardrobe* (1950), in which children go through their wardrobe into a magic world and meet a talking lion who is sacrificed but who returns to life; Philip K. Dick's "We Can Remember it for you Wholesale" (1966), which is set in a future world in which false memories can be purchased and implanted in the mind so that they are believed to be real; and Angela Carter's *The Bloody Chamber* (1979), which contains short stories that blend fairy-tale elements with real-world settings. How can you claim that the novel is to be distinguished from medieval romance because it presents us with our familiar, everyday world rather than impossible situations and enchanted worlds?'

I think that my response to this challenge would go something like this.

- ↩ Some of the works cited are generally categorized in a way that draws attention to their divergence from mainstream fiction – for example: 'the gothic novel', 'the ghost story', 'science fiction', 'magic realism' (see the Glossary for more on some of these terms). The very need so to categorize them suggests that we do not expect such elements in the mainstream novel.
- ↩ Many of the works referred to are short stories or novellas, and shorter fiction does seem more likely to contain fantastic or non-realistic elements (see p. 59 for a discussion of this issue).
- ↩ *The Lion, The Witch and the Wardrobe* is a story written for children, and romance and fantastic elements have survived in much stronger form in children's literature. Fairy stories, for example, are nowadays told mainly to children.
- ↩ In a number of the works named, the supernatural or fantastic occurrence is hinted at or presented as a possibility, but alternative, realistic explanations are possible (Golyadkin is actually going mad and imagining his double, just as the governess imagines the ghosts in *The Turn of the Screw*; Dr Jekyll's transformation is caused by science not magic; the

implantation of memories could be possible in a future, technologically advanced world).

↔ Finally, even where the events are fantastic, they may cause us to think about very this-worldly things. 'Metamorphosis' shows how people respond to chronic illness; 'We Can Remember it for you Wholesale' causes us to consider whether illusions can be as satisfying as reality; the stories in *The Bloody Chamber* remind us how many attitudes to gender are based on the highly stereotyped and discriminatory models found in the traditional fairy stories that are told to children. These stories thus still refer back to the everyday, rather than constituting an escape from the everyday in the manner of the medieval romance.

Life and pattern

Arnold Kettle has suggested that most novelists show a bias towards either 'life' or 'pattern' in their approach to writing: towards, in other words, either the aim to convey the vividness, the particularized sensations and experiences of living, or that of conveying some interpretation of the significance of life. According to Kettle, the novelist who starts with pattern often tries to 'inject' life into it, while the novelist who starts with life tries to make a pattern emerge out of it. He relates these two very general tendencies to, on the one hand, such sources and influences as the parables of the Bible, the morality plays of the Middle Ages and the sermons which common people listened to every Sunday ('pattern'), and on the other hand, the seventeenth- and early eighteenth-century prose journalism and pamphleteering of such as Thomas Nashe and Daniel Defoe (who, we should remember, was a political journalist before he wrote prose fiction). As Kettle says of such writers, the germ of their books is never an idea, never an abstract concept; they are 'less consciously concerned with the moral significance of life than with its surface texture' (Kettle, 1967, 20). Michael McKeon makes a similar point, arguing that in tracing the emergence of the early modern novel we detect a recurrent formal tension between 'what might be called the individual life and the overarching pattern' (McKeon, 1987, 90).

In her essay 'Phases of Fiction', Virginia Woolf uses terms similar to those to be found in Kettle's later comments in explaining what she sees to be a fundamental tension within the genre of the novel:

> For the most characteristic qualities of the novel – that it registers the slow growth and development of feeling, that it follows many lives and traces their unions and fortunes over a long stretch of time – are the very qualities that are most incompatible with design and order. It is the gift of style, arrangement, construction, to put us at a distance from the special life and to obliterate its features; while it is the gift of the

novel to bring us into close touch with life. The two powers fight if they are brought into combination. The most complete novelist must be the novelist who can balance the two powers so that the one enhances the other. (Woolf, 1966b, 101)

It is perhaps the mark of the greatest novels that with them it is most difficult to say whether or not the novelist has tried more to convey what Kettle calls 'life' and 'pattern' and Woolf calls 'design and order' and 'life', for both seem so consummately present.

The 'rise of the novel'

Let us return to the issue of that disputed birth date. Most of those concerned to map and to explain the development of the modern novel are agreed in singling out certain factors crucial to this development. Of these the following are perhaps the most important.

Literacy

The modern novel emerged, and has developed, as a written form – unlike poetry, which existed for centuries prior to the development of writing and still flourishes in oral cultures today. There have been cases of illiterate people gathering to hear novels read; part of Dickens's audience was of this sort. It is also the case that many novels and short stories are presented as if they were written transpositions of oral deliveries, of spoken tellings. (See the discussion of the term *skaz* in the Glossary.) Nonetheless, the novel is typically *written* by one individual in private and *read silently* by another individual who has no personal relationship with the author. Michael McKeon points out that the development of literacy helps to encourage the growth of 'empirical attitudes' which in their turn encourage 'a more skeptical approach to the authenticity of saints' relics and a more rationalistic interpretation of the figurative status of the Eucharist' (1987, 35). Equally if not more important, I suspect, is the fact that silent reading is private and non-collective and thus helps the novel to mediate and express the new individualism of early capitalism while at the same time allowing easier access to the fantasy life.

There was a rapid growth of literacy in the English-speaking world from 1600 to 1800, and whereas it is estimated that in 1600 about 25 per cent of adult males in England and Wales could read, by 1800 the figure is probably between 60 and 70 per cent (Hunter, 1990, 65–6). Although the figures for female literacy lag behind those for male literacy, more and more women too could read during this period.

Tony E. Jackson's recent study *The Technology of the Novel: Writing and Narrative in British Fiction* (2009) represents a sustained investigation into the complex and intimate ways in which writing enables and forms the genre of the novel while also providing significant subject matter for its scrutiny. Jackson takes a standard distinction in narrative theory, that between 'showing' and 'telling' (see p. 135), and suggests that while the oral story unites showing and telling, in modern narrative '[t]he novel is, relatively, all telling and no showing; film and drama are, relatively, all showing and no telling' (2009, 20). Among the many other rich observations contained in Jackson's book is the following.

> One of the thrills of a good experience of reading fiction is the sense of verbal communication that is more direct than speech. Speech can only come from other humans, and since there is no human present as we 'hear' the words, we seem to receive another's thoughts without their having passed through even the intervening medium of speech. We seem to 'hear' another's thoughts, just as we 'hear' our own. This can establish a unique sense of intimacy. (2009, 21)

Paradoxically, then, the distance of writing (the person who writes and the person who reads can be separated in both time and space) leads to a greater intimacy than is experienced between a co-present oral teller and listener. Moreover, the novel is read *in private* by an individual. When we attend a play's performance it is hard to be unaware of how other members of the audience are reacting, and our own reactions are visible to those around us. J. Paul Hunter has noted the novel's liking for the confessional and the exhibitionistic (Hunter, 1990, 37); the problem pages of popular magazines will remind us that confession and self-exposure are often easier through the impersonal medium of writing and, especially, of print.

Printing

The modern novel is the child of the printing press, which alone can produce the vast numbers of copies needed to satisfy a literate public at an affordable price. Note the two-way process here: more people are literate so that the market for books is bigger and publishers and printers have a reason to produce more books, while more books are produced so that more people have an incentive to learn to read. Michael McKeon points out that a number of different factors conspire to assist the development of printing – technological, social and legal:

> By the close of the seventeenth century England had become a
> major producer of paper, type, and various kinds of publication, a
> development that could not have occurred without the abolition
> of protectionist printing legislation. By the middle of the
> eighteenth, licensing laws had been replaced by copyright laws; the
> commodification of the book market as a mass-production industry

had become organized around the mediating figure of the bookseller; and the idea that a writer should get paid for his work was gaining currency on the strength of the perception that there was a growing mass of consumers willing to foot the bill. On the other hand, these new consumers of print were also produced by print – most obviously by the early modern 'educational revolution', which received a great stimulus from the invention of the press and played the central role in raising the levels of literacy in England. (McKeon, 1987, 51)

J. Paul Hunter sums up as follows: 'From the beginning, moreover, novels were artifacts of the world of print. They had been conceived that way, and they lent themselves readily to the physical, social, and psychological circumstances that affected potential readers of printed books' (Hunter, 1990, 41). Later on in this book I shall consider the argument that it is the design of the physical book that imposes linear narrative on the novel, and that the growth of the electronic media is able to 'liberate' fiction from linear narrative (see p. 96).

Print did not succeed oral delivery in one fell swoop; David Margolies points out that the manuscript circulation of written work represented a sort of in-between stage, and 'provided a model for the literary relationships of the early novelists' (Margolies, 1985, 23). Margolies notes that writing for anony-mous readers presented writers with a new set of problems, and he quotes from Austen Saker's *Narbonus* (1580):

> and he must write well that shall please all minds: but he that planteth trees in a Forest, knoweth not how many shall taste the Fruit, and he that soweth in his garden divers Seeds, knoweth not who shall eat of his Sallets. He that planteth a Vine, knoweth not who shall taste his Wine: and he that putteth any thing in Print, must think that all will peruse it: If then amongst many blossoms, some prove blasts, no marvel if amongst many Readers, some prove Riders. (Margolies, 1985, 24)

Compare this to the opening words of Chapter 1 of Henry Fielding's *Tom Jones* (1749): 'An author ought to consider himself, not as a gentleman who gives a private or eleemosynary [i.e. charitable] treat, but rather as one who keeps a public ordinary [i.e. a public house], at which all persons are welcome for their money.' The relationship between the writer of a novel and its reader is, then, typically impersonal and commercial, rather than one based on personal acquaintance and friendship. This is such a familiar state of affairs for us today that we pay no attention to it: for us, it is a matter of note if we *do* know the author of a book we are reading. We should remember that this situation is historically new and is associated with the development of printing. With prose fiction the issue of the relationship between *writer* and *reader* is complicated by the fact that the reader's immediate relationship is with a *narrator* rather than an *author*, and I will have more to say about this in Chapter 6. What I can say here, however, is that novelists had to learn how to become adept at convincing their readers that they were in intimate contact with a narrator who was interested in them as individuals. As J. Paul Hunter argues:

> [The novel's] rejection of familiar plots, conventional mythic settings, and recognizable character types represents a recognition that its future lies in developing a new kind of relationship with new combinations of readers.
>
> ...
>
> One audience-related feature involves the novel's tendency both to probe and promote loneliness and solitariness, rather ironic in view of the novel's expressed design to portray people in their societal context. If the tendency to expose secrets of personal life points one way, the tendency to enclose the self, to treat the self as somehow inviolable and insistently separate in spite of the publication of secrets once thought too personal to articulate, points the other. (Hunter, 1990, 39)

Hunter makes the astute point that this may well be why the novel, although born in another time, is so well placed to represent some central experiences that emerge in a more widespread and dominant form in the twentieth century: a concern with subjectivity, isolation and loneliness (Hunter, 1990, 41–2).

As David Margolies claims, writers did not necessarily learn the new ways of writing that we associate with print without difficulty; early printed works often show signs of a still-flourishing oral tradition, and J. Paul Hunter has argued that the first modern novels 'had their relevant contexts – ultimately even their origins – in a culture that was partly oral and partly written, where functions traditionally performed in communal and family rituals and by oral tradition more and more fell to the impersonal processes of print' (Hunter, 1990, xvii). We should not look upon this as a disadvantage: the novel still owes much of its richness to the importation of techniques and perspectives from oral delivery. From its earliest days the novel has been able to make readers think that they are hearing a voice when they are actually reading print, and the gains of verisimilitude and dramatic immediacy that this has enabled are considerable. One of the striking characteristics of many novels written in the twentieth and twenty-first centuries by writers from the working class of industrialized societies and by writers from newly independent ex-colonies is that oral rhythms and structures are taken from a rich heritage of non-literary traditions. Take the opening of Jack Common's semi-autobiographical novel, *Kiddar's Luck* (1951):

> She was a fool, of course, my mother. Her mother said so: 'Bella is a fool, I'm afraid, a weak fool. Here she is marrying a common workman, one who drinks and is not a good Christian. She will never know

happiness now.' You would think the old lady was great shakes herself to hear her. And she was in her way. Not that she had any money ever, but she made poverty respectable.

The intimate relationship established here between narrator and reader feeds off a living tradition of oral storytelling at the same time as it exploits the potentialities inherent in the privacy and anonymity central to the narrator–reader relationship associated with the novel.

Market economy

Michael McKeon argues that 'the novel' is:

> a deceptively monolithic category that encloses a complex historical process. It attains its modern, 'institutional' stability and coherence at this time because of its unrivaled power both to formulate, and to explain, a set of problems that are central to early modern experience. (McKeon, 1987, 20)

These problems, according to McKeon, encompass both generic and social categories: questions about how to tell the truth in narrative ('questions of truth'), and questions about 'how the external social order is related to the internal, moral state of its members' ('questions of virtue'). McKeon sees a double process in the emergence of the novel: on the one hand, the change from what he calls 'romance idealism' or 'a dependence on received authorities and a priori traditions' to a 'naive empiricism' based upon a more empirical epistemology; on the other hand, the change from 'a relatively stratified social order supported by a reigning world view' that McKeon calls 'aristocratic ideology' to what he refers to as a more 'progressive ideology' which is itself later challenged by a 'conservative ideology' (1987, 21).

These comments relate the birth of the modern novel to the changed social conditions experienced by its earliest practitioners. But if McKeon sees the impact of these social conditions in terms of the ideological problems and solutions they engendered, he and others have also related them to specific social institutions. Most commentators agree that crucial to the 'sociology of the modern novel' is a *market relationship* between author and reader mediated through publishers. In contrast to earlier methods of financing publication or supporting authors such as *patronage* (a rich patron would support a writer while a book was being written) or *subscription* (wealthy potential readers would subscribe money to support a writer in order that a particular work might be written), a market economy increases the relative freedom and isolation of the writer and decreases his or her immediate dependence upon particular individuals, groups or interests (although, of course, it makes him or her *more* dependent upon publishers and, especially, sales). The growth of a market economy is an integral aspect of the rise of capitalism – the socio-economic system which had displaced feudalism in Britain by the eighteenth century. In his book *The Rise of the Novel* (1957), Ian Watt argued that there is a close relationship between the rise of the novel and the rise of the middle class – the class most involved in the triumph of capitalism in Britain. In different ways literacy, printing and a market economy can all be related to the growing dominance of capitalism in the period during which the novel emerges.

Michael McKeon draws attention to the debate in Cervantes's *Don Quixote* between Don Quixote and Sancho Panza about whether the latter should receive 'favours' or 'wages', suggesting that the relationship between these two characters thus 'mediates the historical transition from feudalism to capitalism' (McKeon, 1987, 283). J. Paul Hunter has gone further and has suggested that crucial to the development of the new genre in England is the confrontation between 'a Protestant, capitalistic, imperial, insecure, restless, bold, and self-conscious culture' and 'a constrictive, authoritarian, hierarchical, and too-neatly-sorted past' (Hunter, 1990, 7).

Capitalism is of course founded on competition, and from its earliest days the novel is concerned with conflict. The novel's portrayal of confrontations between individuals very often has a representative quality, pointing in the direction of larger social, historical or cultural rivalries. This is significant in terms not just of the content of novels but also (and this of course is not a separate issue) of their readership. Novels appealed to groups of individuals who were emerging into new prominence and increased power: women and young people, for example. Hunter points out that from its earliest days the novel has been particularly concerned with 'the crises of the decisive moments in adolescence and early adulthood' (Hunter, 1990, 43). A novel such as Jane Rule's splendid *Memory Board* (1987), which focuses on characters who are old and tackling senility, has few parallels before the twentieth century.

The novel and the individual

Ian Watt sees as typical of the novel that it includes 'individualization of ... characters and ... the detailed presentation of their environment'. Unlike many of the narratives that precede it, the novel does not just present us with 'type' characters; we are interested in Tom Jones, David Copperfield, Maggie Tulliver and Paul Morel as distinct individuals with personal qualities and idiosyncrasies. As Ralph Fox puts it:

> The novel deals with the individual, it is the epic of the struggle of the individual against society, against nature, and it could only develop in a society where the balance between man and society was lost, where man was at war with his fellows or with nature. Such a society is capitalist society. (Fox, 1979, 44)

Fox exemplifies his argument by contrasting the *Odyssey* with *Robinson Crusoe* (1719), pointing out that, whereas Odysseus lives in a society without history and knows that his fate is in the hands of the gods, Robinson Crusoe is prepared to make his own history. Furthermore, whereas Odysseus's efforts are directed towards returning *home*, for Crusoe it is the outward and not the homeward trip that is important; he is 'the man who challenges nature and wins'. Crusoe is thus, for Fox, representative of that spirit of expansionism, self-reliance and experimentation that characterizes early capitalist man.

It certainly seems to be the case that the new spirit that accompanies the early development of capitalism infuses the emerging novel. Along with a stress on individualism goes, too, a growing concern with the inner self, the private life, subjective experience. As the individual *feels* him- or herself a unique individual rather than just a member of a static feudal community with duties and characteristics which are endowed at birth and shared with others, then he or she starts more to think in terms of having certain personal rather than shared communal interests. This gives the individual something to *hide*. Without wishing to oversimplify an extremely complex and far from uniform historical development, we can say that in a certain sense the private life as we know it today is born with capitalist society, and that the novel both responds and contributes to this development.

It doubtless seems very odd to many readers to claim that people have not always felt themselves to be individuals in the way that modern men and women from developed societies do, and indeed this assertion has been challenged by a number of recent writers, including Margaret Anne Doody in her *The True Story of the Novel*. Other commentators have detected Eurocentric and even racist attitudes behind the assumption that those from non-literate cultures are not 'individuals' in the way that those from modern developed cultures are.

Fictional works do nevertheless offer strong evidence to support the view that people from non-literate cultures perceive themselves and their individuality rather differently from the way in which those from literate cultures do. (A classic case for this view is made by A.R. Luria in his book *Cognitive Development* [1976].) In an important study, *Form, Individuality and the Novel* (1990), Clemens Lugowski examines a number of much earlier fictional works dating from the sixteenth and early seventeenth centuries, including the anonymous *Eine schöne Historie von den vier Heymonskindern*, Georg Wickram's *Amadis*, the stories known as *Thyl Ulenspiegel* and the novellas of the *Decameron*. He concludes that these works contain nothing that might be referred to as an 'individual'.

This of course begs the question: 'What is an individual?' Nowadays there is a common assumption that all adult human beings are persons, and that they are individuals. But our sense of what an individual is – our sense of what it means to be a specific human being – is not necessarily one that we share with all other human beings. Moreover, we need to pause and ask ourselves: who are 'we'? A complicating but fascinating factor here is that how modern people understand individuality is something to which the novel has undoubtedly both responded and contributed. For example: one of the things that the novel both reflects and helps to establish – in the form which it assumes from Defoe onwards – is a fundamental belief that what a person *is* goes beyond what that person *says* or *does*. We believe, today, that our identity exceeds what is observable to others. According to both Lugowski and Luria, not all human beings share or have shared this belief, and Lugowski argues that prior to the emergence of the modern novel, a view of fictional individuals as more 'components of a whole' than 'genuinely autonomous individuals' (what we might call types rather than real characters) means that fictional characters as we understand them did not exist (Lugowski, 1990, 83). Lugowski's argument assumes that the ability to distinguish oneself from the world in which one lives is not universal, and that its gradual emergence encourages and takes support from the emergence of the novel in its modern form. He argues that 'when the autobiographer explicitly *wishes* to describe his own life, and yet then describes the world outside, then what this means is that his life really *is* the world' (Lugowski, 1990, 155; compare Luria, 1976, Chapter 7: 'Self-Analysis and Self-Awareness'). Moreover, Lugowski suggests that it is when human beings begin to question their 'position in and profound commitment to the world' that an individuality that involves seeing oneself as separate from the world can emerge (Lugowski, 1990, 176).

Similarly, in his essay 'Forms of Time and of the Chronotope in the Novel', Mikhail Bakhtin says of the work of Rabelais (which he much admires) that in it 'life has absolutely no *individual* aspect. A human being is completely external.' He continues:

> For indeed, there is not a single instance in the entire expanse of Rabelais' huge novel where we are shown what a character is thinking, what he is experiencing, his internal dialogue. In this sense there is in Rabelais' novel no world of interiority. (Bakhtin, 1981, 239)

While we might assume that pre-modern novelists had not yet learned how to portray the interior life, then, we have to consider the possibility that it is rather the case that for them the interior life as we know it did not exist. Characteristic of the modern novel, in contrast, is its exploration of *both* the subjective and the social, of *both* the private and the collective. It is this combination of the broadest social and historical sweep with the most acute and penetrating visions of the hidden, private life, *and their interconnections*, that is characteristic of the modern novel and at the heart of its power and continuing life. Paradoxically, although the novel is both written and read in private, it relies upon a highly organized society and industry to produce and circulate it. Even in its sociology it combines the personal and the social, that combination that is at the heart of its aesthetic.

This is not to say that the novel is able critically and analytically to portray all human organizations and groups as well as it can represent and explore the individual. Brook Thomas has, indeed, suggested that 'the generic demands of the novel seem to guarantee that novelistic representations of corporations will lag behind the way in which other forms of discourse have been able to respond to the rise of corporations' (Thomas, 1991, 150), implying that the novel is generically unfitted to portray and examine human beings in certain of their collectivities.

The novel and secularism

When we say that *secularism* is crucial to the development of the novel this is not to imply that a novel may not explore religious themes or be underpinned by a religious imperative. It does mean, though, that the modern novel emerges in a world in which people were more and more likely to try to find non-supernatural explanations for the problems which they faced, and that this cast of mind is reflected in the novel. Milan Kundera remarks: 'As God slowly departed from the seat whence he had directed the universe and its order of values, distinguished good from evil, and endowed each thing with meaning, Don Quixote set forth from his house into a world he could no longer recognize' (Kundera, 1988, 6).

Even today, when a novelist wishes to make a religious point, he or she is typically encouraged by the conventions of the genre to set it in a context of secular explanation. Thus, when a character in David Lodge's *Small World* (1984) prays for help in confronting the imminent task of delivering a conference paper which he has not yet written, his prayer is answered by a sudden outbreak of Legionnaires' Disease that requires that the conference be abandoned. The reader is allowed to read this as either divine intervention or a fortunate coincidence. It is true that there are novels which encourage the reader to imagine supernatural occurrences and fantastic worlds different from our own (the gothic novel, science fiction, magic realism – see the definitions in the Glossary), but it is striking how consistently such novels hedge their bets by allowing for non-supernatural explanations or interpretations of what happens. It is for this reason, among others, that modern readers tend to find the novels of Ann Radcliffe more acceptable than her near-contemporary William Beckford's *Vathek* (1787), in which the supernatural interventions allow for no natural explanation.

The novel and urban experience

The early association of the novel with town rather than country life is also significant. There are novels set in the country, of course, but from its earliest days the novel appears to have had a special relationship with town life, and in the eighteenth century both the readers and the writers of novels were more likely to be town dwellers than country dwellers. If we look at what has a fair claim to be one of the first modern novels – Daniel Defoe's *Moll Flanders* (1722) – we can see that the town and the novel form have much in common. Both involve large numbers of people leading interdependent lives, influencing and relying upon one another, but each possessing, nevertheless, a core of private thoughts and personal goals. Modern readers may need to be reminded that the growth of large towns and of urban life ushers in new forms of loneliness and privacy at the same time that, paradoxically, these large collectivities depend upon and bear witness to collective planning and human cooperation.

Consider the following four passages, each written in a different century. The first is from *Moll Flanders*, and it concludes the scene in which Moll robs a young child of a necklace:

> Here, I say, the Devil put me upon killing the Child in the dark Alley, that it might not Cry; but the very thought frighted me so that I was ready to drop down, but I turn'd the Child about and bade it go back again, for that was not its way home; the Child said so she would, and I went thro' into *Bartholomew Close*, and then turn'd round to another Passage that goes into *Long-lane*, so away into *Charterhouse-Yard* and out into *St. John's-street*, then crossing into *Smithfield*, went down *Chick-lane* and into *Field-lane* to *Holbourne-bridge*, when mixing with the Crowd of People usually passing there, it was not possible to have been found out; and thus I enterpriz'd my second Sally into the World.

The second is from Charles Dickens's *Oliver Twist* (1837–8), and describes Oliver's entry into London in the company of the Artful Dodger ('John Dawkins'):

> As John Dawkins objected to their entering London before nightfall, it was nearly eleven o'clock when they reached the turnpike at Islington. They crossed from the Angel into St. John's Road; struck down the small street which terminates at Sadler's Wells Theatre; through Exmouth Street and Coppice Row; down the little court by the side of the workhouse; across the classic ground which once bore the name of Hockley-in-the-Hole; thence into Little Saffron Hill; and so into Saffron Hill the Great: along which the Dodger scudded at a rapid pace, directing Oliver to follow close at his heels.

The third is from Samuel Beckett's *Murphy*, which was first published in 1938.

> She took the Piccadilly tube from Caledonian Road to Hyde Park Corner and walked along the grass north of the Serpentine. Each leaf as it fell had an access of new life, a sudden frenzy of freedom at contact with the earth, before it lay down with the others. She had meant to cross the water by Rennie's Bridge and enter Kensington Gardens by one of the wickets in the eastern boundary, but remembering the dahlias at Victoria Gate she changed her mind and bore off to the right into the north, round the accident house of the Royal Humane Society.

Finally, the following passage is taken from W.G. Sebald's *Austerlitz* (first published in German 2001).

> For over a year, I think, said Austerlitz, I would leave my house as darkness fell, walking on and on, down the Mile End Road and Bow Road to Stratford, then to Chigwell and Romford, right across Bethnal Green and Canonbury, through Holloway and Kentish Town and thus to Hampstead Heath, or else south over the river to Peckham and Dulwich or westward to Richmond Park.

How well the world of London – rendered 'real' by the detailing of actual streets – and the world we now associate with the novel fit! In all four passages we observe rapid mobility in a well-known world, that everyday world with which so many readers are familiar, alongside a sense of one's private self that, even in the place where so very many people live, is one's own alone (and the reader's). Moll Flanders's comment that by mixing with a crowd of people 'it was not possible to have been found out' may be less true in an age of electronic surveillance, but it remains the case that sometimes we are most alone when surrounded by other people (this odd fact of urban life is much exploited in modernist fiction: see p. 35). *Secrecy*, and *movement* in a location crammed with other people: this mixture has remained central to the novel for over 300 years. (See also the discussion of travel on p. 34.)

Public world and private life

From its earliest days the novel seems often to split not just between novels where the author starts with 'life' and those in which the author starts with 'pattern' – to use Arnold Kettle's terms – but also between novels in which the author is more interested in the public world and novels in which the author is more interested in private life. Again, it is only the very greatest novels that seem to combine the two such that we feel no sense of subordination of either. Henry Fielding's *Tom Jones* (1749) and Samuel Richardson's *Clarissa* (1747–8) can be taken as representative here, with the former's greater interest in a masculine, public life of movement, action and life in the larger social world in sharp contrast to the latter's concentration upon a feminine, more inward life of feeling, personal relationships and personal moral decision. This is not to deny that Fielding's novel includes a concern with feeling and moral duty and Richardson's with the larger social context of the inner world. Nonetheless there is a very significant difference between the two writers and their respective fictional works, and one of which their contemporaries were well aware. J.A. Downie has agreed that the creative dialogue between Richardson and Fielding was a significant factor in the growing popularity of 'the novel' (Downie, 2000, 325), and in his *The Life of Samuel Johnson*, which was first published in 1791, James Boswell shows how attitudes towards these two writers could cause serious dissension. Talking to Johnson and Thomas Erskine, Boswell expressed surprise at Johnson's calling Fielding a 'blockhead' and 'a barren rascal', and continued:

> 'Will you not allow, Sir, that he draws very natural pictures of human life?' JOHNSON. 'Why, Sir, it is of very low life. Richardson used to say, that had he not known who Fielding was, he should have believed he was an ostler. Sir, there is more knowledge of the heart in one letter of Richardson's, than in all Tom Jones. ... ERSKINE. 'Surely, Sir, Richardson is very tedious.' JOHNSON. 'Why, Sir, if you were to read Richardson for the story, your impatience would be so much fretted that you would hang yourself. But you must read him for the sentiment, and consider the story as only giving occasion to the sentiment.' (anecdote from 1772)

We do not need to accept Johnson's value judgements to feel the force of the distinction made here, between a primary interest in drawing very natural pictures of life – albeit low life – and in revealing knowledge of the human heart.

The female voice

I refer above to Fielding's interest in the masculine and Richardson's in the feminine sphere, and I should make it clear that this is a historical rather than a universal judgement; 'masculine' and 'feminine' as they were defined by eighteenth-century English society, in which men alone were able to live a public as well as a domestic life, a public life of travel, work, exploration and adventure. As I have already indicated, the relationship of women to the novel is a very important one. This importance is both as writers and as readers (and, of course, as characters). Towards the end of the eighteenth century in England, more and more women were writing novels, and even male novelists recognized the importance of female readers. The anonymous but probably male author of *The Amicable Quixote; or, The Enthusiasm of Friendship*, published in London in 1788, mentions in his preface 'the commendations of the ladies, *for whom works of this kind are generally written*'. Because of the market economy on which novel production depended, the increasing importance of female readers inevitably had an appreciable effect upon the sort of novels that were written, and there is evidence that some male authors experienced this as an unwelcome pressure. Here for example is a comment from the narrator of Richard Graves's *The Spiritual Quixote or The Summer's Ramble of Mr. Geoffry Wildgoose. A Comic Romance*, which was published in 1773:

> Should any of my amiable country-women, I say, smit with the love of novelty, carry home this trifling volume from some Circulating-library; and throwing herself negligently upon her settee or sopha – or even

on the feet of her truckle-bed – have patience to attend two such odd
fellows thus far; she will probably be disgusted that she has not been
entertained with a single love-tale, which are generally looked upon as
essential to works of this kind; and not only make a principal part of
every episode, but are usually interwoven with the body of the fable.
(Graves, 1967, 77)

This felt tension between what male authors wanted to write and what they
perceived that female readers wanted to read clearly alters in important ways
as more and more women themselves write novels. But even though women
were a dominant force not just as readers but also as writers of the novel by the
nineteenth century, this does not mean that within the world of the novel all
the inequalities of the time miraculously disappear. No novel can totally escape
the ideological bounds of its time. Interestingly, it is often the experience of
colonialism and imperialism that throws up issues of gender in sharp relief in
the modern novel. I will return to this issue below.

It is arguable that the novel's success in exploring the private world, the
subjective self, could never have been accomplished without the contribution
to the genre of that introspective self-knowledge and sensitive perception of
interpersonal relations that women's domestic imprisonment had trained them
to be so expert in. No man could have written Jane Austen's novels.

The international life of the novel: the novel and travel

From its first appearance in the world, the novel is associated with movement and travel – with *mobility*, both geographical and social. In the passages
I quote above from *Moll Flanders* and *Oliver Twist* we are reminded how
important being able to move from place to place was for Moll and for Oliver,
but we should remember, too, that for both characters *geographical* movement was closely linked to a desire for *social* movement or advance. And in
all four of the quoted passages concerning movement in London the reader
needs to be sensitive to the social significance of the locations associated with
different streets.

It is certainly arguable that this stress upon mobility is one of the points at
which the socio-historical conditions of the novel's emergence and the social
tensions which contribute to its birth are transposed into generic and formal
features. The very name 'novel', of course, directs our attention to what is
new, and we typically discover the new by changing our location and by seeing
either new things or old and familiar things from an unusual perspective.

Peter Burke has suggested that travel is one of the factors that can help
to explain the emergence of what he refers to as 'the autobiographical habit'
in the sixteenth century. As he reminds us, this 'was the age not only of the
rise of the autobiography or journal but also of fictional narratives in the first-
person story, such as the picaresque novel in Spain or the sonnet-sequences

of Sidney, Shakespeare and others', and he proposes three likely reasons for this development. First, the fact that this is the age in which print becomes a part of everyday life, which means that the diffusion of printed models can create a new or sharper sense of self. Second, urbanization, because the alternative styles of life offered by the city encourage a sense of individual choice. Third, travel, because travel 'encourages self-consciousness by cutting off the individual from his or her community' (Burke, 1997, 22). While we remain in familiar surroundings we receive more regular confirmation of our identity from those who expect us to continue to be what we have been in the past, but in a strange situation, surrounded by people we do not know, we become aware that to a certain extent we are able to choose who we are, and indeed it is easier to *change* who we are. Those who want to make a fresh start typically move to a new place.

Even that basic component of prose fiction – the linearity of narrative – models progression and movement for us. Some writers have attempted to 'de-linearize' the novel. Brian McHale (1987, 193) refers to two of the best-known examples – Julio Cortázar's *Hopscotch* (1963), which invites the reader to choose between two different routes through its text, and B.S. Johnson's *The Unfortunates* (1969), published in a box of twenty-seven stapled gatherings which can be read in any order. In both cases, one should note, any individual reading is still a linear progression from beginning to end through a finite text. (See also the later discussion of the impact of the electronic media on linear narrative in Chapter 5, which returns to the case of *The Unfortunates*.)

In the mainstream novel, as the line of prose snakes its way ahead from page to page, pressing on in the direction our culture calls 'forward' and always moving away from its point of birth to that last line where it will stop for ever, it constantly reminds us not just of the individual human life journeying from birth to death but also of the typical fictional hero or heroine: progressing ever forward, continually encountering new blank pages in the book of life untouched by the pen of experience. As Michael McKeon puts it, by arranging events in a certain linear order, that 'progressive narrative' which is integral to the emerging novel

> automatically invests personality with the distinct moral qualities that are implied in the condition of being either in decline or on the rise. These qualities imply, in turn, an explanatory rationale whose force is unmistakable. On one side are the extravagant and licentious older sons of nobility, sunk in decay and corruption; on the other, the industrious and virtuous younger sons or tradesmen, hard at work in their honest and quasi-Calvinist callings. (McKeon, 1987, 220)

McKeon's argument links a specific type of narrative with a particular sort of social mobility, but these two forms of directed movement are also and typically associated with geographical progression and movement in the novel.

The stranger, the intruder, the traveller – whether the terrain crossed is geographical or social – are all familiar inhabitants of this 'novel' genre.

There is, then, a relationship of mutual dependency between the novel's concern with the new, its questioning of laws and conventions, its curiosity about the strange and unusual, and its stress on geographical mobility.

Imperialism and gender

'Geographical mobility' is a rather suspiciously abstract and bloodless term. When people move around the world they meet and interact with other people with whom they may have a range of different sorts of relationship: collaborative, subservient, antagonistic, competitive or exploitative. The travel experiences of a tourist are not those of a refugee; those of a soldier are not those of an ambassador. The modern novel emerged in a world in which relationships between peoples were certainly not of an exclusively collaborative or equal type; by the end of the seventeenth century, Europe was already some way into those processes of exploitation and repression which we know as colonialism and imperialism.

Firdous Azim has pointed out that from the moment of its birth the novel enjoyed an 'imperialist heritage', one which is visible both in its themes and in the problematic nature of its status: '[t]he novel becomes a form dealing with adventures in far-off lands, Oroonoko and Robinson Crusoe on the one hand, and the sexual adventures of bold and courageous women at home – Zara, Rivella, Moll Flanders and Roxana, on the other' (Azim, 1993, 21). (We might add that Moll Flanders's adventures are not just 'at home': she also travels from England to America, where a significant portion of Defoe's novel takes place.)

'Imperialist heritage' may sound somewhat tendentious, but it is nevertheless a fact that the modern novel emerges in Western Europe at a time when this part of the world is in the early stages of a long process of imposing its will and influence – by both peaceful and non-peaceful means – on other peoples. Thus the master–slave relationship in, for example, *Robinson Crusoe* has to be seen as more than just an interesting plot detail or method of exploring character. Defoe's hero explores his own individuality in a number of ways, but one that is of defining importance to this novel, as well as to the experience of its author and his or her fellow citizens, is the imposition of an individual and collective will on the inhabitants of other lands. Crusoe discovers who he is – *makes* his identity – in part by establishing Friday's subordination to himself.

One of the most interesting chapters in Judie Newman's book *The Ballistic Bard: Postcolonial Fictions* (1995) looks at a range of recent novels that have attempted to confront, expose or reject the novel's perceived 'imperialist heritage'. Newman focuses on Jean Rhys's novel *Wide Sargasso Sea* (1966) and its attempted settling of accounts with Charlotte Brontë's *Jane Eyre* (1847), and in so doing shows how closely imperialism is related to issues of gender in the novel.

Brontë's novel has served as a mine of hidden or repressed cultural information for feminists: the very influential study, *The Madwoman in the Attic* (Gilbert and Gubar, 1979), takes its title from the situation of Rochester's concealed and incarcerated first wife, and the book presents her situation as in many ways emblematic of a much wider repression and denial of female oppression – and not just in Brontë's culture.

Jean Rhys's interest in the Caribbean aspect of Brontë's novel was doubtless related to her own problematic upbringing in Dominica and even more problematic travel to England, but her taking what has generally been experienced as a marginal or peripheral element in Brontë's novel and making it a central issue in her own intertextual reworking of *Jane Eyre* has had the effect of allowing modern readers to approach the earlier work from a revealingly different perspective.

Newman points out that Charlotte Brontë's portrayal of Bertha is designed to obliterate all sympathy for her:

> [Bertha] is described ... in terms which appeal to both racial and sexual prejudices. Her hereditary madness, which is supposedly accelerated by sexual excess, clearly reflects Victorian syphilophobia. (The nineteenth century had shifted the point of origin of syphilis to Africa.) Brontë's Bertha has 'a discoloured face', 'a savage face' with 'fearful blackened inflation' of the features: 'the lips were swelled and dark'. Successively described as a demon, a witch, a vampire, a beast, a hyena, and even an Indian Messalina, Bertha unites in one person all the available pejorative stereotypes. (Newman, 1995, 14)

Newman draws attention to the description by (Brontë's) Rochester of Jamaica as 'hell', its sounds and scenery those of 'the bottomless pit'. She also notes that when Rochester contemplates suicide he is saved by a 'wind fresh from Europe', and she reminds us that 'Penny Boumelha has observed that in *Jane Eyre* all the money comes from colonial exploitation' and that 'Jane herself gains her financial independence as a result of a legacy from an uncle in Madeira who is connected to the same firm which Mr Mason, Bertha's brother, represents in Jamaica'. Finally, Newman quotes again from Penny Boumelha, and provides us with a phrase very similar to one already taken from Firdous Azim. For Boumelha, Rhys's vindication of Brontë's 'madwoman' serves to display and to criticize 'the legacy of imperialism concealed in the heart of every English gentleman's castle' (14; for Penny Boumelha's comments, see Boumelha, 1988, 111–22). It also serves to demonstrate that inequalities associated with imperialism and colonialism are intertwined with inequalities of gender.

Cultural imperialism and the novel

There is another, rather different, way in which the novel can be seen as an 'imperialist' genre. William B. Warner has noted that, as the producer of the greatest number and variety of fictions, 'France of the seventeenth and early eighteenth centuries is positioned as something of a "Hollywood" for romances and novels'. Europeans, Africans and Asians are today generally much more familiar with parts of the culture of the United States than Americans are familiar with European, African or Asian culture. In like manner, as the novel conquered European culture in the late eighteenth and nineteenth centuries, so too did ideas, attitudes – ideologies – associated not now solely with France but with England too, succeed in influencing and even dominating the cultures of Europe. Franco Moretti puts it thus:

> [I]n the crucial century between 1750 and 1850 the consequence of ccntralization is that in most European countries the majority of novels are, quite simply, *foreign* books. Hungarian, Italian, Danish, Greek readers familiarize themselves with the new form through French and English novels: and so, inevitably, French and English novels become *models to be imitated*. (Moretti, 1998, 187)

In his *Atlas of the European Novel 1800–1900* (1998), Moretti provides powerful evidence in support of the thesis that by the nineteenth century the novel had consolidated a cultural dominance that was based in the centres of political and economic power in Europe – France and Britain. Not only does the novel come to dominate the bookshelf both in the private house and in the public library from the late eighteenth century onwards (to the dismay, as Moretti reports, of nineteenth-century library committees), but novels set in, and emanating from, the powerful urban centres of major European powers – especially France and England – tend to dominate that increasingly large amount of shelving set aside for fiction. Moretti comments:

> Be it mid eighteenth-century Britain ... or mid nineteenth-century Italy ... the message is the same: the novel is *the most centralized of all literary genres*. And its centralization increases with the passage of time. ...
>   Because, first, the novel closes European literature to all external influences: it strengthens, and perhaps it even establishes its *Europeanness*. But then this most European of forms proceeds to deprive most of Europe of all creative autonomy: two cities, London and Paris, rule the entire continent for over a century, publishing half (if not more) of all European novels. It's a ruthless, unprecedented *centralization* of European literature. (Moretti, 1998, 165, 186)

We must conclude that if the novel is significantly the *product* of social change on the national level and cultural influence on the international one, at the same time it becomes one of the most important and powerful *tools* of cultural influence both nationally and internationally.

For whom does the novel speak today?

Although I will consider the impact of the electronic media on fiction later in this book, most works of fiction are still read in printed form, and even if this situation changes (as it seems very likely it *will* change), many of the points following apply as much to electronic as to printed texts. Indeed, access to books presents at present far fewer problems to the very poor than does access to electronic texts. Printing involves not just the technical and economic means to produce and circulate books but also a universal or at least widespread literacy that comes from a highly developed system of public education. Generally speaking, where literacy is not universal in a culture, more men than women are taught how to read and write. In those countries which have recently emerged from colonial rule not only may education be closed to many, but much of the publishing business is controlled by foreign, often multinational, companies. Even when high levels of literacy are established in postcolonial countries, education systems have frequently been built up by colonial or imperialist powers and modelled upon European or North American lines. It is not so very long ago that little of the literature read by the student of English in many newly independent African countries was actually written by Africans.

Issues such as these have led a number of commentators to ask not just whether the novel as a genre is non-collective, 'Western' and masculinist, but whether the novel is or has been used as a weapon of ideological propaganda or control by those cultures within which it emerged and from which it allegedly took its defining characteristics. These questions – or accusations – are of course linked: the implication is clearly that the novel can be used as an ideological or political weapon precisely because those characteristics which distinguish it reflect and even celebrate a pattern of human relationships first identified and acclaimed in the late seventeenth and early eighteenth centuries in Western Europe.

What force does this challenge to the novel have? It seems to me that it is quite wrong to treat a novel written today in Africa or India as just no more than a European import. As a starting point, consider the following words by the Indian novelist Mulk Raj Anand. They compose part of his introduction to a collection of Indian fairy tales:

> The stories contained in this volume were told me by my mother and
> my aunts during my childhood. The primary inspiration to retell them,
> therefore, came from the nostalgic memories of the hour when 'once
> upon a time' began and when one's eyes closed long before the story
> had ended.
>
> But I also had in mind the fact that in the old stories of our country
> lay the only links with our broken tradition. I fancied that only by going
> back to the form of these stories, told by mother to son, and son to
> son, could we evolve a new pattern for the contemporary short story.

Of course, the modern short story is a highly developed folk tale if it is a folk tale at all. But a revival of the short story form ... seemed a fit occasion to relate it to its more primitive antecedents which, surprisingly enough, seem to lie in the sources of the sheaf of tales which I have gleaned. At any rate, I must confess that although I have taken in much new psychology into my own writing of the short story, I have always tried to approximate to the technique of the folk tale, and the influence of these fairy stories has always been very deep on my own fiction.

These fairy stories can, therefore, be read not only by children, but by those adults who have not forgotten the child in them. And, however foreign they may seem to non-Indians, in their atmosphere and effect, I offer them here, not as something completely alien to the Western peoples, but as familiar and well known themes to set beside the fairy tales which they have read in their childhoods, because there has been much international traffic in folk lore between India and the West through traders, travellers, gypsies, craftsmen and crusaders, and many of the stories current abroad have their source in the same springs in which these stories have their origin. (Anand, 1946, 7–8)

The comments are interesting for a number of reasons. First, because they remind us that just as a tradition of fictional tales emerged and established itself in Europe before literacy became widespread, so too can comparable traditions be found in those cultures and societies which were on the receiving end of colonialism and imperialism. Second, because, as Anand points out, the stories with which he is concerned strike non-Indian readers as both 'foreign' and familiar. Oral prose fiction traditions may all share some common or familial features, but they are also possessed of that which is culture-specific, and thus, to the extent that such traditions inform a new tradition of novel writing and reading, this new tradition will also have something that is its alone, something native to its own culture. Third, because, as Anand also points out, 'there has been much international traffic in folk lore', and although the emerging novel may reflect the inequalities and injustices of its mother-culture, it is also the resting place for many perspectives which are critical of that mother-culture and its dominant values. Indeed, as the phrase 'dominant values' may remind us, the societies from which the early novel emerged were by no means monolithic; they contained minority views, 'faultlines', opposi-tions and contradictions.

Anand's collection of fairy tales was published in 1946, in the dying years of British India. (Indian readers of the collection were probably more imme-diately aware of what the discreet term 'broken tradition' referred to than are present-day European readers.) Anand knew as well as anyone what imperialism and colonialism were capable of, but he also knew that in addition to the crusad-ers and the traders there were also travellers, gypsies and craftsmen moving from country to country, and that the commerce was not all one way. The gypsies came originally from India, and were certainly part of Western European culture by the eighteenth century, although of course neither a dominant nor a privileged part.

In short, not only can a novelist writing in newly independent lands incorporate powerful elements of native storytelling tradition into his or her work, but in important senses the European tradition of the novel is itself by no means exclusively European.

Where does this leave us in our quest to determine the extent to which the genre of the novel is or is not value-neutral? It seems to me to be arguable that the novel is probably less well suited to the expression of collective or communal experiences and beliefs than are some other forms such as orally delivered poetry or drama. Not only do such performance arts involve a direct contact between artist-performer and audience, thus allowing both for collective response and for collective feedback from audience to creator, but the drama also allows for the dramatized presentation of distinctive voices – often simultaneously. Now the skilled novelist can resist the individualistic and monologic tendencies of the genre, and indeed I have already referred to Mikhail Bakhtin's belief that the novel is naturally dialogic (see p. 13). In my comments on the narrative technique used by Lewis Grassic Gibbon in his *A Scots Quair* (see p. 158), I suggest that this technique is designed to help us to experience a working-class collectivity and that it largely succeeds. Nevertheless, it is arguable that the representation of such collectivity is more difficult for the novelist than it is for the dramatist. What is more, a culture whose vital life is more closely associated with oral expression and an oral tradition than with written expression and a written tradition may find more natural expression in the drama or poetic recital than in the printed pages of a book.

Having said all this it seems to me that, if we are asking the crude question 'Is the novel essentially a bourgeois, individualist and "Western" (or imperialist) genre?', it is perhaps more productive to look at issues of tradition and economic control than of innate generic identity – in other words, to focus more upon differences of culture and on socio-economic issues than on the inherent formal or technical qualities of the genre. Indeed, so far as the latter are concerned I should repeat that although the novel does seem to be generically predisposed in the direction of representing individual experience, especially when that experience is that of a socially and geographically mobile individual, it is also the case that the novel is a genre which seems to survive by permanently revolutionizing itself, in the light of which fact it is dangerous to talk of what the novel cannot do because of any innate generic identity.

Snatching the pen

If we turn to the issues of tradition and economic control we do I think see how particular values and perspectives may be associated with the genre. To explore this issue I would like to take two novels by the Kenyan novelist Ngũgĩ

Wa Thiong'o: his first published novel, *Weep Not, Child*, which appeared in 1964, and *Devil on the Cross*, which was published first in Gĩkũyũ in 1980 and then in the author's own English translation in 1982. In fact, when *Weep Not, Child* was first published, its author's name was given as 'James Ngugi'. Both books were published by Heinemann, now a part of the Reed Elsevier conglomerate.

Weep Not, Child is a wonderful first novel and was welcomed as such on its initial publication. Re-read today from the perspective of Ngũgĩ's later work, the novel nonetheless gives the sense of a writer having to adapt to the requirements of a tradition and a publishing situation which are partly alien to him and which restrict his freedom of movement. Take the following short passage from the opening pages of the novel:

> There was only one road that ran right across the land. It was long and broad and shone with black tar, and when you travelled along it on hot days you saw little lakes ahead of you. But when you went near, the lakes vanished, to appear again a little farther ahead. Some people called them the devil's waters because they deceived you and made you more thirsty if your throat was already dry. And the road which ran across the land and was long and broad had no beginning and no end. At least, few people knew of its origin. Only if you followed it it would take you to the big city and leave you there while it went beyond to the unknown, perhaps joining the sea. Who made the road? Rumour had that it came with the white men and some said that it was rebuilt by the Italian prisoners during the Big War that was fought away from here.
> (Ngugi, 1972, 5–6)

It seems clear that this passage attempts to present the reader both with the consciousness of Njoroge, the main character of the novel, and with a sense of the, as it were, collective consciousness of Njoroge's people, as well as of the immediate history of his land and culture. Such multiple perspectives are not uncommon in the novel, especially in novels which deal with 'suppressed' or oppressed groups whose lives and experiences are sharply different from those of the writer's intended or expected readers. (Again, my comments on Lewis Grassic Gibbon's narrative technique on p. 159 are relevant to the present discussion, not least with regard to both writers' use of the collective 'you' to affirm and represent shared and communal knowledge.) What the passage gives us is a statement of what, because it is shared cultural knowledge, is actually unlikely ever to be *stated* unless an outsider asks the right questions, and so putting it in Njoroge's unspoken but verbalized thoughts is slightly jarring.

Who is the implied reader (see the Glossary)? Ngũgĩ seems very conscious of the fact that many of the first readers of this novel would know nothing about Kenya or Kenyans, nothing about the history or culture of this part of Africa. Passages such as the one which I have quoted seem in part designed to impart knowledge to such individuals. Writing a novel, in English, for an international publisher, Ngũgĩ must have felt the pressure of his potential readers' ignorance in a way in which a middle-class European of his age and generation would not have done. This may help to explain a stiffness at certain points of the narrative of *Weep Not, Child*.

> Ngotho often wondered if he had really done well by his sons. If he and his generation had failed, he was ready to suffer for it. … But whatever Ngotho had been prepared to do to redeem himself in the eyes of his children, he would not be ordered by a son to take an oath. Not that he objected to it in principle. After all, oath-taking as a means of binding a person to a promise was a normal feature of tribal life. But to be given by a son! That would have violated against his standing as a father.
> (Ngugi, 1972, 83–4)

In this passage it seems to me that the sentence 'After all, oath-taking as a means of binding a person to a promise was a normal feature of tribal life' also jars somewhat: it is sandwiched by sentences which are in Free Indirect Discourse, specifically in represented thought (see p. 126), but it cannot itself be read in this way. This is an authorial interpolation, an explanatory detail provided for the benefit of the reader who is not familiar with the 'tribal life' in question. Writing about that part of Charles Dickens's novel *Bleak House* which is narrated by Esther Summerson, E.M. Forster comments in his *Aspects of the Novel* (first published in 1927) that even when Esther is ostensibly telling the story Dickens may snatch the pen from her and take notes himself (Forster, 1962, 86). I have a sense of something similar happening in Ngũgĩ's first novel.

By the time of Ngũgĩ's *Devil on the Cross* (1982) we feel that this writer is possessed of much greater self-confidence. It is neither accidental nor irrelevant to the argument in hand that this is a novel that is thematically very much concerned with the issues of cultural independence and cultural subservience. In the author's own English translation, words which appeared in English in the original Gĩkũyũ version of the novel are italicized, so that the text of the novel gives a sense of cultural struggle, as the author's very language is invaded by English words and phrases. One of the characters – Gatuĩria – actually finds it hard to speak in Gĩkũyũ without peppering his speech with English words: ironically enough he is a 'junior research fellow in African culture', and to double the irony he uses English in order to describe his post.

This is a novel in which we feel that the novelist's technical assurance is directly related to his sense of who he is writing for and why. Where culture-specific details have to be provided for European readers they are given in foot-notes rather than being smuggled into the thoughts or speech of the characters. The novel speaks freely from within a culture to those sharing the culture: its dedication 'To all Kenyans struggling against the neo-colonial stage of imperialism' provides convincing evidence concerning the readers for whom Ngũgĩ intended the work. The whole theme of cultural imperialism is foregrounded in the novel, and this allows Ngũgĩ the freedom to use the resources of his own culture without self-consciousness or a concern that this might not be proper or understood. For all that he is presented as a victim of cultural imperialism, Gatuĩria is aware of the process that is oppressing him and he bemoans the loss of an indigenous cultural tradition: 'Our stories, our riddles, our songs, our customs, our traditions, everything about our national heritage has been lost to us' (Ngũgĩ, 1987, 59).

Devil on the Cross does not just propose such a case in abstract terms: by incorporating the force and vitality of such indigenous cultural and narrative traditions into its own telling, the novel also enacts a process of cultural self-assertion and revolt. It is very difficult to illustrate this by means of selective quotation, because the shifts between more traditional realism and the fantastic, which are mediated through a range of narrative techniques including 'standard' third-person narrative, riddles and sayings, dance-songs and verses, and other forms unfamiliar to European readers such as that of the 'verse-chanting competition', have a cumulative effect which is lost in brief extracts. The result is to revolutionize the genre within which Ngũgĩ is working and to open the novel to traditions which are certainly 'un-Western', collective rather than individualistic, holistic rather than fragmented. What the novel is today it is partly because of its enrichment by writers such as Ngũgĩ. This is not to deny that literary forms such as that of the novel are involved in international processes of economic, political and cultural conflict, repression and domination, nor that the novel may be better suited to the representation of the individual than the collective consciousness, and to processes of linear development than to complexities of simultaneity and reciprocal interaction. Nor is it to deny that a print-based genre is better adapted to the expressive needs of a literate culture than it is to those of an oral one. But the example of a magnificent novel such as *Devil on the Cross* goes to show that the novel can adapt to and incorporate the strengths of rich oral and communal traditions – whether these are those of Kenya or of the Scottish peasantry and industrial working class about whom Lewis Grassic Gibbon writes.

Topics for discussion

↪ If the novel rises with the middle class, is it a middle-class genre?

↪ To what extent do romance traditions survive in the novel?

↪ Must the novelist choose between 'life' and 'pattern'?

↪ How does silent, private consumption condition novel-reading?

↪ Is the novel one of the first examples of cultural imperialism?

Chapter 3
Shorter fiction

Preview

This chapter deals with:

- ↪ the short story and the novella as recent categories
- ↪ the taint of commercialism and 'definition by length'
- ↪ the 'anecdotal' and the 'epiphanic' short story
- ↪ compression, suggestiveness and the short story
- ↪ the distinctiveness of the novella

I have already suggested that our familiar tripartite division of prose fiction into the novel, the short story and the novella is one that simplifies a more complex and varied reality, and it is as well to start this chapter with a warning against allowing a use of these categories (more popular perhaps with academics than with writers or the common reader) to obscure the variety of forms open to the writer of prose fiction – both today and in the past. Moreover, the terms 'short story' and 'novella' are by no means as widely used or as unambiguous as is the term 'novel'. Although the term 'novella', from which the English 'novel' descends, can be traced back to the Italian, use of this term today to designate a prose fiction that is shorter than a novel but longer than a short story descends from nineteenth-century German usage. The term is little used outside schools and universities. The term 'short story' is more widely understood, but it too is problematic in ways that – for all of the issues of definition that I have discussed in the previous chapter – the term 'novel' is not. Graham Good provides a useful summary of these terminological problems:

> Short fiction terminology is extremely varied and often inconsistent. The word 'novella' is gradually gaining acceptance in English among publishers, writers, and latterly critics, to denote a fictional prose narrative of 'medium' length. This usage is supplementing rather than supplanting 'short story,' which has been firmly established since the turn of the century. The older terms 'tale' and simply 'story' were still employed by writers like [Henry] James and [Joseph] Conrad to refer to any narrative shorter than a novel, from about five to a hundred or more pages. (Good, 1994, 148)

In fact, Conrad used the term 'tale' rather more promiscuously than this suggests: his longest novel, *Nostromo*, is sub-titled 'A Tale of the Seaboard'. One of the reasons why the terms 'short story' and 'novella' were pressed into use by writers and critics from (especially) the early days of the twentieth century is almost certainly because alternative terms such as 'tale' were just too elastic.

In an essay published in 1998, 'Beginnings: The Origins and Art of the Short Story', Joyce Carol Oates comments directly on the dangers of too restrictive or too numerical a definition of types of short fiction.

> Formal definitions of the short story are commonplace, yet there is none quite democratic enough to accommodate an art that includes so much variety and an art that so readily lends itself to experimentation and idiosyncratic voices. Perhaps length alone should be the sole criterion? Whenever critics try to impose other, more substantial strictures on the genre (as on any genre) too much work is excluded.
>
> Yet length itself is problematic. No more than 10,000 words? Why not then 10,500? 11,000? Where, in fact, does a short story end and a novella begin? (Tolstoy's 'The Death of Ivan Ilych' can be classified as both.) (Martin, 2006, 1563)

Behind the search for terms is a sense that length does make a difference, and that although the cake of fiction can be cut into slices of varying sizes, a tripartite division accords well with our experience of reading fictional works varying from (say) the 1,824 words of James Joyce's 'Eveline' through the 42,700 words of Henry James's *The Turn of the Screw* to the 168,000 words of *Nostromo* (and there are many novels that are longer by far than *Nostromo*). Although not all commentators are happy with these terms or the categories they propose, I will use them in what follows to structure my comments since the general acceptance of the tripartite division between novel, novella and short story is indicative of a certain utility and convenience. To take a random but not unrepresentative example, Hortense Calisher's *Extreme Magic: A Novella and Other Stories* (1964) consists of six stories ranging from 12 to 25 pages, and the title story 'Extreme Magic' which is 83 pages long.

Most if not all of the novels written since 1800 that you are asked to study will have been written by authors who had a relatively clear sense of what a novel was. But the same cannot be said of the short story or, especially, the novella. I suggest below that it can be helpful to think of works such as D.H. Lawrence's *The Fox* and Joseph Conrad's *Heart of Darkness* as novellas, but to the best of my knowledge neither of these writers actually used the term 'novella', certainly not to describe these works. Mary Doyle Springer has suggested that '[t]he kinds of works which are now recognized as novellas began to arise in the nineteenth century' (1975, 8), but the application of the term 'novella' to these works only becomes common in English-speaking cultures in the 1970s.

A letter written on 7 January 1902 by Conrad to his publisher illustrates some of these terminological issues. In the letter Conrad outlines a plan for a new piece and comments: 'Of course it shall be "fiction" in the same sense that *Youth* is fiction. Some critics, at the time, called it a short story!' (Karl and Davies, 1986, 368). 'Youth' is only about 13,400 words long, and my guess is that when it is included on a school or university reading list today it is categorized unproblematically as a short story. Conrad clearly views this term with disdain, and the titles of his shorter works are given a range of other sub-headings: 'a tale', 'a story', 'a narrative', 'a sketch', 'a memory', 'an episode' – but never 'a short story'. It is very likely that Conrad liked the term 'tale' because it linked works of shorter fiction with a tradition of oral narrative (many of his works are presented as oral tellings), and that he disliked the term 'short story' because of its association with the commercial and the popular.

Conrad's contemporary and friend Henry James introduces questions about the nature of fiction into his own works in an indirect and relatively unintrusive manner on occasions. His evocatively entitled story 'The Story in it', for example, has a Mr Voyt comment to two female conversational partners: 'Behind these words we use – the adventure, the novel, the drama, the romance, the situation, in short, as we most comprehensively say – behind them all stands the same sharp fact that they all, in their different ways, represent' (Edel, 1964, 319). Voyt may not be the voice of Henry James, but he does seem to reflect his creator's view that what these different sub-genres have in common is more important than what distinguishes them from one another. According to Dieter Meindl, James generally preferred the greater length of the novella (which he termed the nouvelle) to the short story, but he adds:

> James did not care for the designations now commonly used for the intermediary narrative genre: long short story, novella, or novelette. For him, a short novel would be something still longer, an affair of some 200 pages like *The Spoils of Poynton* (1897). As witnessed by the title of the New York Edition, he used the term 'tale' for all his short fiction,

including several texts exceeding one hundred pages, such as 'The Turn of the Screw.' A really short story or short story proper – for example his darkly comic, Boston-based 'Europe' (1899; 19 pages nevertheless) – would be called an 'anecdote' by James. For James, however, the anecdote is nonetheless generally entwined with the nouvelle, as the latter has for him an anecdotal basis. (Meindl, 2008, 32)

Not surprisingly, the idiosyncratic (although not thereby uninteresting) terminology preferred by Conrad and James has not been generally accepted. Nevertheless, we have to be aware that behind the simplicity of our own tripartite division many other distinctions and divisions can be found.

The short story

Commercialism and size

Two spectres haunt the short story. The first of these involves a reaction against what the critic Norman Friedman, in an article entitled 'What Makes a Short Story Short?' (first published in 1958), has called the taint of commercialism – the belief that the short story is a debased form to which writers descended only in order to earn money (Friedman, 1976, 131). (Short works of fiction published in magazines in the late nineteenth and early twentieth centuries generally earned far more per word for their authors than did long novels.) The second involves the fear that perhaps all that distinguishes the short story from longer works of prose fiction *is* its shortness, rather than any more aesthetically interesting characteristic. Both of these spectres have made serious writers and serious critics – those who share an interest in raising the status and the dignity of short fiction – suspicious of the term. The now celebrated short-story writer Elizabeth Bowen, introducing in 1949 a new edition of her first collection *Encounters*, which was first published in 1923, makes a representative comment.

> Decision to fall back upon the short story, on the part of a poet *manquée*, would today seem obvious. In those days, the retreat was more uncertain; the position of the short story was anomalous. It was not yet – I think I am right in saying – recognised as 'a form.' There had appeared so far, that is to say, little constructive-critical interest in the short story's possibilities and problems. (Bowen, 1949, viii)

Behind such attitudes lies a strong tradition of usage that links the short story with more unambiguously commercial works of the sort associated with the American writer O. Henry, works that appealed to a popular market and that were characterized by, among other things, unexpected endings of an ironic or whimsical variety. One recent commentator – William O'Rourke – has commented on the revealing fact that 'as fewer commercial magazines publish it and the general public continues to avoid it, the short story rises in critical favor, not only among professors but among literary reviewers' (O'Rourke, 1989, 199). Then there is shortness. Norman Friedman has stated the problem bluntly, referring to 'the only observable commonality which all short stories share and which does indeed separate them from novellas and novels – their shortness' (Friedman, 1989, 24).

However, beyond such debates about terminology there are other arguments about types of shorter fiction, and I would now like to turn to some of these.

Oral or written? Traditional or modern?

Arguments as to whether the short story is the product of a long tradition of oral storytelling or a modern form associated with magazine publication are clearly intertwined with arguments about whether it is a very old or a very modern genre. In a commentary entitled 'Writing Short Stories', Flannery O'Connor suggests that '[l]ike a river fed by countless small streams, the modern short story derives from a multiplicity of sources' (Martin, 2006, 1563), and the fact that some of these sources are very old and others more recent may make it hard to fix the short story's date of birth unequivocally.

If, as I have claimed, the novel is very much the child of print, one might assume that at least superficial resemblances between the short story and oral narratives – tales, anecdotes and so on – might suggest that the short story has much older parents, which is in part what Mulk Raj Anand implies (see p. 40). It is certainly the case that the length of the typical short story makes it possible to associate it with a single oral telling, and there is no doubt that many writers have seized upon this possibility. (Note that this also means that the typical short story can be *read* without pause.)

In an essay entitled 'A Theory of the Short Story' that was first published in 1917, James Cooper Lawrence confidently asserts that '[t]he more we look into the matter the more evident it becomes that the limits and distinguishing characteristics of the short story as we know it today are the limits and distinguishing characteristics of the spoken story as it has existed from the beginning of time' (Lawrence, 1976, 61). Certainly the man or woman talking to a group of listeners, the individual reminiscing to friends, the *speaker* rather than the *writer*, the tale as heard rather than the tale as read – all of these admittedly fictional narrative devices have appealed to writers wishing to conceal or qualify the situation of the lonely writer reaching out through the mediation of print to a similarly lonely reader. The ostensibly spoken narrative allows the writer access to colloquial speech, to those hesitations and unwilling disclosures that writing conceals, to the collectivity of a listening group, and to exchanges between teller and (fictional) listeners (see the discussion of *skaz* in the Glossary). Longer novels can be presented as spoken rather than written, but the conventions start to creak as the pages mount up. Joseph Conrad reacted to criticism of the impossibility of most of *Lord Jim* being delivered as one continuous oral account, but his protestations are not wholly convincing.

Many recent commentators have, however, argued that the short story is a modern form rather than one with a venerable history. Introducing *The Faber Book of Modern Short Stories* in 1936, Elizabeth Bowen states bluntly that the short story 'is a young art: as we know it, it is the child of this century. Poetic tautness and clarity are so essential to it that it may be said to stand at the edge of prose; in its use of action it is nearer to drama than to the novel' (Bowen, 1976, 152). Frank O'Connor, one of the most influential theorists of the short story, also resists associating the short story with the centuries-long tradition of the spoken tale. He argues that the short story, like the novel, 'is a modern art form; that is to say, it represents, better than poetry or drama, our own attitude to life'.

This is not to say that O'Connor believes the short story to be merely a truncated novel: 'even from its beginnings, the short story has functioned in a quite different way from the novel' (O'Connor, 1963, 13). In his attempt to describe the nature of this difference, O'Connor is thought-provoking if, on occasions, eccentric. He suggests that, unlike the novel, the short story does not encourage identification between the reader and a character, claiming that the short story has never had a hero but has, instead, had 'a submerged population group'. He further claims that there is always in the short story a 'sense of outlawed figures wandering about the fringes of society' along with 'an intense awareness of human loneliness' (1963, 17–18, 19). This argument implicitly extends the claim that the short story is a modern form, as the outlaw figure and a concentration on human loneliness are both very much part of the modernist movement (about which I will talk more in the next chapter).

Fragments and wholes

Another Irish critic, Sean O'Faolain, argued in a book on the short story first published in 1948 that there can be no development of character in the short story – a point of which Henry James was, O'Faolain proposes, unaware (O'Faolain, 1972, 221). Of course, characters in a short story may undergo shocking experiences and they may experience dramatic illuminations, but these are, nonetheless, different from that gradual development of character that we can observe in a full-length novel. For O'Faolain, at the heart of the short story has to reside the writer's ability to make fragments of experience speak for the whole of life (185). The suggestion is an interesting one, and it again associates the short story with the development of literary modernism, from let us say around the start of the twentieth century. Valerie Shaw links 'the rise of the short story in England' with 'the emergence of the characteristic figure of the modern artist, and with anti-Victorianism in its widest sense' (Shaw, 1983, 4), while Suzanne Ferguson, in an article entitled 'The Rise of the Short Story in the Hierarchy of Genres', argues that 'the preeminence of the short story as a modernist genre grew out of the modern, highbrow audience's acceptance of fragmentation as an accurate model of the world, with a concomitant focus on "being" – as in Woolf's "moments of being" – rather than the "becoming" that characterizes the plot of the Romantic and the Victorian novel' (Ferguson, 1989, 191).

Discussion of such Woolfian 'moments' very often involves use of the word 'epiphany'. In the Christian tradition this word has been used to signify the manifestation of God to humanity; the feast of the Epiphany on 6 January celebrates the manifestation of Christ to the Gentiles. The term developed a specific literary sense in the course of the nineteenth century, and in his initial version of *A Portrait of the Artist as a Young Man*, then named *Stephen Hero*, James Joyce used the term in a secular sense to denote those experiences in which the full identity of the commonest object is displayed suddenly and completely.

For a writer such as James Joyce, for example, the depiction of an 'epiphany' can be as effectively achieved in one of the short stories collected in *Dubliners* (1914) as in the over 700 pages of *Ulysses*. The economy of the epiphany inevitably makes it attractive to the writer with limited space at his or her disposal. But do *all* short stories have this intimate relationship with the epiphany?

The 'anecdotal' and the 'epiphanic' short story

In an essay entitled 'The Debunking Rhythm of the American Short Story', Thomas M. Leitch reports that short-story theorists have continued to distinguish between two different kinds of – or structures for – the short story, which he terms the 'anecdotal' and the 'epiphanic':

> The anecdotal story, typified by Hawthorne's 'The Birthmark,' Poe's 'The Gold-Bug,' and the Sherlock Holmes stories of Arthur Conan Doyle, presents an Aristotelian action with a beginning, middle and end; the epiphanic story, represented by Chekhov's 'The Lady with the Dog,' Joyce's 'Ivy Day In the Committee Room,' and Crane's Civil War stories, adumbrates a fictional world not by developing a plot involving purposive agents but by unfolding particular sensations or emotions and proceeding to a climactic revelation that does not necessarily take the form of a complete overt action. (Leitch, 1989, 130–1)

So far as Leitch's two sorts of story are concerned, the much-praised American short story writer Flannery O'Connor, in an essay entitled 'Writing Short Stories', makes it clear that her preference is for what Leitch terms the anecdotal short story.

> A good short story should not have less meaning than a novel, nor should its action be less complete. Nothing essential to the main experience can be left out of a short story. All the action has to be satisfactorily accounted for in terms of motivation, and there has to be a beginning, a middle, and an end, though not necessarily in that order. (1558)

As can be seen, however, there is a kick in the tail of this comment: the short story, O'Connor agrees, must have what Leitch dubs 'an Aristotelian action' with its standard tripartite division, but O'Connor reserves the right to juggle the order of the standard and conventionally successive components.

It is worth thinking about O'Connor's witty (but fundamentally serious) point in relation to one of the examples cited by Leitch – Arthur Conan Doyle's Sherlock Holmes stories. In one of the classic stories, 'Silver Blaze', we do indeed move through a number of apparently conventional stages. The story opens *in medias res* (see the Glossary).

> 'I am afraid, Watson, that I shall have to go,' said Holmes, as we sat down to our breakfast one morning.
> 'Go! – Where to?'
> 'To Dartmoor – to King's Pyland.'
> I was not surprised. (Doyle, 13)

Holmes has read in the newspapers of a mysterious affair involving the apparent abduction of a top racing horse (Silver Blaze), and the murder of the trainer of the stables, John Straker. As Holmes and Watson travel by train to Devonshire they recapitulate the known facts of the case (thus conveniently informing the reader of these). On arrival they talk to the police officer in charge as they travel with him from the station, and to those connected to the stables when they arrive there. Holmes inspects the localities associated with the crime, and visits an unpleasant neighbour, Silas Brown, who is cowed by something that Holmes whispers to him. At this point Holmes announces that he and Watson will travel back to London, thereby convincing the victims of the crime that he has failed to solve it, even though he assures the owner that the horse will run four days later in the Wessex Cup. Before they leave, however, he provides a response to a question from Watson that has become famous.

> 'Is there any other point to which you would wish to draw my attention?'
> 'To the curious incident of the dog in the night-time.'
> 'The dog did nothing in the night-time.'
> 'That was the curious incident,' remarked Sherlock Holmes. (34)

Note how this celebrated exchange focuses the reader's attention not on what is happening *in the characters*, but what happened in terms of *actions* the night of the assumed murder.

A short line break in the text announces a shift of scene, and we are at the Wessex Cup. Colonel Ross the owner has been prevailed upon not to withdraw his horse from the race, and indeed it appears and wins, although the Colonel is not at first convinced that it *is* his horse as its familiar markings have been obscured. After a further line break we find ourselves with Holmes and Watson in the Pullman car back to London, and Holmes explains all, revealing the significance of clues that have been available earlier on to the reader.

Back to Flannery O'Connor. If my summary of Doyle's story does indeed give us a beginning (Holmes's inability to ignore a fascinating case), a middle (his investigation of the scene of the crime) and an end (his successful production of the missing horse and explanation of the trainer's death), it also gives us the same sequence in reverse order: first an end (the unsolved crime), then a middle (the events that occurred immediately before the crime, about which Holmes learns on Dartmoor, next the crime itself, describes by Holmes in the Pullman car) and finally a beginning (the personal situation of John Straker that generated the whole sequence of events). Like all classic detective stories, then, 'Silver Blaze' makes a particular sort of use of the double chronology of prose narrative (see p. 6); it consists of *two* sequences – the one involving the solution of a mystery, and the one involving the sequence of events that constitute the mystery.

Crime scene → Investigation → Solution
Motivation → Planning and crime → Crime scene

It is the laminating of these two sequences in an intriguing manner that constitutes the skill of the writer of detective stories. What satisfies the reader at the end of the story is a sense of having followed a set of cause-and-effect relationships such that everything clicks together, like a successfully assembled furniture flatpack. Indeed, at the end of the story we are able to combine these two sequences into a single, linear sequence.

Motivation → Planning and crime → Crime scene → Investigation → Solution

But actually *telling* the story in such a sequence would furnish the reader with no fun at all. O'Connor is right, that even in the 'anecdotal' short story 'beginning, middle, and end' do not necessarily have to be in that order.

Thomas M. Leitch is also correct in pointing out that this sort of story creates a fictional world for the reader 'by developing a plot involving purposive agents'. These purposive agents do not, as in the 'epiphanic' short story, unfold 'particular sensations or emotions', proceeding then 'to a climactic revelation that does not necessarily take the form of a complete overt action'. Holmes and Watson are the same throughout the story, indeed they are more or less the same throughout all of Doyle's Sherlock Holmes stories. The stories are *formulaic* to the extent that, admittedly with small twists and variations, they present the reader with a pattern that is repeated again and again. And this pattern has little concern with changes or subtleties in the inner lives of the characters.

Not all 'anecdotal' stories are equally formulaic, and I should add that those of Flannery O'Connor are certainly not. But they do tend to present a sharp contrast to the sorts of story that Leitch dubs 'epiphanic'. Significantly, of the examples he gives, two (James Joyce and Stephen Crane) are leading figures in the movement known as *modernism* (see p. 69), while the third, Anton Chekhov, can be seen as a precursor of modernism. Martin Seymour-Smith has noted that as a story writer Chekhov 'depends not on plot or surprise ... but on atmosphere and the captivation of the sense of a whole life in just a single of its moments' (Seymour-Smith, 1973, 937) – the latter quality precisely what we can term an epiphanic focus. In my discussion of modernism in the chapter following I devote some time to analysing a classic modernist story, James Joyce's 'Eveline', a work that exemplifies the epiphanic short story as well as typifies certain key qualities of modernist prose fiction. After you have read this analysis you can consider to what extent Leitch's division between the anecdotal and the epiphanic short story is worth maintaining.

The short-story cycle

Not all short stories are published in magazines – or at least, not only in magazines. Some of the most important examples of the short story owe part of their force to publication in single-volume collections. The title of James Joyce's *Dubliners* (1914), for example, clearly signals that the different stories contained in the volume have something in common, and that the volume as a whole says something about a city and its inhabitants. As many commentators have pointed out, the opening paragraph of 'The Sisters', the opening story of *Dubliners*, has the youthful first-person narrator musing over three words that prepare the reader for themes that recur throughout the collection as a whole. All of the stories collected in Angela Carter's *The Bloody Chamber* (1979) offer disturbing blendings of traditional fairy tales and modern settings and issues. The cycle or collection allows the short-story writer to obtain that sense of an extended investigation into a particular issue or topic that the novelist can achieve in the course of a single work, and authors often plan individual short works as component parts of a larger whole.

Telling and suggesting

If the modernist short-story writer is interested in making a fragment or epiphany imply or display a larger whole, then he or she, according to Sean O'Faolain, must become adept at replacing direct *telling* by *suggesting*:

> Telling by means of suggestion or implication is one of the most important of all the modern short-story's shorthand conventions. It means that a short-story writer does not directly tell us things so much as let us guess or know them by implying them. The technical advantage is obvious. It takes a long time to tell anything directly and explicitly, it is a rather heavy-handed way of conveying information, and it does not arrest our imagination or hold our attention so firmly as when we get a subtle hint. Telling never dilates the mind with suggestion as implication does. (O'Faolain, 1972, 177)

To make his point, O'Faolain presents his readers with a splendid analysis of the opening sentence of Anton Chekhov's short story 'The Lady with the Little Dog' (in his account granted a slightly different title in English translation from the one used by Thomas M. Leitch). O'Faolain concentrates upon this opening sentence because he believes that the openings of short stories in particular demand of the author that he or she be adept at influencing the reader by means of suggestion and implication. The sentence in question reads as follows: 'It was reported that a new face had been seen on the quay; a lady with a little dog.' Here is O'Faolain's commentary:

> The amount of information conveyed in that sentence is an interesting example of the shorthand of the modern short-story. What do we gather from it? …. We gather, altogether by implication, that the scene is laid in a port. We gather that this port is a seaside resort, for ladies with little dogs do not perambulate on commercial docks. We gather that the season is fine weather – probably summer or autumn. We gather that this seaside resort is a sleepy, unfrequented little place: for one does not observe new faces at big, crowded places like Brighton or Deauville. Furthermore, the phrase 'it was reported' implies that gossip circulates in a friendly way at this sleepy resort. We gather still more. We gather that somebody has been bored and wakes up at this bit of gossip; and that we shall presently hear about him. I say 'him', because one again guesses, when it is a question of a lady, that the person most likely to be interested is a man. (O'Faolain, 1972, 177–8)

As he adds (perhaps redundantly, in view of the contrast between the length of his commentary and the length of the sentence in question!), 'we may imagine how much time it would take, and how boring it would be, to have all that told at length'.

Much of the skill of the short-story writer has to be devoted to making characters appear three dimensional in spite of the fact that we see them for only a very short period of time. In addition, care has to be taken to render atmosphere and situation convincingly. Very often the short-story writer will use something akin to shock tactics to make the reader think and respond: an unexpected ending, a dramatic unveiling, a surprising twist of plot. Many consider these to be artistically inferior techniques, less sophisticated than other means of creating depth and body in the short story. What are these means?

We have already mentioned *suggestion*, and clearly there are a number of techniques whereby we get people's imaginations racing. We should probably remember that there are two sorts of suggestion: the first when we know exactly what it is that we want the target person to think (as Iago gets Othello to imagine that Desdemona has been unfaithful without actually stating as much), and the second when a person's imagination is stimulated to be innovative and to think of things that the suggester him- or herself may never have intended. A much-quoted example of this second sort is to be found in Henry James's comment in his 'New York' Preface to a collection of tales including *The Turn of the Screw*:

> Only make the reader's general vision of evil intense enough, I said to myself – and that already is a charming job – and his own experience, his own imagination, his own sympathy (with the children) and horror (of their false friends) will supply him quite sufficiently with all the particulars. Make him *think* the evil, make him think it for himself, and you are released from weak specifications.

There seems little doubt that the second of these alternatives is potentially richer and more aesthetically rewarding, as it gives the reader's imagination a genuinely creative function.

A classic example of such suggestiveness used to full aesthetic effect is to be found at the end of James Joyce's 'The Dead' (started 1907, published 1914), the final story in his *Dubliners*. At this point of the story, the character Gabriel, in a hotel room with his sleeping wife after the annual dance held by Gabriel's aunts, is sinking into sleep. The final lines of the story read:

> A few light taps against the pane made him turn to the window. It had begun to snow again. He watched sleepily the flakes, silver and dark, falling obliquely against the lamplight. The time had come for him to set out on his journey westward. Yes, the newspapers were right: snow was general all over Ireland. It was falling on every part of the dark central plain, on the treeless hills, falling softly upon the Bog of Allen and, farther westward, softly falling into the dark mutinous Shannon waves. It was falling, too, upon every part of the lonely churchyard on the hill where Michael Furey lay buried. It lay thickly drifted on the crooked crosses and headstones, on the spears of the little gate, on the barren thorns. His soul swooned slowly as he heard the snow falling faintly through the universe and faintly falling, like the descent of their last end, upon all the living and the dead.

The suggestiveness of this very rich passage is partly a matter of inexplicitness: what for example does 'The time had come for him to set out on his journey westward' mean? We have earlier learned that Gabriel does not want to accompany his wife on a visit to the west of Ireland. Has he changed his mind, or is the reader supposed to recall that the idiom 'to go west' means to die, and to associate this with sleep as proleptic of death? This is my second sort of suggestiveness, one that is creative and open-ended rather than closed and with a single, fixed objective.

Those who have read 'The Dead' will recognize that in this final paragraph a shift to what we can call a different mode takes place; the language becomes more poetic, and the more literal meanings of certain statements are hard to determine, while at the same time there is uncertainty as to who is making them.

The ending makes extremely difficult demands on the reader, and is suggestive in a number of different ways (to take a simple example, the mention of 'crosses', 'spears' and 'barren thorns' inevitably calls the Passion of Christ to mind, a very different passion from the one experienced by Michael Furey, although one which also ended in death and which thus fixes a certain association between passion and death that has already been implied).

In addition to being suggestive, the ending is also evocative. It calls up particular states of mind and forms of experience, very often in their concrete particularity. Having said this, it is less easy to say exactly what it is that is evoked. There is a general movement in the paragraph towards a greater and greater universality, fixed in the actual mention of the word 'universe' in the last sentence. It is as if we leave Gabriel (whose consciousness we abandon as the vision becomes more and more general), and take more and more in our view. As this shift coincides with Gabriel's falling asleep, one of the experiences evoked is precisely that of falling asleep, leaving more rational, specific topics of thought and entering into a dream state that deals with more general and universal topics. Note that what I have written about this passage is necessarily tentative; if one is dealing with suggestion then interpretive certainty is no longer possible.

The last paragraph of 'The Dead' illustrates other important techniques. The use of poetic devices such as repetition and chiasmus (reversal involving the pattern 'ab ba', as in the opposition of 'falling faintly' and 'faintly falling'), symbolism (see the discussion of symbol and image starting on p. 150, which pays particular attention to the repeated references to snow in 'The Dead') and other techniques are not limited to the short story, but they very often have to carry a heavier weight in this genre to compensate for the limitations that a restriction of length places on the development of plot and character.

The novella

The novella has had less theoretical attention devoted to it than has the short story, and this is especially so in its modern and its Anglo–Saxon manifestations. In my first chapter I suggested that the novella was typically between about forty or fifty and a hundred pages long, and Mary Doyle Springer proposes a word count between 15,000 and 50,000 (Springer, 1975, 8). Use of the term 'novella' in Britain and the United States is, as I have said, relatively recent; during three years of undergraduate study of English in the early 1960s I never encountered the term at all. When I studied D.H. Lawrence's *The Fox* (1923), it was described by my lecturer as a 'short novel'.

The Fox is just over 27,000 words long – 62 printed pages in the standard edition of Lawrence's *Collected Stories*. It offers us a good test case for the need for a third generic term in addition to 'novel' and 'short story'. A 62-page work of fiction seems too short to be dubbed a novel, and of those characteristics that we associate with the short story – a lack of character development, a focus on epiphanic enlightenment or revelation rather than slow change, coverage of a very limited time span – only the moment of epiphany is to be found in *The Fox*. There is restriction: there are essentially only three characters involved in Lawrence's story, and their interaction takes place exclusively in one place. But to call *The Fox* a short story seems as misleading as to call it a novel.

In *The Fox* we meet two women in their late twenties – Banford and March – who are trying to make a success of running a farm in the years immediately following the First World War. They are not well equipped for this task, and the farm is going badly.

> One evil there was greater than any other. Bailey Farm was a little homestead, with ancient wooden barn and low-gabled farm-house, lying just one field removed from the edge of the wood. Since the war the fox was a demon. He carried off the hens under the very noses of March and Banford. Banford would start and stare through her big spectacles with all her eyes, as another squawk and flutter took place at her heels. Too late! Another white Leghorn gone. It was disheartening.

Early on in the work, March, who we have been told in the second paragraph of the tale 'would be the man about the place', goes out with a gun and falls into a sort of musing trance.

> The trees on the wood-edge were a darkish, brownish green in the full light – for it was the end of August. Beyond, the naked, copper-like shafts and limbs of the pine trees shone in the air. Nearer the rough grass, with its long, brownish stalks all agleam, was full of light. The fowls were round about – the ducks were still swimming on the pond under the pine trees. March looked at it all, saw it all, and did not see it. She heard Banford speaking to the fowls in the distance – and she did not hear. What was she thinking about? Heaven knows. Her consciousness was, as it were, held back.
>
> She lowered her eyes, and suddenly saw the fox. He was looking up at her. Her chin was pressed down, and his eyes were looking up. They met her eyes. And he knew her. She was spellbound – she knew he knew her. So he looked into her eyes, and her soul failed her. He knew her, he was not daunted.
>
> She struggled, confusedly she came to herself, and saw him making off, with slow leaps over some fallen boughs, slow, impudent jumps. Then he glanced over his shoulder, and ran smoothly away. She saw his brush held smooth like a feather, she saw his white buttocks twinkle. And he was gone, softly, soft as the wind.

Soon after this epiphanic, revelatory episode occurs, a young man – Henry Grenfel – chances upon the farm and ends up staying to work for the women. As soon as she encounters him, March sees him in a particular way.

> The youth stared at them without changing colour or expression. If he had any expression, besides a slight baffled look of wonder, it was one of sharp curiosity concerning the two girls; sharp, impersonal curiosity, the curiosity of that round young head.
>
> But to March he was the fox. Whether it was the thrusting forward of his head, or the glisten of fine whitish hairs on the ruddy cheek-bones, or the bright, keen eyes, that can never be said: but the boy was to her the fox, and she could not see him otherwise.

As this identification is strengthened, so too is another one: 'Meanwhile he was talking softly and smoothly to Banford, who loved nothing so much as gossip, and who was full of perky interest, like a bird.'

I will stop at this point, and suggest that if my account has whetted your appetite then you get hold of Lawrence's tale and read it. The desire to read on is aroused less by what any of the characters have said or done overtly and more by the sense Lawrence's narrative creates of a parallel plot taking place below the surface of the work's realistic detail. Our impression of a mystical or super-natural identification of human characters with animals – fox, bird – creates a sense of profundity, as if the realistic plot detail is but the visible part of the iceberg. And in this way, if I can extend my spatial metaphor, the very limited *length* of the work is supplemented by a sense of greater *depth*. The critic Mary Rohrberger, incidentally, suggests that 'perhaps more than any other narrative structure, the short story veers toward what Joseph Frank calls "spatial form," a set of narrative techniques and processes of aesthetic perception that works to impede linearity' (Rohrberger, 2004, 6). (For discussion of linearity, see p. 96.) We can extend the scope of this observation to the novella.

Although the typical novella is more limited in its concerns than the novel, often restricting itself to a single state of affairs, collection of relationships, or setting, it characteristically compensates for this limitation by means of a greater reliance on implied or suggested secondary meanings. Hence it has some of the concentrated power of the short story, but without the frequent one-dimension-ality that characterizes many short stories.

Probably the most-studied work of short fiction in English is Joseph Conrad's *Heart of Darkness*, at just under 39,000 words somewhat longer than *The Fox*. It is hard to imagine many short stories that could have generated the enormous body of interpretative responses that *Heart of Darkness* has done, and its force has once again something to do with its symbolic richness. I have warned that generalizations are dangerous, however, and the attentive reader will spot that what I have just said is difficult to reconcile with my earlier comments about the suggestiveness of the short story and my comments on the ending of Joyce's 'The

Dead'. I would venture, however, that 'The Dead' probably is unusual among short stories in terms of the richness and intensity of its symbolism, and it will also be noted that it is relatively long for a short story (about 15,600 words). Mary Doyle Springer treats it as a novella rather than a short story in her *Forms of the Modern Novella* (1975, 4), and it is clearly near the borderline between the two forms. Furthermore, although a short story may be suggestive in O'Faolain's sense, and this may lead to a rich reading experience, it does not necessarily involve the same potentiality for interpretative complexity that we find in a major novella such as Joseph Conrad's *Heart of Darkness*.

The actual events of *Heart of Darkness*, like those of *The Fox*, could be summarized in a few lines; whatever we read this work for it is not primarily for complexity of plot development. It is true that in his *The Deceptive Text: An Introduction to Covert Plots* (1984), Cedric Watts argues that *Heart of Darkness* has a dual plot structure consisting of both an overt and a covert plot. But the covert plot is implied or suggested only by means of the occasional hint and comment. Equally important are such things as Conrad's use of symbol and image in the work, the complexities of narrative technique (the 'tale within a tale' and the interplay between the frame and framed narrative, each of which has its own narrator) and the texture of the prose.

The novella is dominated by Marlow (narrator of the framed narrative), and his fascination with, and search for, the mysterious figure of Kurtz. Early on in the story Marlow comes across a painting that Kurtz has executed:

> Then I noticed a small sketch in oils, on a panel, representing a woman, draped and blindfolded, carrying a lighted torch. The background was sombre – almost black. The movement of the woman was stately, and the effect of the torch-light on the face was sinister.

We see here, I think, how a relatively short work can be given a complex unity by means other than those involving the intricacies of plot development. The picture is one of a number of symbolic 'moments' in the work which draw various threads together in a masterly way. We note a relationship between the blindfolded woman carrying a lighted torch and those Europeans (including Kurtz) who have claimed that they are bringing light to Africa but who are actually 'going at it blind', either self-deceived or dishonestly plundering. We are reminded of Kurtz's fiancée, 'the Intended', whom we meet at the end of the tale and who is as blind metaphorically as the painted woman is literally. (As Marlow's account makes clear, European women have to be left in the dark about what their men are doing in Africa at this time – including what they are doing with African women such as the one who we may assume is Kurtz's mistress.) The references to light and blackness link up with a repetitive pattern of black–white images in the work which have an intricate relationship to sets of moral judgements indicated by Conrad in indirect ways.

Writers of short stories and novellas do not just produce truncated novels. These different fictional genres require a different use of the resources of prose, and they should not be read or judged in the way that we read or judge a 500-page novel.

Topics for discussion

↦ Does the short story have any other distinctive characteristics apart from its length?

↦ Imagine what a favourite short story would be like extended to novel length – or a novel compressed into a short story. What are the gains and losses? Does the novel have all the advantages?

↦ How significant is it that we can read a whole short story in one session?

↦ 'Neither one thing nor another.' Is the novella more than a failed novel or a short story that has got too long?

Chapter 4
Realism, modernism, postmodernism

Preview

This chapter deals with:

→ the problems of defining realism, modernism and postmodernism
→ realism as content or realism as effect on the reader
→ modernism and postmodernism as periodizations and as generic classifiers
→ modernism and the inner self
→ fragmentation and 'realities' in modernism and postmodernism
→ the use of fiction to explore extreme experiences in recent history

The three terms mentioned in the title of this chapter occur so frequently in discussion of the novel that they merit separate consideration at this point. All three terms are used not just in relation to literature or fiction, but in order to isolate important cultural tendencies associated with periods within (primarily) the past three centuries.

So far as prose fiction is concerned, the use of all three terms is complicated by the fact that each can be used to indicate both *historical periods of literature* and *trans-historical types of literature* or *specific literary characteristics* (although the term 'modernism' is not normally applied to literature written before the final years of the nineteenth century). Indeed these terms are increasingly used to denote particular literary genres or sub-genres, as in 'the modernist short story' or 'the postmodernist novel'. And if this were not confusing enough, it needs to be added that very often the terms are invoked to specify a particular philosophical outlook or position.

To attempt to reduce the confusion, let us list these different ways in which these terms may be used.

- ↪ periods or schools of literature
- ↪ literary schools with their associated conventions
- ↪ literary genres or sub-genres
- ↪ philosophical positions

In some respects the problems associated with the use of these terms are not dissimilar to those attached to the use of the term 'romanticism', another word that can also be used to denote a tightly delimited historical period of literature, a more general variety of literature with its associated conventions, or a set of trans-historical cultural attitudes or beliefs. And just as not all literature written during the romantic period is necessarily romantic in a generic or philosophical sense, so too not all fiction written in the early twentieth century is modernist, and neither is all the fiction written today necessarily postmodernist.

'Enough!' you may feel like saying: 'given all these complications let us agree to avoid using any of these terms'. This tempting solution is not, alas, a viable one. The history of the novel is so intimately bound up with the issue of realism that we can hardly talk about the novel without addressing it. Moreover, that there is a family of new characteristics to be found in significant works of art and literature produced at the end of the nineteenth century and the beginning of the twentieth century can scarcely be disputed, and the term 'modernism' helps us to isolate these characteristics and to distinguish between radically different lines of development in the art and literature of the twentieth and twenty-first centuries. Finally, although theories of the postmodern have come into major prominence only during the last three decades, they are so central to discussion not just of recent experimental fiction but also of many much older works that they cannot just be ignored. So we have to grit our teeth and engage with the difficult task of producing at least working definitions of these three terms.

Realism

We saw in our earlier discussion of the emergence and development of the novel that the genre is distinguished by what we can call its 'formal realism': it is stocked with people and places that *seem real* or *evoke a familiar, everyday reality* even if they are imagined, whereas genres such as the romance or the epic were peopled with people and places that seem (and were meant to seem) unreal and that do not turn the attention of present or past readers to everyday reality. We can note, furthermore, that 'realism' and its cognates are terms that a large number of novelists have felt the need to use in connection with their work.

On a simple level it can be said that something – a character, an event, a setting – is 'realistic' if it resembles a model in everyday life. The matter becomes more complex, however, when we remember that a novelist can make us think seriously and critically about the real world by creating characters, events and settings that in many ways diverge from what we would expect in everyday life – in 'reality'. Peter Lamarque has noted that a 'fiction is realistic if it describes characters with combinations of properties that would not be strange or out of place if exemplified in individuals in the real world', but he goes on to discuss the problems raised by a novel such as George Orwell's *Animal Farm* (1945) which, in spite of the fact that it contains farmyard animals which speak, think and reason exactly like human beings, also strikes us as 'realistic' or 'true to life'. He suggests that what we need in order to explain this apparent contradiction 'is an appeal to levels of interpretation or understanding' (Lamarque, 1996, 38). In other words, it is difficult to arrive at a concept of realism which is not trivial unless one goes beyond a concern with simple one-to-one resemblance and proceeds to consider not just the ways in which characters and events in a novel may be like characters and events in the real world, but also *how a reader responds* to these characters and events and to their presentation.

This is a shift of emphasis that opens up a set of new problems. William B. Warner, for example, has argued that, because what he calls 'the realist effect' can be provoked by a given novel at one time and not at another, the whole association of the novel with realism is thus rendered suspect: 'Because history undermines the naturalness and self-evidence of received modes of representing the real, it has proved difficult to sustain any "realist claim" made by or for a novel' (1998, 35). This I feel casts out the baby with the bathwater, for even though readers may find the same novel more, or less, 'realistic' at different periods of history, as conventions become stale and apparent rather than invisible, such changes seem to me to involve relative rather than absolute shifts of response. We still find Dickens's novels more realistic than William Beckford's *Vathek*, even though we are perhaps more conscious of many conventional elements in them than were Dickens's first readers.

Warner's point does serve to remind us that a novel seems realistic to readers even when it charts events and describes characters that are far from typical or everyday: think how many unusual coincidences and extraordinary events there are in those novels which are normally described as highly realistic. (George Eliot's *Middlemarch* (1871–2) is a good example.)

Lamarque's mention of *Animal Farm* should also draw our attention to the issues raised by parody and satire, both of which can be used by the novelist to make us think about the real world we inhabit. A parody is often very unrealistic in one sense, depending upon such extremes of exaggeration and such pointed selection that it cannot be said to give us anything that can be compared to our everyday world *in terms of direct, one-to-one resemblance*. Even so, parodies and satires clearly *do* cause us to see our everyday world very differently – otherwise their targets and victims would not be annoyed by them. The paradox, then, is that sometimes that which distorts what the real world is like may actually lead us to see the real world more accurately.

Brecht, Lukács and the realism debate

One of the most influential debates about the nature of realism in the twentieth century involved a critic very much associated with the novel – the Hungarian Marxist Georg Lukács. For Lukács, who saw realism as the contemporary artist's necessary, even ultimate, aim, the artist was required to represent the totality of reality at any given point in history, to penetrate surface appearances and to reveal processes of change. This sounds a tall order, and of course Lukács accepted that 'the totality of reality' could only be displayed by the writer through representative selection. For Lukács, the artist's task was similar to that set for himself by Marx: to understand world history as a complex and dynamic totality through the uncovering of certain underlying laws. In practice this led Lukács to place a supreme value upon certain works of classical realism in the novel – the names of Tolstoy, Balzac and Thomas Mann are frequently on his lips or at the tip of his pen – and to wage an unceasing campaign against different aspects of what he classified as modernism (see below). At the end of his *The Historical Novel* (written 1936–7), Lukács referred to the 'misunderstanding' of his position as one entailing 'a formal revival, an artistic imitation of the classical historical novel' (Lukács, 1969, 422), but in spite of this disclaimer many commentators have seen his opposition to modernism as so all-embracing that this is actually what would have been required in order to satisfy his requirement that a literary work be realistic.

When the German dramatist Bertolt Brecht, writing about the concept of realism, stated that we 'must not derive realism as such from particular existing works' (Brecht, 1977, 81), the unstated target was clearly Lukács (especially as Brecht goes on to refer to Balzac and Tolstoy). Brecht's argument is, in a nutshell, an anti-essentialist one. In other words, realism for him is not intrinsic to a literary work, born with it like a genetic code and remaining unchanged through all its vicissitudes, but a function of the role the work plays or can play – the effect it has on a reader's (and not necessarily *all* readers') view of the world. Brecht's realism focuses on questions not of form or content, but of function and consequence.

In other words, Lukács and Brecht exemplify the two fundamentally different ways of understanding realism that I have already outlined – as a quality that is *innate* in a text, or as one that is measured in terms of a text's changing *effect* on its readers or audiences. From Lukács's perspective a text either is or is not realistic; from Brecht's perspective it may be realistic at one time, but not at another. The important point to bear in mind is that when a critic discusses whether or not a novel is realistic, he or she can be referring either to what it is or contains, or to what it does. Now very often critics and lecturers use the term in a loose sense and restrict it to the question of verisimilitude, but we should remember that a novel can be unrealistic in the former sense but realistic in the latter – or vice versa.

Think of it this way: if what we read in a novel seems just like the world we experience every day, it may be unlikely to encourage us to examine that world critically, to see it in a new light, to ask whether its appearance is deceptive. In contrast, if a novel presents us with a world that seems extremely unusual, it *may* encourage us to ask to what extent our familiar world perhaps really *is* like this, in ways we have not previously considered.

The term 'realism' very often implies that the artist (and not just the literary artist) has tried to include a wider and more representative coverage of social life in his or her work, and in particular that he or she has extended the coverage of the work to include 'low life' and the experiences of those deemed unworthy of artistic portrayal by other artists. The apparent realism of the early novel was intimately related in the public mind to the fact that it often concerned itself with the lives of the sort of human being who would not only never have been portrayed by the romance but whose depiction was clearly out of bounds too for the genteel eighteenth-century poet. Fielding's Joseph Andrews, Defoe's Moll Flanders, Smollett's Humphry Clinker – none of these characters or their real-life equivalents could have entered into the polite world of Alexander Pope except in certain forms of satire or burlesque. This is one of the reasons why *Joseph Andrews* (1742), *Moll Flanders* (1722) and *Humphry Clinker* (1771) are generally taken to be more realistic works than *The Rape of the Lock* (1711).

'Realism' also has a specific reference to a particular literary movement which started in France in the early nineteenth century, and flourished in the latter part of the century. The names of the novelists most associated with this movement are those of Balzac, Stendhal and Flaubert. These writers made enormous efforts to ensure that 'factual details' in their works were 'correct' – that is to say, capable of being checked against an external reality by empirical investigations. They achieved this accuracy by lengthy and painstaking research. 'Realism' in connection with these writers is thus both a term denoting a group of novelists and also a term referring to a particular method of composition. (See also the comments on naturalism in the Glossary.)

One conclusion that can be drawn from the foregoing is that the term 'realistic' should be used only with extreme care in connection with a novel; it is a problematic rather than a self-obvious term and raises complex questions about what 'reality' is (our fantasies are after all real in the sense that they really exist and are related to our experiences in the real world), and about the means whereby a novelist explores the real. Having said all this it remains important to be able to distinguish between novels that – in however complex and indirect a way – cause us to think about reality critically, and those that encourage us not to try to do this but rather to escape from our everyday reality into a world of illusory imaginings.

The 'classical realist novel'

A term that is increasingly encountered in discussion of fiction is 'the classical realist novel' (sometimes rendered as just 'the classical novel'). Generally
speaking we can say that this term emerges to denote and classify canonical
novels of the nineteenth century, such as those by the Brontë sisters, Elizabeth Gaskell, Charles Dickens, William Makepeace Thackeray, Leo Tolstoy,
Nathaniel Hawthorne, Herman Melville, (the early) Henry James and others.
What is it that these works are seen to have in common? A short list in answer to
this question might include the follow elements.

- ↔ A belief in the knowability of a unified world which, however many
  secrets it contains, can be explored and studied.
- ↔ A similar belief in the knowability of the self which, like the external
  world, is conceived as unitary except in certain significant exceptional
  cases (doubles, split selves).
- ↔ A plot based on cause-and-effect that has a clear beginning and normally
  an even clearer ending.
- ↔ A commitment to 'the reality illusion' – in other words, a 'contract' with
  the reader that the world of the novel will be treated as real, and that the
  reader's immersion in this world will not be broken by the author's or
  narrator's admission that it is only make-believe (see the quotation from
  Henry James below, p. 77.)

A crude but helpful test here is the ease with which one can respond to the
unacademic question: 'What's this novel about?' Asked this question of, say,
Charlotte Brontë's *Jane Eyre* the 'common reader' (to use a phrase coined by
Samuel Johnson) will most likely reply along the following lines. 'It's a story
about Jane Eyre, told by herself, that traces her growth and development from a
deprived childhood though her attempts to build a life for herself in spite of her
poverty. In particular it traces her relationship with two potential husbands, who
offer her the prospect of very different sorts of married life. After many complications (including her finding out that the second of these men is married), Jane
is able to find contentment with this man, Rochester.'

Now if your response to such a summary is: 'So what?', imagine how you
would respond to this inquiry were the novel in question Virginia Woolf's *The
Waves* (1931) or Angela Carter's *The Magic Toyshop* (1967). If I had to answer
the question with regard to Woolf's novel, I might end up saying something like
this. 'It's a novel that traces the lives of seven characters, six of whom become
known to the reader through monologues that represent their thoughts and their
sense of the world and of themselves. These monologues are interlaced with
sections printed in italics that represent not the perceptions of any individuals
but a reality that is, paradoxically, not observed by anyone.' Even at this point it
is possible to make two observations concerning what I have written. First, that it

is not uncontroversial, especially with regard to the italicized sections in Woolf's work. But second, that while the summary I gave of *Jane Eyre* could have been said of a real person, or an autobiography, in order to explain what *The Waves* is 'about' I have to engage with its fictional and conventional characteristics, even in a short two-sentence summary.

Now this is not to say that any classical realist novel could be mistaken for a biography, and autobiography, or a work of history if the cover and title page did not announce it as a novel. As I note on p. 65, there are certain aspects of even the most realist novel that announce the work as fictional. But it does mean that the classical realist novel typically presents its characters and events according to conventions that may not coincide, but that certainly overlap, with those conventions that we apply to the telling of stories about real people and events. When the novel stops presenting characters and events in such a way, a new term is needed to indicate the importance of this shift, although it has taken time for such a term to come into more general use.

Modernism

Modernism is a term that (at least so far as its general acceptance is concerned) is younger than the works that it describes. During five years as a student of English at a British university in the 1960s I cannot recall ever having come across it once. It is now widely used to refer to those art works (or the principles behind their creation), produced since the end of the nineteenth century, that decisively reject many of the key artistic conventions of the previous age. Foremost among such rejected conventions are those associated with realism in a generic sense. In particular, modernist works tend to be *self-conscious* in ways that vary according to the genre or art form in question; in different ways they deliberately remind the reader or observer that they are art works, rather than seeking to serve as 'windows on reality'. Whereas one may forget that one is reading a novel when immersed in, say, *War and Peace* (1865–8) – responding to characters and events as if they were 'real' – this is not a reading position invited by a modernist work such as Virginia Woolf's *The Waves*. Thus Picasso's rejection of representational art and of the conventions of perspective in his early paintings can be compared with the rejection of the 'tyranny of plot' by novelists such as Joyce, Woolf and Marcel Proust. This shift in attitudes from realism to modernism can be witnessed in the work of Joseph Conrad. In 1898 Conrad wrote to his friend Cunninghame Graham, 'You must have a *plot*! If you haven't, every fool reviewer will kick you because there can't be literature without plot' (Karl and Davies 1986, 5). Four years later, in 1902, he wrote to Arnold Bennett (one of Woolf's 'materialists' and thus far from what we now call modernism), 'You just stop short of being absolutely real because you are faithful to your dogmas of realism. Now realism in art will never approach reality' (Karl and

Davies, 1986, 390). What we see here is a writer beginning to question 'dogmas of realism' and to search for alternatives to the well-made plot, the rounded and lifelike character, the knowable world wholly accessible to reasoned and rational enquiry.

Modernism and the inner self

The modernist novel typically focuses proportionally greater attention on the states and processes *inside* the consciousness of the main character(s) than on public events in the outside world. If the twentieth century was the century of Freud and Marx then we can say that the modernist novel has much more in common with the outlook of the former than that of the latter (which explains, incidentally, why an orthodox Marxist critic such as Georg Lukács argued so bitterly for realism and against modernism during his long life). Moreover, as I will go on to argue in greater detail in Chapter 6, the emergence of modernism involves profound changes with regard to novelists' conception of *character*. Michael Levenson opens his book *Modernism and the Fate of Individuality* as follows:

> This thing we name the individual, this piece of matter, this length of memory, this bearer of a proper name, this block in space, this whisper in time, this self-delighting, self-condemning oddity – what is it? who made it? Ours may be the age of narcissism, but it is also the century in which ego suffered unprecedented attacks upon its great pretensions, to be self-transparent and self-authorized. (Levenson, 1991, xi)

For the great modernist novelists (Levenson pays particular attention to Conrad, James, Forster, Ford Madox Ford, Wyndham Lewis, Lawrence and Woolf), character can no longer be taken to be self-transparent – more than one character in a modernist novel asks 'Who am I?' without receiving a clear answer. Nor is the self any longer its own source of authority – which does not necessarily mean that any alternative source of authority is readily available.

This focussing upon the problems of the self and of the inner life has encouraged the development of new *methods* of fictional expression. If modernism can be defined negatively in terms of its rejection of realist conventions and assumptions, its positive side can be seen in its remarkable development of techniques such as *stream of consciousness* and *internal monologue*, its challenging of traditional conceptions of story and plot, its markedly greater emphasis upon what Joyce calls 'epiphanies' and Virginia Woolf 'moments' (see p. 51) and its revolutionary use of various forms of what we can call 'poetic expression' in the novel. (Witness my earlier discussion of the final paragraph of Joyce's 'The Dead' on p. 56.) Such techniques will be discussed in Chapter 6.

A brief comment should be added concerning the philosophical underpinnings of modernism. These are very often implicit rather than overt, but frequently we find that modernist novels are pessimistic in tone, unsure about the sense or logic of the world, and look on human beings as isolated and alienated. The philosophical corollary of the rejection of perspective in art, and of an omniscient view of a knowable world obeying certain laws in fiction, seems to be a view of reality as lacking any unifying logic, to the extent that one should perhaps talk rather of 'realities' than of reality. (Again risking a generalization, we can say that modernists have a monist view of reality but accept that complete knowledge of this reality is impossible, while postmodernists adhere to a pluralist view and deny that it makes any sense to talk of a single reality.) Thus, for the modernist, different perspectives have to be combined because although what they reveal may appear contradictory, there is no 'super-perspective' from which to rank their validity.

A modernist short story: James Joyce's 'Eveline'

The Irishman James Joyce wrote one of the longest works of modernist fiction – *Ulysses* – and also one of the shortest, the 1,824-word-long story 'Eveline', which appeared in his collection *Dubliners* (first published in 1914, but written from 1905). What the Irish critic Vivian Mercer said of a later central modernist work – Samuel Beckett's play *Waiting for Godot* (1953) – could also be applied to 'Eveline': in it, 'nothing happens, twice'. The entire story is limited to two scenes. In the first of these the reader meets the title character Eveline sitting at the window of her home, musing about the past and looking forward to her forthcoming elopement with her young man Frank, who is to take her away from Ireland to Buenos Ayres. In the final, even shorter scene she is waiting on the quay for the ship that is to take both of them to a new life, but it appears that Eveline is, when the point of decision comes, unable to break her ties with her family and her past.

The story thus exemplifies well two of the characteristics that I have suggested are typical of modernist fiction: its focus on the inner self, and its abjuration of a traditional plot in which characters interact through involvement in events that succeed one another in a cause-and-effect manner. The important things that 'happen' in 'Eveline' happen *inside* Eveline, although they are related to things that have previously happened around and outside her. Interaction between characters occurs only in retrospect, in Eveline's memory, and the events that are planned for the future seem doomed not to occur.

This is how 'Eveline' opens.

> She sat at the window watching the evening invade the avenue. Her
> head was leaned against the window curtains and in her nostrils was the
> odour of dusty cretonne. She was tired.
>
> Few people passed. The man out of the last house passed on his way
> home; she heard his footsteps clacking along the concrete pavement
> and afterwards crunching on the cinder path before the new red houses.

One time there used to be a field there in which they used to play every evening with other people's children. Then a man from Belfast bought the field and built houses in it – not like their little brown houses but bright brick houses with shining roofs. The children of the avenue used to play together in that field – the Devines, the Waters, the Dunns, little Keogh the cripple, she and her brothers and sisters. Ernest, however, never played: he was too grown up. Her father used often to hunt them in out of the field with his blackthorn stick; but usually little Keogh used to keep *nix* and call out when he saw her father coming. Still they seemed to have been rather happy then. Her father was not so bad then; and besides, her mother was alive. That was a long time ago; she and her brothers and sisters were all grown up; her mother was dead. Tizzie Dunn was dead, too, and the Waters had gone back to England. Everything changes. Now she was going to go away like the others, to leave her home. (Joyce, 2000, 29)

Initially the reader is presented with Eveline, and told certain things about her that may represent her conscious thoughts but may well not (she may not be aware of the smell or of her tiredness). But in the second paragraph we are taken into Eveline's mind and we follow her perceptions and thoughts, both those that are prompted by what she observes, and those that she retrieves from her memory. The movement in these two paragraphs is almost cinematic: it is as if the camera moves nearer and nearer to Eveline, until we stop looking *at* her and start looking – and thinking – *with* her.

Fixing the reader as it were inside Eveline's head, the head of a person who is on her own and who seems to be better at communicating with herself than with other people, has the effect of forcing the reader to experience and share the character's isolation. Speaking personally, I find the experience of reading this story to be one that merits the adjective 'claustrophobic'; it is if, for the duration of one's reading, one is imprisoned in Eveline, in her mind and in her alienated life, and unable to escape.

This sense of alienation is very typical of much modernist literature. A lonely person reading a Jane Austen novel might well find relief in the sense of belonging to a world in which characters interact and engage with one another – not always successfully or in a positive manner, of course, but in a manner that confirms their existence in a social world of connections and influence. The same lonely person reading 'Eveline' might find some comfort in the sense that others had been there before, but the story engenders a pessimistic and depressing sense in the reader, one that suggests, perhaps, that our lives are more cut off from the lives of others than we would like to admit. Even the memories of human contact in the past are qualified: 'they *seemed* to have been rather happy then'; 'Her father was *not so bad* then'. And those with whom Eveline shared a childhood vitality are either dead or have left Ireland for England.

A couple of words of warning are necessary here. First, the fact that Joyce locates the reader so firmly in the isolated consciousness of Eveline should not be taken to imply a lack of interest in the outside world, or in the specific social and historical characteristics of the Dublin setting of the collection of stories to which 'Eveline' belongs. Indeed, if *Dubliners* is read from cover to cover the reader builds up a sense from story to story that the characteristics of inertia, alienation and non-communication are very intimately related to this setting. In *Ulysses* the character Stephen Dedalus expresses his frustration at being the servant of two masters, the imperial British state and the holy Roman catholic and apostolic church, and this sense of political and ideological enslavement forms too a constant background in the stories that make up *Dubliners*. Second, the fact that the reader is imprisoned so securely in Eveline's consciousness in this story does not mean that Joyce is unable to insert levels of meaning in the story that are independent of her understanding.

Even in the second of the two paragraphs I quote, for example, the name 'Waters' is unlikely to have been chosen at random given the motifs of aridity that run through the story: at the end of 'Eveline' the title character feels that 'All the seas of the world tumbled about her heart. He [Frank] was drawing her into them: he would drown her', and this fear of water and of drowning is, in the context of *Dubliners* as a whole, symptomatic of the inability of the people of early twentieth-century Dublin to renew themselves and throw off their oppressors. (That this fear of renewal was not limited to either Ireland or to modernist fiction can be confirmed by its centrality to another classic modernist text: T.S. Eliot's poem 'The Waste Land' [1922].) The other names listed in this paragraph may also have a specific resonance: 'the Devines, the Waters' has a half suggestion of water diviners, so that Eveline's choice is between searching for something new, some new source of life, and admitting that her life is 'Dunn' and dead.

In the previous chapter I referred to Thomas M. Leitch's report that commentators on the short story continued to distinguish between the 'anecdotal' and the 'epiphanic' story, and I noted that the use of the term 'epiphany' with reference to modernist literature was particularly associated with James Joyce's writing. According to Leitch, the 'epiphanic' short story 'adumbrates a fictional world … by unfolding particular sensations or emotions and proceeding to a climactic revelation that does not necessarily take the form of a complete overt action' (Leitch, 1989, 130–1). This definition fits the end of 'Eveline' perfectly. In the story's short final scene Eveline waits on the quay to board the ship that will take her and Frank to Buenos Ayres. But although he calls to her, she seems frozen – paralysed.

> – Come!
> All the seas of the world tumbled about her heart. He was drawing her into them: he would drown her. She gripped with both hands at the iron railing.

– Come!

No! No! No! It was impossible. Her hands clutched the iron in frenzy. Amid the seas she sent a cry of anguish. (Joyce, 2000, 34)

The waters that at the start of the story have seemed to hold out the promise of life and renewal are here experienced as a threat, the danger of existential drowning. As in Leitch's comment, we are not given 'a complete overt action' – rather the reverse: an inability to act, a panic-filled paralysis on Eveline's part. But nonetheless we are given a 'climactic revelation': Eveline's life has been invaded by the paralysis of her surroundings. She, and the reader, perceives that she is lost. In this final epiphany we see the full extent of her inner hopelessness.

Modernism's familiar association with inwardness and alienation, in other words, does not entail a lack of concern with social, political and historical contexts. Sometimes these contexts are invoked more directly, as with *Dubliners*, and sometimes they are less explicit, as in the fiction of Kafka where alienation and meaningless, life-denying bureaucracy are presented more as the universal lot of humanity than as the conditions of life of those living in a particular place at a particular time.

Postmodernism

With the term 'postmodernism' we move on to other terminological problems. One perhaps inevitable confusion has arisen from the fact that although one commentator has traced this term back to the mid-1930s (Hassan, 1985, 119–31), it has only really come into more common use in Europe and the United States in the last three or four decades. Thus works which before this time were categorized as either 'experimental' or 'modernist' have in some cases received a new, often disputed, categorization as postmodernist. As Andreas Huyssen puts it, 'one critic's postmodernism is another critic's modernism' (Huyssen, 1988, 59). A sharper critique comes from John Frow who, in a chapter of his book *Time and Commodity Culture: Essays in Cultural Theory and Postmodernity* (1997) entitled 'What Was Postmodernism?', argues that the concept of postmodernism is incoherent. He gives two reasons to back up this claim. First, those who use the term either give no examples of what or who falls into the category, or alternatively one person's examples are quite different from another's. Second, there is no agreement concerning the period associated with the term (Frow, 1997, 26–8).

Other commentators have argued that the term does not really isolate any significant characteristics (in art, literature or culture) that cannot be covered by the term 'modernism'. Such individuals frequently make what amounts to a political gesture by pointedly referring to 'late modernism' rather than 'postmodernism': behind the debate is the issue of whether we now inhabit a new sort of reality – the 'postmodern world' – which is fundamentally different from the world, or social systems, that produced the great modernist art. This political edge to the debate is worth noting, as the term 'postmodernism' is typically used in a rather wider sense than is 'modernism', referring to a general human condition, or society at large, as much as to art or culture (a usage which was encouraged by Jean-François Lyotard's book *The Postmodern Condition: A Report on Knowledge*, the English translation of which was published in 1984).

Postmodernism, then, can be used today in a number of different ways: (i) to refer to the non-realist and non-traditional literature and art of the post-Second World War period; (ii) to refer to literature and art which take certain modernist characteristics to an extreme stage; and (iii) to refer to aspects of a more general human condition in what is tendentiously referred to as the 'late capitalist' world of the post-1950s which have an all-embracing effect on life, culture, ideology and art, as well as (in some but not all usages) to a generally welcoming, celebratory attitude towards these aspects.

Those modernist characteristics which may produce postmodernism when taken to their most extreme forms include the rejection of representation in favour of self-reference – especially of a 'playful' and non-serious, non-constructive sort; the willing, even relieved, rejection of artistic 'aura' (sense of 'holiness') and of a view of the work of art as organic whole; the substitution of confrontation and teasing of the reader for collaboration with him or her; the rejection of 'character' and 'plot' as meaningful or artistically defensible concepts or conventions; even the rejection of meaning itself along with the belief that it is worth trying to understand the world (or that there is a world to understand).

Postmodernism takes the subjective idealism of modernism to the point of solipsism, but rejects the tragic and pessimistic elements in modernism in the apparent conclusion that if one cannot prevent Rome burning then one might as well enjoy the fiddling while the flames rise. It has been argued that there are affinities between postmodernism and the philosophical positions to be found in the work of various post-structuralist and deconstructive critics such as Jacques Derrida, Michel Foucault and Jacques Lacan (see Chapter 9 for discussion of these critical positions).

Postmodernism is characterized in many accounts by a more welcoming, celebratory attitude towards the modern world. That this world is one of increasing fragmentation, of the dominance of commercial pressures and of human powerlessness in the face of a blind technology is not a point of dispute with modernism. Even so, whereas the major modernists reacted with horror or despair to their perception of these facts, some have claimed that it is typical of postmodernism to react in a far more accepting manner to them. The extent to which postmodernism is mimetic of recent and new social, economic and political practices in the societies in which it appears is a matter of some debate. Thus the different but uncommunicating worlds with which many a postmodern novel faces the reader reflect, it has been claimed, the fact that more and more people in the modern world live in self-contained ghettoes about which outsiders know little or nothing. Moreover, in the developed ('late capitalist') countries the advances of the communications and electronics industries have (it is argued) revolutionized human society. Instead of reacting to these changes in what is characterized as a Luddite manner, the postmodernist may instead counsel celebration of the present: enjoyment of that loss of artistic aura or 'holiness' which follows what Walter Benjamin (one of the most important theorists of modernism and to a certain extent also a prophet of postmodernism) called 'mechanical reproduction'. In common with some much earlier avant-gardists, many postmodernists are fascinated with rather than repelled by technology, do not reject 'the popular' or the commercial as beneath them, and are very much concerned with the immediate effect of their works: publication is for them (allegedly) more a strategic act than a bid for immortality.

David Harvey's *The Condition of Postmodernity* (1989) initiated much discussion around such issues, and subsequent debates involving (among others) Terry Eagleton and Fredric Jameson further helped to create a wider awareness of the issues involved.

A postmodernist novel: Jeannette Winterson's *Lighthousekeeping*

To exemplify some of the points that I have made about postmodernism, I would like to focus for a few pages on a recent (2004) novel by Jeanette Winterson: *Lighthousekeeping*. Winterson herself has been, as Sonya Andermahr puts it, 'resistant to postmodernism ... believing it to be a faddish phenomenon compared to the gravitas of the modernist canon' (Andermahr, 2009, 17). Andermahr agrees that we must take seriously the view that Winterson is a modernist writer, not least because this is how Winterson views her own work.

> However, she is also indubitably a postmodernist engaged in a playful and parodic rescripting of popular and canonical genres, and in the construction of reality as precisely an intricate web of fictional worlds, of endless stories. Winterson's novels clearly exemplify a postmodern aesthetics, demonstrating high levels of temporal dislocation, self-reflexivity, intertextuality and pastiche. (19)

Andermahr's comments, while reminding us that there is no Berlin wall between modernism and postmodernism, also I think legitimize my using *Lighthousekeeping* – which is by no means the most obviously postmodernist of Winterson's novels – as a representative example of postmodernist fiction.

Lighthousekeeping was first published in 2004. In 2005 the novel was reissued in paperback under the Harper Perennial imprint, and I would like to focus on this particular 'textual manifestation' of Winterson's novel in the comments that follow. Note that this is the only time in this book that I direct attention towards one particular *edition* of a work of fiction, and this unusual focus has something to do with the postmodernist features of the work in question.

At first sight this book may look much like any other recent paperback edition of a novel. It has a striking front-cover illustration (which we are able to discover, from the small print on the back cover, is a 'digitally enhanced' detail of an 1897 painting entitled 'Pot-Pourri'), and a back cover that includes a very brief description of the novel along with four very brief quotations from reviews in national British newspapers. If we open the book, we find even more extracts from reviews in the opening pages of the novel. These are followed by a list of other works by the author, the title page, the 'Publication details' page that includes a copyright declaration and the book's ISBN number, a dedication (to Deborah Warner), a page thanking six named individuals and other unnamed individuals associated with the publisher Harper Perennial, a page with two short 'epigraphs' by Muriel Spark and Ali Smith, and finally a page giving the title of the novel's first section.

There are a number of unusual features about the actual text of the novel, but let us skip over these for the time being. After the novel's final page a new section follows entitled *P.S. Ideas, Interviews and Features*. This section is repaginated – in other words, the first page of this section is numbered 1. It is divided into three sub-sections: 'About the author'; 'About the book'; and 'Read on'. Some of the material in these sections is written by journalists and others, some is written by Jeanette Winterson herself. There is even a final sub-sub-section entitled 'Find out more' that provides information about books and web pages, ranging from Virginia Woolf's novel *To the Lighthouse* to web pages on the (actual) Cape Wrath Lighthouse, about Jeanette Winterson and about holidays in a Scottish lighthouse.

None of this, I admit, is earth-shattering. Indeed, it is to a large extent the sort of material that we have come to *expect* in 'academic' issues of older works of literature – editions aimed at the student market. But it marks a substantial change from the way in which a *new* novel would have been packaged a couple of decades ago. In particular, devoting attention to the figure of the *author*, to *actual places* mentioned in the novel and to *writers* whose lives and works are alluded to in the novel may seem to weaken that conventional boundary between 'the world of the fiction' and 'our normal, everyday world'.

Elsewhere in this book I have argued that it is important for the reader to be able to experience the 'world' of a work of fiction as consistent and in a sense self-enclosed. In a very influential essay on the novel entitled 'The Art of Fiction' (1884, revised 1888) the novelist Henry James insisted that the novelist-as-real-person should not appear within the pages of his or her creation and expose its fictionality to the reader.

> Certain accomplished novelists have a habit of giving themselves away which must often bring tears to the eyes of people who take their fiction seriously. I was lately struck, in reading over many pages of Anthony Trollope, with his want of discretion in this particular. In a digression,

a parenthesis or an aside, he concedes to the reader that he and this trusting friend are only 'making believe.' He admits that the events he narrates have not really happened, and that he can give his narrative any turn the reader may like best. Such a betrayal of a sacred office seems to me, I confess, a terrible crime; it is what I mean by the attitude of apology, and it shocks me every whit as much in Trollope as it would have shocked me in Gibbon or Macaulay. It implies that the novelist is less occupied in looking for the truth (the truth, of course I mean, that he assumes, the premises that we must grant him, whatever they may be), than the historian, and in doing so it deprives him at a stroke of all his standing-room. (James, 1984, 46–7)

Much postmodernist fiction challenges James's position head-on, and Winterson's novel is representative of this refusal to treat the created fictional world as sacred territory, into which the novelist can venture only by disguising his or her real self and assuming an identity that – like a person in church who feels in a spiritual space that is set apart from everyday reality – accepts as real that which is actually an imitation of the real.

All of the 'surrounding material' in *Lighthousekeeping* to which I have referred has been given a descriptive name: 'paratext', a term which has filled a gap in critical terminology. The term is a coinage of the French narrative theorist Gérard Genette, used in his work *Seuils* (1987; English translation *Paratexts: Thresholds of Interpretation* [1997]). According to Genette, 'Paratext' refers to 'those liminal devices and conventions … that mediate the book to the reader: titles and subtitles, pseudonyms, forewords, dedications, epigraphs, prefaces, intertitles, notes, epilogues, and afterwords'. Genette even distinguishes between such material found within the text, which he calls *peritext*, and material found outside it, which he calls *epitext*. In the former category in our case might come such things as the section headings that we find in the novel.

We might say that the bits of paratext that come at the front of *Lighthousekeeping* detail the novel's *effects* – the responses and evaluations it has produced – while many of the bits of paratext at the end of the book detail the materials used to *create* the book – historical characters, geographical locations and events (the Great Exhibition of 1851), and works of fiction and their characters. (So: what comes first in the book is what came last in time, and some of what comes at the end of the book is what preceded the writing of the novel. However, although these are in a sense *sources*, as the heading 'Read on' suggests, this part of the book also contains suggestions to the reader about what to read after he or she has finished the novel.)

My point in detailing all this is to draw attention to the fact that this is a book constructed in a manner that actively encourages the reader to link the world depicted in the novel with the real world of places, events, individuals, reviews – and author. Instead of the sharp division between the world of the real-life author and the created world of the fictional text recommended by Henry James, we have very blurred boundaries between these two worlds – so blurred, in fact, that we may wonder whether the world of the novel *is* separate from the everyday world of the author (and the reader). Reading this book, then, is almost like watching a film or a TV play in which the director and cameras are in constant view.

However, if this blurring of boundaries might suggest that the world depicted in the fiction and the world of real-life author and reader are similar or identical, we find that quite the opposite is the case. The world of *Lighthousekeeping* is a strange, surrealistic one, in which bits of our real world co-exist with fantastic people and events. Let us now turn to the actual text of the novel.

Fictional and real people and places

In *Lighthousekeeping* we find the same encouragement to the reader to link the people, places and events of the fiction with both real-world people, places and events, and people, places and events taken from other novels that I located in the book's 'peritext'. Like many novels – realist and modernist, as well as postmodernist – *Lighthousekeeping* is populated with both fictional and real-world people and places. Thus there really is a lighthouse at Cape Wrath, and it really was built by the father of the novelist and traveller Robert Louis Stevenson, who appears as a character in Winterson's novel. Moreover, Robert Louis Stevenson's novels *Treasure Island* and *The Strange Case of Dr Jekyll and Mr Hyde* are referred to both directly and indirectly throughout *Lighthousekeeping*.

Dr Jekyll and Mr Hyde is named in the text, initially when the protagonist Silver finds a copy of the book.

> I took them out. Two first editions: Charles Darwin, *On the Origin of Species*, 1859, and *The Strange Case of Dr Jekyll and Mr Hyde*, 1886. The other books were the notebooks and letters that had belonged to Babel Dark. (124)

Note here the move from the historically real to the fictional: Darwin and Stevenson and their books existed in the everyday world; Babel Dark exists only as a character in this novel. So far as *Treasure Island* is concerned, there are many allusions to this work in *Lighthousekeeping*. The novel opens with two characters: a lighthouse keeper named Pew, and his helper, the narrator Silver. One of the characters in *Treasure Island* is named Blind Pew, while the hero is the boy named Jim – the name of Silver's dog. And the villain of *Treasure Island* is a Pirate named Long John Silver – thus hinting that Silver is herself descended from him. References such as this are called *intertextual* references (see the Glossary), and the topic of intertextuality is raised explicitly on the second page of the P.S. section of the book, in an interview with Winterson.

Now at this point you may protest that many novels contain passing allusions to other works (Scott and Cowper are discussed by the characters early on in Jane Austen's *Sense and Sensibility*, for example). But *Lighthousekeeping* is packed full of intertextual references to which the reader's attention is drawn by both the characters and the narrator – and, in the peritext, by the author. Thus in case we might not have realized that in reading the novel we need to bear in mind Virginia Woolf's *To the Lighthouse*, this novel is listed in the additional material in the sub-section 'Find Out More' in the P.S. section of the book. It is almost as if Winterson is acting as her own critic. Let me pause here in order to make some provisional summarizing points.

We can I hope agree that *Lighthousekeeping* is possessed of many characteristics typical of *postmodern* fiction.

- ↔ self-reference
- ↔ 'ludic' or playful games with the reader; teasing the reader
- ↔ the rejection of artistic 'aura' or seriousness
- ↔ the rejection of conventional ideas of character and plot
- ↔ blurring the boundaries between the factual and the fictional

Let me consider these features one at a time.

- ↔ So far as self-reference is concerned, I will come back below to the way in which a discussion about the nature of stories and storytelling – of *narrative* – threads its way through the whole novel.
- ↔ So far as the novel's ludic qualities are concerned, we can trace a jokey quality throughout the work.

> I lived in a house cut steep into the bank. The chairs had to be nailed to the floor, and we were never allowed to eat spaghetti. We ate food that stuck to the plate – shepherd's pie, goulash, risotto, scrambled egg. (3)

> My mother was a single parent and she had conceived out of wedlock. There had been no lock on her door that night when my father came to call. So she was sent up the hill, away from the town, with the curious result that she looked down on it. (4–5)

> Pew – why didn't my mother marry my father?

> She never had time. He came and went. (85)

This ludic quality has the effect, among other things, of undermining artistic seriousness and 'aura' – although, importantly, there are moments of passion, intensity and insight that are powerful and moving in the novel.

- ↔ It is clear, too, that it is hard to find a conventional plot in the novel – not least because it spans such a long period of time. Moreover, the characters in it are sometimes strange – like the succession of Pews, all blind, who pass the job of lighthouse keeper on from generation to generation. Furthermore the intertextual references to *Dr Jekyll and Mr Hyde* undercut the idea that a character – either fictional or real – is consistent and integrated, and what is called 'self-transparent', because the two characters named in the title are two personalities or identities that are contained in a single individual. (You may note, however, that because Stevenson's novel is indeed first published in 1886, this means that the novel's attack on a belief in the unity of the individual and the individual character is something that predates postmodernism by a long time.)

↔ So far as blurring the boundaries between the factual and the fictional is concerned, consider these two quotations:

> Storytelling is a way of establishing connections, imaginative connections for ourselves, a way of joining up disparate material and making sense of the world.

> The continuous narrative of existence is a lie. There is no continuous narrative, there are lit-up moments, and the rest is dark. (134)

The first quotation comes from the end of the book, and is Winterson talking in her own voice in an interview; the second comes from the text of the novel and it is given to us as delivered by Silver. It is hard, surely, to say that the first belongs to a world of fact and the second to an enclosed world of fiction.

Text and peritext

In my comments above I noted that the section headings in the novel could be considered to be an aspect of what Gérard Genette terms the work's *peritext* – that is, of paratextual material 'inside' the novel proper which is not strictly part of the fictional world of the novel, but material that represents structurally ordering and categorizing information that we attribute to either the narrator or the author. It is important to remember that even the most realist of nineteenth-century novels include such material, even if it is just limited to chapter divisions and numbering. But if we look at such peritextual material as it appears in what we now consider to be standard nineteenth-century novels, we can see that it is different from what we encounter in *Lighthousekeeping*.

Here are a couple of examples from nineteenth-century novels.

CHAPTER XXVI

I fall into Captivity

XI

THE ARCHED WINDOW

The first of these is from Charles Dickens's *David Copperfield* (1849–50) while the second is from Nathaniel Hawthorne's *The House of the Seven Gables* (1851). The two chapter headings are representative of the novels in which they appear: those in Dickens's novel are presented as if they were written by the character narrator David Copperfield himself, while those in Hawthorne's novel seem to emanate from a categorizing intelligence that is apart from the world in which the characters live. Henry James, we should not be surprised to discover, had a preference for minimalist chapter and part headings that consisted merely of a number, and many of his modernist successors reduced chapter-division markers to textless space. Virginia Woolf's *The Waves*, for example, reduces such markers to page breaks – although the novel's alternation between roman and italic typeface also plays an important rôle in denoting perspectival shifts and thus divisions between sections, as it does too in Winterson's novel. In Woolf's last-published novel, *Between the Acts*, there are no conventional part or chapter divisions, but occasional line spaces are used to suggest a movement from one scene to another.

Now even though it seems to make sense to attribute the chapter heading from *David Copperfield* to David himself, it is a David who is as it were standing back from the action, separated from what is told both by time and by tone. If we return to *Lighthousekeeping* we become immediately aware that the neat division between (to use Genette's terms) text and peritext is hard to maintain. For example, the normal division between a chapter or section heading and the text that follows is often omitted in a manner that draws attention to this challenging of conventions. Note that if the headings in bold in the examples below were set in roman and closed up with the text that follows them, we would be hard put to see where the shift from heading to text occurred.

> **A beginning, a middle and an end is the proper way to tell a story. But I have difficulty with that method.**
> Already I could choose the year of my birth – 1959. (23)

> **As an apprentice to lighthousekeeping my duties were as follows:**
> 1) Brew a pot of Full Strength Samson and take it to Pew.
> 2) 8 am. Take DogJim for a walk. (37)

> **Dark was looking at the moon.**
> If the earth's history was fossil-written, why not the universe? The moon, bone-white, bleached of life, was the relic of a solar system once planeted with earths.
> He thought the whole of the sky must have been alive once, and some stupidity or carelessness had brought it to this burnt-out, warmless place. (147)

In the first two of these examples the headings appear to be written by the narrator Silver, and to merge into the subsequent first-person text. (And the year in which Silver is born is also the year in which her creator, Jeanette Winterson, was born.) But the third example details actions that took place years before Silver's reported birth, and so both the heading and the following text have to be attributed to a source other than that of Silver herself.

The postmodernist novel: some observations

It is tempting to suggest that a neat way of answering the question, 'What is postmodernism?' is by means of the reply: 'Everything that Henry James would have disapproved of!'. For James, maintaining the reading illusion that the fictional is real is fundamental to the success of the novel. If the novelist intrudes as him- or herself in the pages of the created work, reminding the reader that characters are his or her creation and events could have been decided otherwise, then the reader can no longer take what is read seriously, can no longer become involved with characters and their fates in the manner in which we get involved with real people and their fates.

So it is worth asking whether a novel like Jeanette Winterson's *Lighthouse-keeping* can serve as a sort of Jamesian Awful Warning. Does the intermingling of real-world and fictional-world people and events cause us to lose interest in Winterson's creation? Do we respond to the work as to a sort of one-person show on Winterson's part, one in which because we can see the strings and the puppet mistress, we lose interest in the puppets? Different readers will have to answer these questions themselves, but I have to say this is not how I respond to this novel. What is very striking and not a little strange to me is that in spite of all its postmodernist characteristics, I find myself as much gripped by this novel as by a novel by Henry James, as much involved with the lives of the characters and as concerned with what happens to them. Even the recurrent references to storytelling, to what we can call theories of narrative, do not lead me to disengage from the characters and events about which I am reading. Here are a few short examples.

> It was a long story, and like most of the stories in the world, never finished. There was an ending – there always is – but the story went on past the ending – it always does. (11)

> 'Why can't you just tell me the story without starting with another story?' 'Because there's no story that's the start of itself, any more than a child comes into the world without parents.' (27)

It seems to me that comments like these perform a sort of double function: on the one hand their self-referential nature has a sort of 'alienating' effect on the reader, who is reminded that the neat conventions of the novel beginning on page 1 and ending on the last page may simplify the complex reality of life. But on the other hand they make perfectly good sense as utterances delivered by a narrator who is forced to make choices about – for example – where to start her story.

If we ask *why* the postmodernist novel should have emerged when it did and in the form it has done, then a number of answers can be volunteered. On a personal level, Jeanette Winterson studied English at university and has clearly read and thought a lot about theoretical issues connected to narrative. But in the material included at the end of the book, following the final page of the novel proper, she includes a comment that suggests that her interest in narrative does not just come from books: 'Our mental processes are more like a maze than a motorway. We do not remember our lives chronologically, nor do we reflect on them in neat order.'

The comment provides a useful reminder that some aspects of postmodernism are taken from their predecessors, the modernists – and even from their predecessors, the 'classic realist' novelists. Virginia Woolf's essay 'Modern Fiction' has long been recognized as one of the key theoretical texts of modernist fiction, written by one of its leading practitioners. In this essay Woolf takes issue with what she calls 'materialist' writers such as H.G. Wells, Arnold Bennett and John Galsworthy and, having provided an unsympathetic account of their fiction (from which, in the case of Arnold Bennett, she claims 'life escapes'), she outlines an alternative. Instead of a concern with the objects of the outer world she proposes that we 'look within'. If we do, she suggests, we will see that the mind 'receives a myriad impressions', and that 'as they fall, as they shape themselves into the life of Monday or Tuesday, the accent falls differently from of old; the moment of importance came not here but there; so that, if a writer were a free man and not a slave, if he could write what he chose, not what he must, if he could base his work upon his own feeling and not upon convention, there would be no plot, no comedy, no tragedy, no love interest or catastrophe in the accepted style, and perhaps not a single button sewn on as the Bond Street tailors would have it. Life is not a series of gig lamps symmetrically arranged; life is a luminous halo, a semi-transparent envelope surrounding us from the beginning of consciousness to the end' (Woolf, 1966b, 106). Note that, as I have already suggested, although Woolf's essay represents a key statement of modernist principles, it also reveals the extent to which Woolf aims to represent life more realistically than her predecessors. If for some of them 'life escapes' from their accounts, she clearly hopes that it does not so escape from hers, and if there is more 'life' in her fiction then it is, arguably, in some sense more realistic than fiction from which life has, to a greater extent, escaped.

All new movements in fiction seem to involve a rebellion on the part of writers against conventions that have become so fixed that they end up almost as templates to which the novelist must conform, templates that push the novel in the direction of stereotype, cliché and the formulaic. It is perhaps ironic, in view of the use I have made of it, that Henry James's essay 'The Art of Fiction' was itself a polemic against precisely such a template – a guide to the writing of fiction by Walter Besant. But for Virginia Woolf there is a different template to be rejected, and although postmodernist writers may sympathize with her rebellion, they also see the need to push further.

If Woolf's injunction to 'look within' fixes her moment in history as one that she shares with Freud and the development of both psychology and psychoanalysis, Winterson's perhaps even greater concern to allow a lived experience of the world to determine the form in which that world is portrayed can also be linked to her own moment of history.

Fiction, truth and (recent) history

I would like to discuss briefly and with some hesitation one aspect of a moment of history so far as it impinges on the function and responsibilities of the writer of fiction. To do this, I will look at two short narratives, 'The Death of Schillinger' by Tadeusz Borowski and 'Revenge of a Dancer' by Sara Nomberg-Przytyk. These two very short stories have much in common: both are set in the Auschwitz concentration camp during the Second World War, and both recount a similar event. Amongst a group of prisoners destined for the gas chamber is a beautiful young woman who manages to snatch a revolver from an SS guard and kill him.

What these stories also have in common is that each of them is authored by an individual who themselves survived imprisonment in the Auschwitz concentration camp in the closing years of the Second World War, and that both stories appear in a collection of tales or stories that are either set in Auschwitz or that involve those who survived Auschwitz. Borowski's story appears in *This Way for the Gas, Ladies and Gentlemen*, which contains stories written in Polish between the end of the war and the author's suicide in 1951, and which was first published in English in 1976; Nomberg-Przytyk's story is to be found in *Auschwitz: True Tales from a Grotesque Land*, the Polish typescript of which is dated 1966 but which was first published in English in 1985. I should make it clear that I am not suggesting that either of these stories can productively be read as 'postmodernist', but rather that the reality with which they both engage, and thus disseminate in emplotted form in their stories, comes to constitute part of the historical moment of writers of a subsequent generation who read accounts such as these.

Formally speaking the two accounts also have certain features in common. Both are framed narratives, with the 'I' narrator reporting what a first-hand witness of the event had seen and has told him. This is how Borowski's story opens.

> Until 1943, First Sergeant Schillinger performed the duties of Lagerführer, or chief commanding officer of labour sector 'D' at Birkenau, which was part of the enormous complex of large and small concentration camps, centrally administered from Auschwitz, but scattered throughout Upper Silesia.
>
> Schillinger was a short, stocky man. He had a full, round face and very light blond hair, brushed flat against his head. His eyes were blue, always slightly narrowed, his lips tight, and his face was usually set in an impatient grimace. He cared little about personal appearance, and I have never heard of an incident involving his being bribed by any of the camp 'bigwigs'. (Borowski, 1976, 143)

After having described Schillinger and his actions, Borowski's narrator goes on to report that in August 1943 'we heard the news that Schillinger had died suddenly in unusual circumstances', and he then recounts the story told to him by the '*Sonderkommando* foreman' who was in charge of getting the female victims undressed and into the gas chamber. According to this man, Schillinger drew his revolver, then walked up to one of the women and took her hand. She bent down, scooped up some gravel and threw it in Schillinger's eyes, at which he cried out in pain and dropped his revolver. She then picked up this revolver and shot Schillinger several times in the chest, then also shooting the chief. At this the *Sonderkommando* men drove the victims into the gas chamber with clubs, and called on the SS to release the poison gas.

Borowski's story does not end there. The foreman concludes his account by describing the men of the *Sonderkommando* carrying the dying Schillinger ('not too gently', as he puts it) out to a car.

> 'On the way he kept groaning through clenched teeth: "*O Gott, mein Gott, was hab' ich getan, dass ich so leiden muss?*", which means – O God, my God, what have I done to deserve such suffering?'
> 'That man didn't understand even to the very end,' I said, shaking my head. 'What strange irony of fate.' (Borowski, 146)

In the final paragraph of the story, the 'I' narrator reports that later, shortly before the evacuation of the camp, the same *Sonderkommando* attempted to escape but were all machine-gunned by the SS guards.

In Borowski's story, then, the act of desperate and doomed defiance on the part of the woman serves as a backdrop to the main focus of the story, on an overwhelmingly bleak double irony. Even when Schillinger is given the chance to experience something of what it is like to be on the receiving end of undeserved violence, and even when he is contemplating his own imminent death, he is utterly unable to learn anything from this shift of perspective and he betrays no sense of sympathy for those he has murdered or any sense of having merited his fate. The woman and her fellow victims die, Schillinger dies, and the men of the *Sonderkommando* die – and none of these deaths is reported to have led to any understanding on the part of those who die, or to any sense of having established any sense of worth through their death.

This is how Nomberg-Przytyk's story opens.

> During the summer of 1944 the transports used to arrive at Auschwitz at night as well as in the daytime. We often woke up because of the shouting of the SS men, the barking of dogs, the whistling of trainmen, the stamping of hundreds of feet, and the cries of desperation in different languages. At night the atrocities combined with our sleeplessness to give us a very real sense of existing in a factory of death. And yet, it all appeared unreal.
> This particular July night it was the shouting of the SS men and the barking of the dogs that awakened me. (Nomberg-Przytyk, 1985, 107)

The I narrator of the story – in this case a woman prisoner – is summoned by a friend to the infirmary, where they find a very frightened young girl, who eventually tells them her story. She and her fellow female prisoners had arrived at Auschwitz the previous evening. They were wearing bathing suits because of the extreme heat. They believed that they were going to be put to work and did not respond to warnings that they were heading for death. One of her fellow prisoners was 'an unusually beautiful woman', a young dancer from Paris.

On arrival at Auschwitz they are told to take off their clothes and they are treated brutally by the SS men. The dancer refuses to undress, and is approached by an SS man who is apparently the commandant of the guards.

> 'Beautiful girl, take off your suit,' he said quietly, coming closer and closer to her. Then, all of a sudden, with a rapid movement, she grabbed the pistol out of his holster and shot straight at him. After that, she took three steps backward and shot at the SS men who were running all over the place. She saved the last bullet for herself. (109)

The young girl who tells the story to the narrator is thrown a dress by a German soldier and, in the confusion, pulled behind a gate and taken to the infirmary, where she is subsequently able to assume the identity of a French girl who has died in the camp. One of the listeners to her story comments on the action of the dancer: '"That's how you're supposed to die," said Magda' (109).

Speaking very generally we can say that a comparison of these two stories can serve to show how comparable events can be presented in different narratives in ways that lead the reader to utterly different conclusions. In Nomberg-Przytyk's narrative the act of rebellion asserts certain recognizable human qualities: independence, resistance to oppression, courage, activity rather than passivity. In the most extreme circumstances the young dancer asserts her humanity and reminds her listeners (and the readers of Nomberg-Przytyk's story) of ours. In Borowski's story no such positives are apparent. In this story, as in others by Borowski, the message is that both perpetrators and victims are corrupted and morally destroyed by the degradation of Auschwitz. There is no assertion of a shared humanity, no uplifting message for the listeners, no reported final insight on the part of Schillinger, the young woman, the *Sonderkommando*, the framed narrator or his listeners. For some commentators, this may make Borowski's story the one that engages more truthfully (or 'realistically') with the actuality with which it attempts to engage.

Fiction, fact, truth

In order to engage with this opinion I want, at this point, to discuss something that I have deliberately avoided commenting on up to now – the generic status of these two stories. The collection in which Borowski's story is gathered in English translation is categorized on its back cover as 'fiction', and the translator's note that prefaces the stories describes them as 'stories inspired by his [Borowski's] concentration-camp experiences' (9). The edition of Nomberg-Przytyk's stories at no point describes them as fictional, and indeed the volume title describes them as 'true tales', although there is no unambiguous statement in the volume confirming that this title was chosen by Nomberg-Przytyk herself. The translator's note refers to the original manuscript as 'a readable, dramatically compelling account, not simply of the author's consciousness, but of the people in the camp' (ix). The assumption, then, is that the 'I' of these stories is Nomberg-Przytyk herself rather than a fictional narrator, and that although they can accurately be described as *stories*, they are not *works of fiction* but 'accounts' – reports of real people and actual events.

Two other accounts of this event have been published, one by Auschwitz survivor Wieslaw Kielar in his memoir *Anus Mundi: Five Years in Auschwitz*, which was first published in Polish in 1972, and one by Buchenwald survivor Eugen Kogon in his *The Theory and Practice of Hell: The German Concentration Camps and the System Behind Them*, which was first published in German in 1946. Kielar reports that there are different versions of what happened, but he indicates which version he finds most likely to be accurate. So why should one read a fictional account of a terrible event when there are non-fictional accounts available?

To write fictional accounts of the horrors of the Holocaust, even when the writer is him- or herself a Holocaust survivor, is a very contentious activity. During, immediately following and long after the events of the Holocaust many commentators have insisted that only the truth will do, that fictional accounts of these terrible events betray the writer's duty to give true testimony and may play into the hands of those who deny all or part of the reality of the sufferings and murders inflicted on the victims. However, the editors of Nomberg-Przytyk's stories, Eli Pfefferkorn and David H. Hirsch, note that 'even [Eli] Wiesel has recognized that sometimes it is only fiction that can make the truth credible', and they quote from his imagined conversation with a Rabbi: 'Things are not that simple, Rebbe. Some events do take place but are not true; others are, although they never occurred' (166). The narrator of another work of fiction dealing with Holocaust experiences – Anne Michaels's novel *Fugitive Pieces* – comments: 'Never trust biographies. Too many events in a man's life are invisible' (141). Such events may be invisible to the historian, but some may be exposed by the writer of fiction. Such paradoxes have a postmodernist ring to them, and they may lead us to wonder whether certain of the characteristics that strike us now as postmodernist may have emerged in experiences that in some cases could be represented truly only in fiction. Whether we accept this or not, the act of classification that would in a traditional view place these two stories in absolutely distinct categories is belied by the reader's experience of them as in many ways very similar.

It may be something of a seven-league leap to link this perceived similarity with the postmodern tendency to reject Henry James's view that the fictional world that a novelist creates, and the real world that he or she inhabits, should never be confused, but I think that the thought is worth some consideration. My point, then, is that the historical moment of postmodernism is a moment in which we have become more conscious of the puzzling fact that not only can fictional accounts open up to our scrutiny aspects of experience that are closed to the gaze of the historian, but also that the accounts of the historian contain artifices and arrangements that are shared with the writer of fiction. Remember that in Chapter 1 I quoted Dorrit Cohn's claim that only in fiction can narrators enter the consciousnesses of individuals other than themselves. One implication of this is that the only form of narrative that can present the reader with the inner experiences of those who cannot bear testimony to their own sufferings is fiction.

Wieslaw Kielar's account of the incident has one significant point of interest. He reports that when the story became known, '[t]he news spread through the camp like wildfire and was greeted everywhere with rejoicing' (Kielar, 1982, 178). Moreover

> [t]he incident passed on from mouth to mouth and embellished in various ways grew into a legend. Without doubt this heroic deed by a weak woman, in the face of certain death, gave moral support to every prisoner.
>
> ...
>
> Reaction came swiftly; prisoners straightened up, hope grew once more. (178, 179)

'Embellished accounts', legends – *fictions* even if based on a fundamentally factual and true core, are one of the means whereby people discover their own potentialities and alter their behaviour in the real world.

I hope that I have already made it clear that I would not want to describe either of these stories, or any of the other stories in the two volumes in which they are collected, as 'postmodernist'. For a start, that association of postmodernism with a playful display of writerly virtuosity is utterly at odds with the tone and atmosphere of these two tales. But the stories may conceivably illuminate some aspects of the historical moment of postmodernism, a historical moment in which reality can seem unreal, fiction can depict truths beyond the gaze of the historian, and the truthful account must seek the help of fictional artifice.

Topics for discussion

→ Do you like novels to be 'true to life'? Explain why (or why not). What does 'true to life' mean?
→ Why do governments often fear 'unrealistic' parodies and satires?
→ Is modernism 'the realism of the age of Freud'?
→ What technical innovations are associated with modernism and postmodernism? Why are they needed?
→ Can fiction help us to understand actual historical experiences in a way that history cannot?

Chapter 5

Fiction and the electronic media

Preview

This chapter deals with:

↪ new technology and traditional forms in 'electronic fiction'
↪ electronic texts: the end of the linear narrative?
↪ technology and artistic value

A new sort of fiction?

According to an online newspaper article accessed on 3 August 2004, up to four million players world-wide regularly visit make-believe lands to fight, hunt for treasure or just chat (Meek, 2004, 1). All of these individuals are participants in online fantasy games known by the acronym MMORPG ('massively multiplayer online role-playing games'). Each player adopts an online identity and, using this identity, is able to enter virtual worlds and to interact with other players (who also, of course, have entered the game by means of other adopted identities). Here there is no single plot, no shared beginning and – the companies who earn vast amounts of money from these games earnestly wish – no ending. MMORPGs represent only one of the new fictional experiences currently on offer to those with a personal computer and (ideally but not essentially) an internet connection.

What has this to do with the study of fictional works such as *Wuthering Heights* and 'Fanny and Annie'? In immediate terms, not much, perhaps. The very nature of such online games with their multiple plots and character lists that make a novel by Charles Dickens look underpopulated do not lend themselves to academic study. But the history of prose fiction is the history of a succession of low-status popular forms that are eventually accorded academic respectability (compare Bakhtin's comments on the 'heterogeneous' ancestors of the novel, quoted on p. 13), and it would be rash to suggest that none of the new fictional forms associated with the electronic media will ever produce anything worthy of serious attention. That, however, is a matter for history to rule on; so far as the present is concerned, these new fictional forms deserve some comment for a number of reasons. The first is that many of them are heavily parasitic on certain traditional fictional genres and sub-genres, ranging from the folk tale to fantasy and science fiction, and this survival of such popular and frequently highly formulaic fictional modes prompts us to ask whether these often despised modes answer some essential need in human beings.

The second reason for devoting some brief attention to new forms of fiction associated with the electronic media is that those who have analysed them have often found some of the tools developed by literary critics and, especially, narratologists extremely useful, and this too may tell us something about underlying continuities in the narratives we read and enjoy.

The third reason is the one I find most important. Some of the new possibilities brought to fiction by the electronic media, such as reader/player–text interaction, (permanently) postponed closure and multiple, non-linear plots, oftentimes appear to be counter-productive in terms of artistic quality, however much they may increase reader/player enjoyment on a short-term basis. This may suggest some link between the high artistic achievements of traditional prose fiction and certain of its conventional formal elements. Another way of putting this is to suggest that although it is possible for the writer of fiction to do things in a text that is published electronically that are not possible with traditional book publication, this increased freedom may cut away some of the constraints that have helped to produce novels and short stories of great artistic merit. (Greater technical possibility is by no means a guarantee of greater artistic accomplishment: the advent first of sound, and then of colour, did not immediately result in the production of better films.) It is in particular the *fixity* of the printed text and the *linearity* of the printed narrative that seem to have been instrumental in establishing a set of artistically productive limits for the novel. The reason why there is no universally acknowledged great work of electronic fiction may not merely be that the 'text' followed in various electronic fictional forms is ephemeral and thus hard to subject to collective scrutiny, but also that the loss of the fixed linear narrative may also entail a loss of artistic worth.

In what follows, then, I want to look briefly at some of these new fictional forms, searching them for evidence of new potentialities in fiction while also using them to explore some of the sources of the artistic importance of more traditional forms such as the novel, the novella and the short story. Paying some attention to the typical computer game or to interactive fiction can be productive in much the same way that looking at a film adaptation of a novel can be: it may show what the traditional novel is incapable of achieving, but it may also show what the traditional novel can do that is beyond the reach of film or interactive fiction.

Let us start by reminding ourselves of certain things about traditional fictional forms such as the novel. When we pick up a novel we know that we are expected to start reading at the beginning and read sequentially through to the end, following the single track of what is known as a '(uni)linear narrative' (a telling that follows a single line of written text). Note that even if the narrative is telling us about two or more separate threads in the plot, the actual *telling* still has this quality of 'one thing at a time' – in contrast to a film which can (and generally must) depict a number of things going on at the same time. The 'conventional generic requirements' that I have mentioned sanction pauses to contemplate what we have read, and the reader is also permitted to flick back to pages that have already been read so as to review their content. A reader can also choose his or her own speed of reading, and can vary this from chapter to chapter or paragraph to paragraph. Note that this gives the individual reader a control over his or her own reading experience that the members of the audience of a play or a publicly shown film do not enjoy. Peering at a novel's conclusion before we have read all the pages that precede it, omitting chapters or even deciding to ignore the final chapter printed in the book and writing our own conclusion – such behaviour is in contrast not sanctioned by the unstated but universally agreed conventions of novel-reading; it breaks the established and understood codes that all novel readers have to a greater or lesser extent internalized. Moreover, the fact that a novel is contained in a physical object – a book – means that we have a very clear sense of how much more there is to read as the right-hand collection of pages gets thinner and thinner.

We expect, furthermore, that excepting a few rare and unrepresentative cases, what we read will be the responsibility of a single author, however much he or she may have been influenced by others. (Interestingly, in a number of cases of joint authorship the writers conceal their plurality behind a single pseudonym.) We also assume that this single person is ultimately both author and authority: he or she alone can decide what happens in the world of the novel. We do not expect to open a newspaper and to read a headline that states: 'Readers Reject Conclusion of New Harry Potter Novel: Publisher Sacks Author and Starts Search for a Replacement'. (If that seems a merely silly example, we should remember that this sort of thing actually happens all the time in the world of television soaps and comedies – usually without millions of viewers knowing that it has happened. The high status, visibility and legal authority possessed by the writers of novels are not enjoyed by all writers of fiction.)

It is often assumed that such conventions were faithfully and uncomplainingly adhered to until suddenly the possibilities offered by the new electronic media presented writers and readers with the chance to subvert or ignore them. But in *The Anthology and the Rise of the Novel: From Richardson to George Eliot*, Leah Price shows that subversions were there from the start, and sometimes encouraged by the authors themselves. Thus Samuel Richardson himself published an anthology of 'sentiments, cautions, aphorisms, reflections and observations' taken from his 1747 novel *Clarissa* (and published only three years after the novel) which were arranged in alphabetical order. By 1760 Richardson was responsible for a 'set of entertaining Cards, neatly engraved on Copper-Plates, Consisting of moral and diverting Sentiments, extracted wholly from the much admired Histories of PAMELA, CLARISSA, and SIR CHARLES GRANDISON' (Price, 2000, 17). So much for the modernity of the subversion of linear narrative! But Price also reports that Lady Bradshaigh

> accepted Richardson's invitation for friends to write a sequel to.
> Grandison which he himself would merely edit, so 'that every one
> of my Correspondents, at his or her own Choice, assume one of the
> surviving Characters in the Story, and write in it; and that ... I shall
> pick and choose, alter, connect, and accommodate, till I have completed
> from [the contributions], the requested Volume'. (38)

So much too, then, for the view that interactive fiction was born in and with the necessary help of the electronic age – although it is noticeable here that Richardson does retain for himself the power to decide what to include and what to alter or omit. While these 'subversions' are interesting, what I find more telling is the fact that today we still read *Clarissa* but the entertaining cards and the anthology of sentiments are to be found only in dusty library vaults.

Within a few years of this example, Chapter 20 of the first book of Laurence Sterne's *Tristram Shandy* (1759–67) shows an author attempting to create at least the illusion of interaction with a particular reader. The chapter opens with the following much-quoted lines.

> – How could you, Madam, be so inattentive in reading the last chapter?
> I told you in it, That my mother was not a papist. – Papist! You told me
> no such thing, Sir. – Madam, I beg leave to repeat it over again, that I
> told you as plain, at least, as words, by direct inference, could tell you
> such a thing. – Then, Sir, I must have miss'd a page. – No, Madam, you
> have not miss'd a word. – Then I was asleep, Sir. – My pride, Madam,
> cannot allow you that refuge. – Then, I declare, I know nothing at all
> about the matter. – That, Madam, is the very fault I lay to your charge;
> and as a punishment for it, I do insist upon it, that you immediately
> turn back, that is as soon as you get to the next full stop, and read the
> whole chapter over again. I have imposed this penance upon the lady,
> neither out of wantonness nor cruelty; but from the best of motives;
> and therefore shall make her no apology for it when she returns back:

– 'Tis to rebuke a vicious taste, which has crept into thousands besides herself, – of reading straight forwards, more in quest of the adventures, than of the deep erudition and knowledge which a book of this cast, if read over as it should be, would infallibly impart with them ....

This is a joke, of course: Sterne is pretending that the author can communicate personally about his or her text with each individual reader. But in making the joke, Sterne is also exposing the limits and limitations of print-based fiction and, moreover, making a distinction between two sorts of reading that can be compared both to Samuel Johnson's comment on the two possible ways of reading Richardson's fiction (see p. 33) and to very recent attempts to produce non-linear narratives.

From the start of the modern novel, then, there have been sporadic if not widespread attempts to subvert, expose or submit to pressure some of the most established of fictional conventions: linearity and fixed sequential progression through the text of the novel (which does not, of course, entail a fixed chronological progression through the events of the story; see the discussion of story and plot on p. 140), a fixed text determined by a single author who cannot be interacted with directly by the reader, and a coherent and unitary story-world within which certain laws of irreversibility generally apply. ('Generally', because genres such as fantasy and science fiction do complicate this last element somewhat.) Granted that such precedents can be found, however, it is certainly the case that the electronic media have opened up new possibilities for such subversion – or, to avoid prejudgement, let us say for rewriting the ground rules of fiction. What possibilities in particular do the electronic media offer? Let us consider the most important ones.

Fixity

A book or story once printed cannot be significantly altered. Misprints and mistakes can be indicated in an 'erratum' slip, and new editions can always be produced, but there is a very powerful tendency in print culture to consider printed texts as complete, unalterable and sacrosanct. The dramatist Joe Orton ended up in prison after being caught defacing library books, and even if this is an extreme example, it does show how alterations to written texts have tended to be seen not as creative additions but as violations. In the days of hot-metal typesetting (which only really disappeared in the book trade in the 1970s), publishers used to send out instructions to authors along with proofs warning them that the addition of a single comma could necessitate the re-setting of several pages of print, at very great cost. Today an electronic typesetter is able to make such an adjustment in a fraction of a second, and everyone knows how very easy it is to alter electronic text. But even with electronic typesetting, once a book has been printed it cannot be changed in the way that an electronic text on a computer screen (or an electronic book display unit) can be. It is thus hard to treat an electronic text as 'finished', as complete and unalterable, in the way that a book appears to us to be. Even a text written by someone else can be imported and changed on a computer. One result of this fixity is that whereas traditional books have beginnings and ends, the beginnings and ends of electronic texts tend to have a much more provisional quality to them. When the final page of a book is read, there is no more. With an electronic text, what is the final word today may be followed by additional text tomorrow.

Linearity

According to Milan Kundera, 'since its very beginnings, the novel has tried to escape the unilinear, to open rifts in the continuous narration of a story', and he notes that although Cervantes's Don Quixote travels on a linear journey, he meets other characters who tell their own stories and thus the reader is able to step outside the novel's linear framework (Kundera, 1988, 74). However, even if the line of Quixote's journey may be interrupted, the reader has to follow Cervantes's line of prose wherever it takes him or her.

No one who has surfed the net can be unaware that by clicking on a succession of links one can take a path through a variety of texts that may well be unique to oneself. It is typical of the reading experiences offered by the electronic media that they do not conform to a strict linear pattern. This does seem to represent a fundamental shift in reading possibilities. Of course, we can always say that the person who read a novel and who stopped every now and then to look up a word in a dictionary, or to consult an entry in an encyclopaedia, or even to check what happened in another novel by the same author was exploring 'links' in just the same way as a person who clicks on a link on a computer screen. However, although there is arguably a parallel here, it is a weak and a very restricted one, and cannot obscure the fact that while linear progression characterized most reading experiences – and especially the reading of fiction – from the eighteenth century to about 1990, the growth of the World Wide Web means that nowadays this is no longer the case. We have even coined a new verb to reflect this: 'to surf'. Readers in the past could skim or skip or browse or 'dip into' books (strange that so many of these metaphors are connected to water!), but surfing is arguably different from all of these slightly shameful ways of dealing with printed texts.

Interaction and collective authorship

Generally speaking, although the reader can tell an author what he or she thinks of a novel after having read it, actually influencing how it is written *while* it is being written has until recently been possible only for a few intimate friends of the author. We have two endings for Charles Dickens's *Great Expectations* because Edward Bulwer-Lytton, who read the novel in proof, persuaded Dickens to write a happier ending. And to remain with Dickens: the special circumstances of serial publication meant that readers could plead with him concerning the fate of favoured characters. However, this example is perhaps as well known as it is precisely because it is so unusual and atypical. The resources of the electronic media have enabled the creation of so-called interactive fiction, or IF, based on programs that require 'readers' to make choices that resemble the choices a map reader makes in working his or her way across a town. The program allows for a number of possible 'routes', but a single reading will involve only one such route. Other web-based writing resources allow for more genuinely democratic interaction, where participants are free to submit text that may be voted in to form a part of a constantly evolving collective fiction.

These new resources of the electronic media have been exploited by those claiming to offer revolutionary new forms of fiction. Among these are the following.

The computer game

It may seem odd to introduce discussion of the computer game in a book on the novel. However, in his book *More Than a Game: The Computer Game as Fictional Form*, Barry Atkins argues that 'computer game-fiction is a form of popular fiction' (Atkins, 2003, 9). For Atkins, many of the most popular computer games available today can be linked directly to forms of traditional narrative. Discussing one of these games – the now-dated *Tomb Raider* – he argues that in many ways it 'conforms to the generic conventions of the folk tale, and particularly the quest narrative, and wears many of its folk tale credentials on its sleeve' (42). He explains:

> As in *Tomb Raider* there are few extraneous or irrelevant encounters within the folk tale quest narrative: anyone or anything encountered will prove to be either an adversary or a helper. Overcoming adversaries through violence is virtually mandatory and, as in *Tomb Raider* or any amount of contemporary *Ramboesque* versions of the quest narrative, there is no ethical or moral problem with such violence.
>
> ...
>
> The occasional riddle must be solved. Often an object must be retrieved. (43)

Of course, the riddles to be solved differ in nature from those in the traditional folk tale, and the player of the game must solve problems correctly before being allowed to proceed through the narrative, but the parallels between the computer game and, say, the picaresque novel (see the Glossary) are striking. One important difference, however, is that although the reader of a picaresque novel is able to empathize with the picaro, some of the experiences of the *hero* in the earlier form become the experiences of the *reader/player* in the new one. I should add that many computer games do allow players to shift their point of view – to experience events at one moment through an active 'hero' or 'heroine' and at another moment from a more detached and contemplative perspective.

As Atkins points out, the computer game is only 'interactive' in a very limited way: one cannot stray too far from the 'correct', and circumscribed, path and generally one can only perform actions that have been predicted or allowed for by the game-fiction's designers (41). But then much the same can be said of the experiences offered by different varieties of popular fiction to which the label 'formulaic' has been attached – the folk tale, the picaresque novel, the detective novel and the romance, for example. However formulaic and restricted the choices offered by the computer game may be, they do show how very traditional elements from narrative fiction can be married to the resources of the electronic media in ways that will inevitably become more sophisticated (and perhaps, although not necessarily, more aesthetically productive) as time goes by.

Interactive fiction

It is not a long jump from computer games to what is known as interactive fiction, or IF. Indeed, deciding where the frontier between the two forms is to be drawn is by no means a straightforward matter. According to Nick Montfort, 'IF works are often, among other things, games, with an optimal outcome that the interactor, acting as a player, tries to attain' (Montfort, 2003, 13). Like Barry Atkins, Montfort also comments on the presence of the old in the new, noting that the narratives generated by IF 'are often more trivial and repetitive than even the bluntest folktale' (14). Montfort explains that a work of IF is not itself a narrative: 'it is an interactive computer program' that can, when 'played', generate narratives (25). When we start such a program our initial experience is that we are much more active than we are when we read the printed text of a traditional novel. We have to respond, to make decisions, to interact with the program. Should we take this route or that route, should we do this or do that? My choice of words is deliberate here, because IF programs typically present us with a finite – indeed a small – number of pre-decided options to choose from rather than asking us to come up with a totally new and original plot movement. The experience of IF is thus closer to the experience of finding our way through a maze than to sitting down and reading a novel from scratch – something strongly suggested by the title of Montfort's book: *Twisty Little Passages: An Approach to Interactive Fiction*. This is why I wrote that our *initial* experience is that we are much more active than we are when we read the printed text of a traditional novel – because the sort of activity in which we engage when we play a computer game is actually rather less sophisticated, and less artistically satisfying, than the sort of mental activity generated in us when we read a major novel. When we read *Bleak House* or *The Waves* we do not interact with the text by deciding how the plot will unfold – by choosing between or amongst proffered plot alternatives. But if we search back into our reading experiences we will find, I think, that they are by no means purely passive, and this is one of the reasons why no two readings of an important novel, whether by the same reader or by two different readers, are identical. This is an important point and I would like to suggest that the reader pause here and consider the sorts of 'interaction' that take place when we read a challenging novel. Isn't one of the dangers of establishing a sub-genre known as 'interactive fiction' that this may imply that the reader of a traditional novel does not interact with what the text provides him or her with?

As is the case with the computer game, the artistic or aesthetic worth of such generated narratives is not generally deemed to be high, but interactive fiction is worth commenting on for a couple of reasons. The first is that it is striking how useful the conceptual tools of modern narratology (see p. 198) have been found in describing elements in the IF world. Thus for example Montfort distinguishes between the *commands* keyed in by the IF 'reader' – which are 'diegetic' and refer to an action in the IF world – and *directives*, which are keyed in instructions 'such as those that save, restore, quit, restart, change the level of detail in the room descriptions, or address some entity that is not part of the IF world – for instance, to ask for hints' (26), and which are by implication 'extradiegetic'. Why is this significant? Because it perhaps demonstrates that however modern IF may appear, in narrative terms it is relatively old-fashioned and (to coin a horrific term) 'pre-postmodernist'. By this I mean that, as insisted upon by Henry James (see p. 77), IF involves fictional worlds that are insulated from direct contact with our everyday world.

In her excellent study *Narrative as Virtual Reality: Immersion and Interactivity in Literature and Electronic Media* (2001), Marie-Laure Ryan discusses the tension and the interplay between 'immersion' and 'interactivity' in the reading of fiction. Her discussion has points of contact with my contention in this book that both when reading and when studying the novel we have to alternate between treating the characters and events as in some way real, and recognizing them as creations of the writer's craft (see for example p. 177). Ryan suggests, correctly I think, that 'immersion' in a fictional work of any sort is only possible by means of 'an imaginative relationship to a *textual world*' (Ryan, 2001, 14), and she suggests that our concept of a textual world assumes four features: 'connected set of objects and individuals; habitable environment; reasonably intelligible totality for external observers; field of activity for its members' (91). The word 'external' is important here: it only makes sense to talk about *immersing* ourselves in the world of a fiction if that world is in some way fenced off from our own world. One further important point argued by Ryan is that when we assess the viability of a work of fiction 'as a document of real-world events', we are no longer reading it as fiction but as non-fiction (105). In other words, immersion in a fictional world necessitates some sort of abandonment of our own 'real world'. Readers must decide to what extent such a position is undercut or problematized by my comments on postmodernist fiction in the previous chapter.

This very sharp distinction between the extrafictional world in which the real-life reader lives in his or her everyday life, and the realized world of the fiction that can only be entered imaginatively and interacted with by him or her if its rules are adhered to, is one that is familiar to readers of conventional fiction, although once again it is important to underline that we are talking about two very different sorts of interaction here. Nothing that goes on in my head while I am reading *Wuthering Heights*, or after I have finished reading it, will change the text of that work, although – and this is an important point – it *will* change my perception of that text. Nevertheless, one of the things that traditional print-based novels from *Moll Flanders* to *The Hours* have in common with various modes of electronic fiction is that they offer what Montfort calls 'simulated worlds' that are possessed of an internal coherence and logic that may mimic the coherence and logic of the extrafictional world but that are nevertheless distinct.

The second reason why IF is worthy of consideration, then, is precisely because it reminds us that a fiction is only of interest to the extent that it offers the reader some *resistance*. A generated IF fiction in which the reader-player can change the rules of the fictional world at will would be merely boring; however much we may want certain things to happen when we are reading a novel, a fiction that allows us to realize and enact any desired outcome is neither stimulating nor satisfying. Imagine reading a work of fiction on the screen of an electronic book, and coming across the following message:

> Final chapter: press 1 for happy ending, 2 for tragic ending, 3 for ambiguous ending (advanced users only)

After the previous edition of this book was published I discovered that Julian Barnes had got there before me in his novel *Flaubert's Parrot*, although as the novel was published in 1984 the choices offered were not electronic.

> After all, if novelists really wanted to simulate the delta of life's possibilities, this is what they'd do. At the back of the book would be a set of sealed envelopes in various colours. Each would be clearly marked on the outside: Traditional Happy Ending; Traditional Unhappy Ending; Traditional Half-and-half Ending; Deus ex Machina; Modernist Arbitrary Ending; End of the World Ending; Cliffhanger Ending; Dream Ending; Opaque Ending; Surrealist Ending; and so on. You would be allowed only one, and would have to destroy the envelopes you didn't select. *That*'s what I call offering the reader a choice of endings; but you may find me quite unreasonably literal-minded. (Barnes, 1985, 89)

Note again, however, that even in this example there is a limited choice between predetermined alternatives: the reader cannot write a unique ending to suit him- or herself.

Since 1984 it has become clear that the technological capacity to offer readers such options at the click of a computer mouse is already with us – and electronic texts offering a succession of such choice-points may soon be on offer (if they are not already). But one of the aspects of the extrafictional world that is simulated by fiction is that reality is not something that we can mould at will and to our will. Marie-Laure Ryan expresses the matter with telling economy:

> If the reader or spectator can choose whether Jack will be a hero or a coward, this means that Jack's behavior, and by extension the fate of the entire fictional world, is determined not by any kind of internal necessity but by the decisions of an omnipotent creator located in the real world. Yet the loss of the sense of the autonomy of the fictional world that occurs at every decision point is not compensated by a gain of creative power, because the choices are all prescribed paths. (2001, 283)

If then the fictional world is one into which we can enter, which we can observe and to which we can emotionally respond, but which we cannot act within or change, does not this turn the reader into a sort of voyeur? Ryan would not be dismayed by the question: 'Whether or not we like to admit it, voyeurism has a lot to do with the pleasures we take in narrative fiction: where else but in a novel can we penetrate into the most guarded and the most fascinating of realms, the inner workings of a foreign consciousness?' (149). Note the clear implication that Ryan shares Dorrit Cohn's view that it is only in fiction that a consciousness other than that of the teller may be entered (p. 3).

Modes such as the computer game and IF may thus teach us a negative lesson: the fixity of print-based fiction, the unalterability of a novel published in book form, may actually contribute to its artistic force. Our ability to change the physical and social world is significantly limited in real life, perhaps the unchangeability of the printed text mirrors and models this aspect of our experience of the world. Is not our interaction with a major novel very often of the type: 'What would I have done in this situation?'And is not this a more productive form of interaction than that involved in choosing one of a number of predetermined plot paths or story-lines? One of the easy assumptions into which we can fall is that indulging our fantasy in fiction is pleasant because nothing nasty ever happens and we can control everything. As Ryan puts it, if we feel that things happen in a created fictional world not as a result of 'internal necessity but by the decisions of an omnipotent creator located in the real world' – whether that omnipotent creator is the designer of a computer program or an author who keeps speaking in his or her own voice and reminding us of his or her power – then does not this undermine the crucial ability of fiction to model the problems and experiences of the world in which we live?

Fan fiction

From an academic perspective, fan fiction (otherwise 'fanfic') may perhaps be almost the least respectable form of fiction being written today, but it too is not without its points of interest for the serious student of fiction. Fan fiction is very much a child of the internet, and publication is almost exclusively in electronic format. Its authors are the fans of particular books, films or TV series who use the characters from these sources to create their own extensions of the stories in the originals. Some fan fiction also involves the creation of stories in which real celebrities appear as characters. Fan-fiction stories generally involve accounts of activities barred to the original outlets, especially ones involving sexual activity. Authorship can be individual or collaborative (as in IF – see p. 93). The anonymity of internet publication may be an essential aspect of this form of writing, and it may also make contact between fan-fiction writers less problematic than it would otherwise be. Although it is a disregarded form of writing so far as academics are concerned, it is widespread and fast-expanding.

The genre is worthy of attention because it may make visible an activity in which many readers of more canonical fiction engage: imagining new scenes involving the characters, including scenes in which the reader him- or herself is involved. Beyond this, fan-fiction writing is a very democratic affair, lacking the usual distinction between the few (authors) and the many (readers). It thus serves to remind us how central fiction is to ordinary lives, and how closely related to the everyday exercise of our ability to imagine and to fantasize, and how bound up with our private and secret lives. It offers a relevant example of the way in which a new technology may offer new possibilities for some very ancient human impulses and capacities.

Hypertext fiction

Nick Montfort, to whose book *Twisty Little Passages* I have already referred, provides a neat definition of hypertext fiction:

> A hypertext fiction (as it is most commonly defined and discussed)
> is a system of fictional interconnected texts traversed using links. An
> interconnected text is referred to by George Landow (1992) and others
> as a *lexia*, a term borrowed from [Roland] Barthes (1974), who applied
> it differently as a block of signification or unit of reading that was
> empirically determined, during a reading. ... There is, however, nothing
> in the nature of the lexia or the link, those fundamental elements of
> hypertext, that allows the reader to type and contribute text or provides
> the computer with the means to parse or understand natural language.
> (2003, 12)

The definition does not state whether these varied 'lexia' are written by the same person or by a number of individuals, or whether the 'fiction' is produced with all of its lexia available from the start, or whether it can be added to as time goes on. These are presumably details that vary from fiction to fiction.

Marie-Laure Ryan notes that for some commentators 'Hypertext thus becomes a metaphor for a Lyotardian "postmodern condition" in which grand narratives have been replaced by "little stories," or perhaps by no stories at all – just by a discourse reveling in the Derridanean performance of an endless deferral of signification' (2001, 7). This short comment needs considerable unpacking. One of the characteristics attributed to our 'postmodern condition' by the French theorist Jean-François Lyotard is the replacement of 'grand narratives' by 'little narratives' (see p. 74 and the Glossary for discussion of postmodernism). These 'narratives' are not those that constitute works of literary fiction, but explanatory 'stories' by means of which we make sense of our lives. 'Grand narratives' are ideological systems of belief such as Marxism or religious beliefs such as Christianity, and for Lyotard the postmodern world is characterized by the loss of such all-embracing and comprehensive stories that provide meaning. Instead, we live in a world and at a time when sense and meaning have only a local purchase. Ryan's reference to the French philosopher Jacques Derrida deals especially with Derrida's concept of 'différance', a term that in French combines the meanings 'to differ' and 'to defer'. The concept is part of a much more complex argument on Derrida's part, but the important point for our purposes is that it builds upon a vision that also rejects some of the formal characteristics of the traditional narratives that we use to make sense of our lives, especially fixity of meaning, cause and effect, and completion (what is often referred to as 'closure').

This somewhat wordy excursion into theory is necessary to explain why for some commentators the technical possibilities displayed by hypertext do no more than actualize already existing elements in the postmodern world: a loss of totalizing systems of meaning, a concern with local, self-contained explanations rather than final answers, and an individually chosen and potentially never-ending route through a maze of possibilities rather than a walk along a broad single highway of meaning in the company of everyone else, until the end of the road is reached. Ryan calls such new modes of organization 'rhizomic', picking up on ideas taken from another French theorist, Gilles Deleuze. The potato plant exemplifies such a connective system, with each potato (in botanical terms a rhizome) connected to other potatoes not in one long linear string, but in a network of interconnections. As Ryan puts it:

> In a rhizomic organization, in opposition to the hierarchical tree
> structures of rhetorical argumentation, the imagination is not
> constrained by the need to prove a point or to progress toward a goal,
> and the writer never needs to sacrifice those bursts of inspiration that
> cannot be integrated into a linear argument. (2001, 8)

Ryan also provides a useful distinction between *multilinear* texts, which are those that offer the reader a choice among many well-charted sequences, and non-linear texts, which are those 'that allow the reader to break her own trail' (209).

From such a perspective the traditional novel with its linear narrative, single fictional world, story-line linked by laws of cause and effect, and an overall meaning relating to a plot with a beginning, middle and end is based upon assumptions that no longer match our experience of, or beliefs about, the world. In contrast, the infant mode of hypertext fiction reflects more accurately the world in which we live, and the ways in which we live in the world.

In very broad terms such a view can be said to be sociological in essence. It argues a broad similarity between the dominant characteristics of an age (both how the age 'works' and how people living at that time perceive their lives and surroundings) and the dominant characteristics of fiction. The argument goes something like this. In the nineteenth century the fiction produced in developed countries was realist because it reflected the way people made sense of the world (a shared sense of what was real, explanatory narratives based on strict rules of cause and effect, unitary characters with an understanding of themselves and their identities, and a commitment to 'grand narratives' that were 'teleological', that is, that were moving towards a predetermined and meaning-conferring goal). In the modern age (that is, for the first three quarters of the twentieth century), in contrast, people yearned to live in this same world but could not, and thus modernist fiction contrasts the tragic gap between the need for a comprehensive system of belief that explained the individual's place in the world, and the recognition that actual experience is meaningless, personality is fragmented and communication between human beings is at best partial. Finally, in the postmodern world of today, an acceptance that meaning can be at best local, and that the movement from experience to experience is largely or completely random and fortuitous, finds expression in postmodernist fiction. And postmodernist fiction is able to be most completely itself when granted the resources of the electronic media, resources that finally allow fiction to shrug off the fetters of the single linear plot, the fixed text and the passive reader.

It should be clear that although I find such arguments interesting, I strongly suspect that they are at best half truths (among other things, the proposed periodization strikes me as too crude and simplistic). But I will allow myself just two final comments that reiterate points that I have made earlier in this discussion. The first is that when one considers the ways in which fictional composition and reading habits have been adapted to the electronic media, one cannot but be struck by the blending of the very old and the very new. Modes such as the computer game and IF, as a succession of commentators have pointed out, wed advanced computer technology to some of the most traditional (and among the lowest-status) narrative and fictional conventions.

The second (and perhaps related) comment is that even sympathetic commentators on the various modes of electronic fiction generally concede that, so far, the great work of electronic fiction remains unwritten. This may of course be because the modes I have been considering do not produce single retrievable texts. But it may also be, as Marie-Laure Ryan concludes, that there is something about linear narrative that makes it indispensable to Western culture and, arguably, to culture in general (2001, 270). A name that frequently comes into the discussion of twentieth-century attempts to subvert or supersede the limitations of the linear narrative of printed prose fiction is one that I have mentioned earlier in this book: that of the novelist B.S. Johnson. As critic Frank Kermode points out in a review article discussing Johnson's work, the most striking instances of such subversion or supersession are to be found in his novel *Albert Angelo* – which has a hole cut in a page so that readers can read a sentence that comes some pages later – and another novel, *The Unfortunates*, which was published in 'a box containing a bundle of unbound gatherings to be read in random order' (Kermode, 2004, 11). We can be forgiven the wistful thought that Johnson, who took his own life in 1973 at the age of 40, was one to whom the cliché 'born before his time' was thoroughly appropriate. Was he not a would-be electronic writer imprisoned in print? Born thirty or forty years later, could he not have produced fictional works not with just a hole in one page, but hypertext links every other line?

Kermode is sympathetic but sceptical, noting that *The Unfortunates* 'is interesting and well written, but it has never been the primary topic of conversation, the sensationally loose gatherings in the box having pre-empted that position' (11). He further suggests somewhat laconically that resonances between remote parts of a story 'can be achieved without cutting holes in pages' (12). The moral, it seems to me, is, first, that the linear narrative of traditional prose fiction does not exclude subtle and artistically productive effects, and second, that technical innovation does not always lead to greater artistic achievement.

Topics for discussion

↪ Do any of the new electronic fictional texts have any artistic merit?

↪ Have computers finally liberated fiction?

↪ Would you like to be able to decide what happens in the novels you read?

Chapter 6
Analysing fiction

Preview

This chapter deals with:

↦ the different ways in which a novel or short story can be narrated
↦ different sorts of narrator; different relationships between narrator and story
↦ stream of consciousness, interior monologue, Free Indirect Discourse
↦ types of character and methods of characterization
↦ story and plot, setting and theme
↦ symbol and image
↦ representing speech and dialogue in the novel

Prose fiction and formal analysis

The association of the novel with realism has meant that there has always been a strong temptation to discuss it as one would discuss people and events in the world and ignore the art (especially the verbal art) that is a necessary part of its existence. Poetry typically calls attention to its verbal art and formal techniques, while performance arts such as drama require the discussion of verbal detail as a part of the planning of performance. There are venerable traditions of theoretical discussion of the art of the dramatist and the poet, starting with Aristotle, that have bequeathed a vocabulary and a set of principles to the critic. Moreover, the very popularity of the novel – something, as we have seen, that since its birth has been found regrettable by various guardians of culture – has meant that it has seemed inappropriate or unnecessary to devote the same analytical attention to novels as has been paid to plays and poems.

I do not want to suggest that detailed analytical concern with prose fiction (as against a scholarly interest in its texts and its history) cannot be found in the eighteenth and nineteenth centuries. However, it is the case that such a concern emerged in its recognizably contemporary form in the late nineteenth century and developed via a number of routes. First, early modernists such as Henry James, Joseph Conrad, Virginia Woolf and James Joyce – and their contemporaries writing in languages other than English – took their art seriously and often wrote about it. Moreover, by frustrating the expectations of their readers, they drew attention to the changing conventions on which the novel was based. Second, the academy began to provide for the study of literatures other than those of Classical antiquity. Third, particular schools of criticism such as the Russian and Czech Formalists and the New Critics (see Chapter 9) significantly extended our understanding of the art of the novelist by means of detailed analyses. Fourth, the recent development of *narratology* as an academic and intellectual discipline (see again Chapter 9) has helped to build up a far more precise vocabulary and conceptual basis for the analysis of narratives in general and prose fiction in particular.

Much of what follows in this chapter is indebted to these sources. This chapter focuses not on the novel's history and its historical identity but rather on those techniques and skills – the craft of the novel – that can be found in novels and shorter works of prose fiction from various cultures and historical periods, and on the methods, concepts and approaches that have been developed by critics and theorists to analyse works of prose fiction. The reader should remember that the craft of the novel has its own history, and different techniques emerge at different times in response to changes in the way people live and think – although they typically outlive the circumstances of their birth and the forces behind their creation.

Narrative technique

In my opening chapter I drew attention to the fact that everything we read in a novel comes to us via some sort of 'telling'. We are told what happens in a novel; no matter how successful the novelist is in making a scene seem dramatic it is never dramatic in the way that a play or a film is. A novel may make us feel that we 'see' characters and actions, but we see as a result of what we visualize in response to a telling, not an enactment. Even in those relatively rare cases in which a novelist makes extended use of the present tense, a technique which gives an added sense of immediacy to the narrative, we are still *told* what is happening rather than witnessing it directly as we can with a play or a film. The fact that when reading a novel we know that we can flip forward a page or a chapter, or look at the last page, is thus worth thinking about: it explains that sense we have that in reading a novel we are going through what *has already happened*, that which is being *re*counted to us. Whereas the last page of a novel is already printed and waiting there for us, in the world of our experience of a play the final scene has not yet been performed as we watch the first scene, even if it has been written and perhaps performed the night before.

In one respect, however, the writing of a novel is comparable to the making of a film. When we watch a film we seem to be seeing 'things as they are' – 'reality'. We need to remember that a director has *chosen how* we see these things, this reality; he or she has decided whether the camera will be placed high or low, whether or not there will be rapid cuts from one camera angle to another, whether a camera will follow one character as he or she walks along a street – and so on. One scene in a film could be shot in innumerable ways, and each of these ways would produce a different effect upon the audience. Even with a simple conversation between two characters the audience's attitude towards each character can be affected by different camera angles, cutting and so forth.

The novelist has a far greater range of choices open to him or her than does the film director, and we conventionally refer to that particular selection which he or she makes as the *narrative technique* of a particular work. Narrative technique includes such matters as the choice of *narrator* and *narrative situation*, the creation of a *plot* with its implied underlying *story*, selection and variation of *perspective and voice* (or 'point of view'), implied *narrative medium*, linguistic *register* (for example, the choice between colloquial or formal language) and techniques such as *Free Indirect Discourse*. All of these I will discuss below. The Glossary can also be consulted for definitions of many of these terms.

Let us start with narrators, with the individuals or voices who (or which!) *tell us* the story. And let us start with two sets of alternatives.

- ↔ personified narrator or unpersonified narrator
- ↔ character narrator or non-character narrator

If this looks like two ways of describing the same distinction, remember that a narrator may seem to have many of the attributes of a human being without being a character in the story that he or she narrates. In other words, it is possible to have a personified, non-character narrator.

Let us turn first to the issue of personification.

Narrators: impersonal or personified

An author may choose to have the story told through the mediation of a *personified narrator*, a 'teller' recognized by the reader as a distinct person with well-defined individual human characteristics. Alternatively, the narrative source can seem so undefined as to make it doubtful whether or not we are dealing with an individualized human source which comes between the author and the reader. (There is no ideal term to describe such a narrator: *authorial, impersonal* and *third-person* all have their drawbacks. The first suggests identification with the real-life author, the second suggests a lack of intimacy which may be misleading and the third excludes those first-person narrators on whom we are unhappy to bestow 'personhood'.)

Consider the narrator of Laurence Sterne's *Tristram Shandy*, whose distinct personality is thrust at us in the opening words of the novel: 'I wish either my father or my mother, or indeed both of them, as they were in duty both equally bound to it, had minded what they were about when they begot me.' The opening of D.H. Lawrence's *Sons and Lovers* (1913), in contrast, strikes us as far more impersonal; whereas the opening of Sterne's novel focuses our attention on the narrator, who is talking about himself, the narrative of *Sons and Lovers* focuses our attention on *what* is told rather than *who* tells or how: '"The Bottoms" succeeded to "Hell Row". Hell Row was a block of thatched, bulging cottages that stood by the brookside on Greenhill Lane. There lived the colliers who worked in the little gin-pits two fields away.' Note that a narrator who can penetrate into the consciousnesses of other characters who share his or her world – as many narrators can – is by definition not conventionally human, as this is something that ordinary human beings cannot do.

Some narrators may even have names and detailed personal histories, as does Nick Carraway, the narrator of F. Scott Fitzgerald's *The Great Gatsby* (1925). Other narrators merely suggest to us that they are persons – perhaps by the occasional use of 'I' in their narrative – but tell us no more about themselves than this. We thus have a continuum of possibilities: (i) personified, named and with a full human identity; (ii) human but anonymous; (iii) not corresponding to any recognizable human entity.

Narrators: character or non-character

One obvious distinction between the narrative of *Tristram Shandy* and that of *Sons and Lovers* is that the first of these novels is narrated in the first person, while the second is what is often referred to as a third-person narrative – it is a narrative told from a source external to the world of the novel by a narrator who is not one of the characters in the novel. As I suggest above, two different issues are involved here: (i) is the narrator personified? (ii) is the narrator presented as an individual who lives in the same world as the characters? While it is the case that there is a conventional association of personified narrators with life inside the world of the novel, and of third-person narrators with a perspective on characters and events from outside the world of the novel, there are exceptions. The narrator of Henry Fielding's *Tom Jones*, for example, is personified and makes first-person comments but he appears to live in a different world from Tom and the other characters, and he is able to comment upon their fictionality. He is thus outside of this world even though he can see into it, like God looking down on (and into the hearts and minds of) mankind.

The standard technical terms used by structuralist narratologists (see Chapter 9) to define narrators get at some of these distinctions. The basic term here is that of *diegesis*, which is used by narrative theorists to refer to the 'story level' of a narrative as against its 'narrating level'. This basic distinction is refined in a set of more specific terms. Generally speaking, structuralist narratologists are interested in such 'levels' more than in the question of whether a narrator does or does not belong to the same fictional world as his or her characters, or whether the narrator is or is not personified, although of course to be a character in the story one tells generally requires that one lives in the same world as its characters.

An extradiegetic narrator is in some sense or other 'superior to', or on a higher level from, the story he or she narrates – like the narrator of D.H. Lawrence's *Sons and Lovers*. But as Shlomith Rimmon-Kenan puts it, further explicating a terminology that stems from the work of structuralist narratologist Gérard Genette, 'if the narrator is also a character in the first narrative told by the extradiegetic narrator, then he is a second-degree, or intradiegetic narrator' (1983, 94), and she cites Marlow in *Heart of Darkness* as an example.

Note that an extradiegetic narrator may, or may not, be a frame narrator. In Joseph Conrad's *Heart of Darkness* the extradiegetic narrator is a character who listens to Marlow's narrative and transmits it to the reader. He is thus also a frame narrator. But in Conrad's *Lord Jim*, in which the first four chapters are told by a non-personified and (on occasions) omniscient narrator, this narrator is extradiegetic but he is not a frame narrator and neither, in this case, is the Marlow who takes over the mantle of narrator in the fifth chapter a frame narrator.

Rimmon-Kenan further notes that a narrator who does not participate in the story is called heterodiegetic, whereas one who does so 'at least in some manifestation of his "self", is "homodiegetic"' (1983, 95). Finally, an autodiegetic narrator is him- or herself the main character in the story he or she tells (thus, in her own narrative but not in the narrative of the anonymous frame narrator, the governess in *The Turn of the Screw* plays an autodiegetic role).

These basic terms can then be combined to produce a range of compounds. I list some of these below, but at this point I feel the need to stress that these more abstruse terms enter into more general discussion of literary fiction only rarely. Unless you wish to develop a specialist interest in structuralist narratology you are unlikely ever to need to memorize and use them.

↪ extra-heterodiegetic narrator: a 'first level' narrator who narrates a story in which he or she is not present
↪ extra-homodiegetic narrator: a 'first level' narrator who narrates a story in which he or she is present

↔ intra–heterodiegetic narrator: a 'second level' narrator who narrates a story in which he or she is not present

↔ intra–homodiegetic narrator: a 'second level' narrator who narrates a story in which he or she is present

You may well be relieved to hear that in recent years a more self-explanatory set of terms have been proposed by rhetorical narratologists (again see Chapter 9) to mark some of these distinctions – for example 'character narrator' and 'non-character narrator'. There seems every chance that these more user-friendly terms (if the users are English-speaking!) will replace the hard-to-remember terms used by structuralist narratologists even if they do not so precisely specify all the distinctions covered in Genette's terminology. As I suggest in Chapter 9, if even academics confronted with such terms have on occasions to reach surreptitiously for their dictionaries and glossaries, then it may be simpler just to spell out what the terms mean. (Try innocently asking your lecturer what the difference between intra–heterodiegetic and intra–homodiegetic is!)

'Omniscient' is also a term about which many recent commentators have expressed reservations (see the entry for omniscience in the Glossary). 'Omniscient' means 'all-knowing', and the word implies that the narrator knows everything: what has happened and what will happen, what the characters are thinking and so on. One objection to the term is that it has been applied rather loosely to any non-character narrator, many of whom actually profess ignorance about their characters and the events with which they are involved. Another objection is that it seems odd to talk about some narrators knowing 'everything' when there is nothing more to know in a work of fiction than that which is created by the author. Such objections are unlikely to get rid of the term, and indeed many sophisticated narratologists still have recourse to it, and to handy if illogical compounds such as 'semi-omniscient'.

As ordinary human beings are not all-knowing it is conventional for omniscient narrators to be unpersonified, although this convention is sometimes broken, as in the case of *Tom Jones*. The term 'omniscient' is often used in a loose way to indicate any work in which the narrative has access to that which – like a character's secret thoughts – is normally concealed to observers in our everyday world. Thus a so-called omniscient narrator may not, actually, be completely all-knowing. The first sentence of Joseph Conrad's *Lord Jim* reads: 'He was an inch, perhaps two, under six feet, powerfully built, and he advanced straight at you with a slight stoop of the shoulders, head forward, and a fixed from-under stare which made you think of a charging bull.' The word 'perhaps' reveals that however much this narrator may later on appear to 'see all', it is not quite all that is seen – maybe because Conrad wants the reader to respond to the narrator more as a personified individual than as an omniscient source of information at this stage of the novel.

It should be remembered that, just as novelists may decide to give a narrator more knowledge than is possessed by an ordinary human being, so too they may decide to restrict this knowledge when it suits them. Complete omniscience is not only unfamiliar to human beings; it may work against the creation of that tension and uncertainty that exercise the reader's mind in a creative fashion. It is also extremely important to remember that novelists may vary what a narrator knows from page to page. In his study of Conrad's narrative technique, Jakob Lothe (1989) has discussed two examples of the sudden intrusion of the first person into a previously unpersonified narrative, in *The Secret Agent* and *Nostromo*. One of the things at which the student of the novel has to become adept is recognizing when such a shift of overt or implied narrative source takes place in a work of fiction. Such shifts can be either marked or unmarked; that is to say the author may or may not draw attention to them.

Why?

What leads an author in his or her choice between personified and non-personified narrator, and between character and non-character narrator?

Dieter Meindl makes some interesting points about the relative advantages of the first set of choices, although in his terminology the choice is between a first-person or a third-person narrator.

> First-person narration is limited in scope: the narrator cannot simply state the inner world (thoughts, feelings) of others. Conversely, the first-person narrator – a real person or subject – is unlimited in manner, commanding as s/he does the whole range of subject discourses – erring, deceiving oneself and/or others, etc., as well as telling the truth: s/he is (un-)reliable. The narrative agency ('narrator') of third-person narrative is not a person or subject; hence, third-person narrative can hardly be subjective or unreliable, but is basically reliable in the sense of being authorial. (Meindl, 2008, 35)

You may notice that this goes against what I argued above when talking about the narrator of Henry Fielding's *Tom Jones*, in which novel I claimed that we had a personified narrator who did have access to the inner lives of other characters: Meindl is here talking about the most usual variants of these alternative types of narrator. His comments are, nonetheless, useful. Reading the account of a personified narrator we react in some ways as we do to the account of a real person telling a true story (or a false one!), whereas when reading the account of an unpersonified narrator we have a sense of reliability that we can rarely attach so fully to the stories told by human individuals, while at the same time being unable to share in the narrator's self-deceptions, boastings, humility and so on because an unpersonified 'agency' can hardly be expected to be possessed of such human characteristics.

Framed narratives

One classic technique for combining the advantages of different sorts of narrator is by means of a 'framed narrative'. Examples of this technique can be found in both Henry James's *The Turn of the Screw* and Joseph Conrad's *Heart of Darkness*. Both of these works start with a group of people talking, and then one of the conversationalists starts to deliver the 'framed' narrative, the main telling contained in the work. In both cases the 'outer' narrator is unnamed, while in Conrad's novella but not James's the inner narrator is named. I shall have more to say about the narrative of *The Turn of the Screw* in Chapter 8 when I discuss film adaptations of works of fiction. Although many film adaptations of framed narratives – including those mentioned by Conrad and James – often drop the framing device, it is possible to retain it even in a film (Woody Allen's film *Broadway Danny Rose* [1984] is remarkably like *Heart of Darkness* with respect to its use of the framing device of a man telling a story that the film then dramatizes).

Narrative medium and language

In addition to choosing a narrator or narrative source, the novelist can (but need not) select a stated or implied *medium* for his or her narrative. Now of course all novels consist of written, normally printed, words in a literal sense, but a novel may well be presented to the reader as if it were spoken or thought rather than written, or it may even be presented in such a way as to suggest that it is a sort of medium-less narrative – something impossible outside the realms of literature.

Thus, to take two very different examples, Agatha Christie's *The Murder of Roger Ackroyd* (1926) and Fyodor Dostoyevsky's *Notes from Underground* (1864) are both presented to the reader as *written* documents. We learn this only towards the end of Christie's story, when the narrator explains how he came to write his account (and that should make us pause for thought: think of the oddness of reading a story and not knowing until the end of the story whether it is a written document we are reading: that is because the written text *we* see stands for another text, about the precise nature of which we can be left in the dark by the novelist). In Dostoyevsky's story we find the following interpolated comment on the first page:

> (A poor witticism; but I won't cross it out. When I wrote that down, I thought it would seem very pointed: now, when I see that I was simply trying to be clever and cynical, I shall leave it in on purpose.)

We may well ask: why should one author want to reveal the implied narrative medium of the story on the first page, and another only towards the end? What difference does it make to the reader's response to the story? (Compare Philip Roth's *Portnoy's Complaint* [1969], in which the fact that the narrative is a spoken one is revealed on the last page along with the precise context of its delivery.)

Where a novelist does not state his or her implied narrative medium, all sorts of variations are possible. Emily Brontë's *Wuthering Heights* opens as if it might be some sort of diary entry: '1801. – I have just returned from a visit to my landlord – the solitary neighbour that I shall be troubled with. This is certainly a beautiful country!' Other parts of the novel, told by Mr Lockwood, as is this opening passage, read more like thought processes than writing. This is the third paragraph of Chapter 10:

> This is quite an easy interval. I am too weak to read, yet I feel as if I could enjoy something interesting. Why not have up Mrs Dean to finish her tale? I can recollect its chief incidents, as far as she had gone. Yes, I remember her hero had run off, and never been heard of for three years: and the heroine was married: I'll ring; she'll be delighted to find me capable of talking cheerfully.
> Mrs Dean came.

There is, I think, a slight clumsiness here. Novelists following Brontë perfected techniques for making such transitions between narrative viewpoints and media less obtrusive.

Closely related to the foregoing issues is the matter of *linguistic register*. (By 'register' is meant a particular sort of language-use that is appropriate to a given circumstance.) Whether a narrative is formal or colloquial, for example, depends a lot upon whether it is told by a personified or unpersonified narrator, and upon whether we are to assume that it is spoken, written or thought. (Conversely, of course, the degree of informality of a novel's language may lead us to infer that a narrative is, for example, a spoken tale by a personified narrator.)

Now in one sense language is the medium of a novel just as paint is the medium of a painting, but this is a misleading comparison as painters do not generally represent paint whereas novelists often represent language: *Heart of Darkness*, for example, is not just *in* language, it *represents* language – the language uttered by Marlow and used by the novella's frame narrator. Thus in one sense the *actual* medium of this novel – language – is also its *implied* medium (although of course the implied medium of most of *Heart of Darkness* is spoken, not written, language). A novel may well have no stated narrative medium: Joseph Conrad's *The Shadow-Line* (1916–7) can be read as if written, spoken or thought in origin. (Interestingly, as a result of gout in his hand Conrad actually dictated rather than wrote a significant section of this work.)

Narrative and representation

The previous comment may seem to contradict what I said earlier about all narrative being a telling: does not a telling necessarily require a medium by means of which the telling takes place? It should be said that this question touches upon a number of very complex disputes within the theory of narrative.

Some theorists prefer to distinguish between *representation* and *telling*, and claim that the novelist can represent – say – a character's consciousness in such a way as gives the reader knowledge of this consciousness without any sense of this information being told or transmitted – something that is, of course, impossible outside the realms of written narrative.

Thus the narrative theorist Ann Banfield has argued that representation is, as the name suggests, a 're-presentation' which makes 'present' what is either absent or past, and which is thus unlike narration, having only a single point of reference with respect to time and place (Banfield, 1982, 268). (A narration has two: the time and place of the narrated events, and the time and place of their narrating – compare my earlier remarks on the novel's double chronology on p. 6.) Banfield accordingly argues that, so far as certain examples of representation are concerned, to enquire into the process of 'telling' bespeaks only the critic's lack of comprehension of what representation involves – hence the title of the book in which she argues this case: *Unspeakable Sentences*. In Banfield's view, the novelist may give us sentences which are not and cannot be spoken by anyone; their function is that of representation, not telling or narrating.

Ways of telling

Let us pause for a moment and ask why all this is important. What difference does it make? Well, in everyday life the fact of *who* tells us a story, and *how*, makes a very big difference. A proposal of marriage uttered directly, in emotional speech, strikes the recipient rather differently from one formally written and received by post. Source and medium affect the *selection*, the *authority* and the *attitude towards what is recounted* of the narrative – and thus, of course, the effect on the reader or listener. (One of the problems involved in Banfield's view of representation is, it seems to me, that even such representation involves selection, and the act of selection implies some form of mediation.)

The same is true with the novel: different narrators, different narrative media *change* a story; they affect not just how we are told something but what we are told, and what attitude we take towards what we are told. Nobody knows this better than novelists themselves, and different novelists have given us some revealing accounts of the problematic processes that deciding upon a narrative technique involves. There is, for example, a fascinating entry in Virginia Woolf's diary dated 25 September 1929, outlining her plans for her novel *The Waves*, which at this stage of her work on it she had provisionally entitled *The Moths*. She writes:

> Yesterday morning I made another start on *The Moths*, but that won't be its title; and several problems cry out at once to be solved. Who thinks it? And am I outside the thinker? One wants some device which is not a trick. (Leonard Woolf, 1972, 146)

Note how the choosing of a particular perspective, a particular centre of perception for the telling, presents itself as a *problem* right at the start of Woolf's work on this novel. Note too her distinction between 'I' and 'the thinker' – in other words, between the creative-moral centre of authority and the perceiving-observing-telling situation, in the novel. It is very important to recognize the fact that these two are not necessarily identical, either in *The Waves* or in any other novel or short story. Finally, that comment that she 'wants some device which is not a trick' also underlines the fact that this sort of choice is not a purely technical one, but has aesthetic and moral implications which demand careful consideration.

A succession of fascinating letters written by Jean Rhys provides relevant evidence concerning her choice of a way of telling her novel *Wide Sargasso Sea* – a novel with complex intertextual links with Charlotte Brontë's *Jane Eyre* (see my comments concerning the links between these two works in Chapter 2, p. 36). 'Way of telling' is a formulation I use which includes both 'perspective' and 'voice' (see the discussion of this distinction on p. 122 and in the Glossary). What Rhys is concerned about here is, strictly speaking, the choice of a particular voice, although this has implications for narrative perspective. To her daughter, in 1959, Jean Rhys writes about her forthcoming novel:

> It can be done 3 ways. (1) Straight. Childhood, Marriage, Finale told in 1st person. Or it can be done (2) Man's point of view (3) Woman's ditto both 1st person. Or it can be told in the third person with the writer as the Almighty. Well that is hard for me. I prefer direct thoughts and actions.
> I am doing (2). (Wyndham and Melly, 1984, 162)

Later on in the same year she writes to Francis Wyndham admitting that the novel has already been written three times, first told by the heroine in the first person, second told by the housekeeper Mrs Poole as the 'I' and now using two 'I's: 'Mr Rochester and his first wife'. According to Rhys it was unsatisfactory to have the heroine tell all the story herself because the result was obscure and 'all on one note', and it was also unsatisfactory to have the housekeeper Grace Poole tell the whole story because although technically this was the best solution, the character 'wouldn't come to life' (172). Before we leave this example, you should think a bit about the phrase 'Man's point of view'. This has both a technical and an ideological or 'sexual political' meaning: a writer's choice of 'point of view' is rarely just a technical matter.

Let us return to the issue of choosing a way of telling in the light of our understanding of the crucial importance of such decisions by the novelist. Many critics have found it useful to distinguish between *reliable* and *unreliable* narrators. We can also note that, reliability apart, we associate some narrative choices more with the views and position of actual authors, and some not at all (or far less) with their creators. In general we can say that a single, consistent, unpersonified voice is more likely to be associated with authorial beliefs than is a personified narrator in a novel with many narrators, although of course in both cases this depends upon the attitudes expressed in and revealed by the narrative.

Thus it is easier to assume that the opinions expressed by the anonymous narrator of Conrad's *The Secret Agent* (1907) are close to those of Conrad himself than it is in the case of his personified narrator Marlow, who appears in a number of his works. Moreover, even if Marlow is a generally reliable narrator, we do not take everything he says on quite the same trust as we do what the narrator of *The Secret Agent* tells us, simply because we see Marlow from the outside and treat him as another person, whereas we adopt the perspective of the narrator of *The Secret Agent* and, as we read, think ourselves fully into his position from the inside.

Consistency is a crucial issue here. An inconsistent narrator cannot, logically, be wholly reliable, although we may recognize in fiction as in life that inconsistency may be the result of a continued and painful attempt to be truthful and accurate. The fact that Gulliver in Swift's *Gulliver's Travels* seems to vary from book to book, being alternatively percipient and obtuse, blindly patriotic and unchauvinistically humanistic, warns us that we cannot relax into unguarded acceptance of his statements or opinions. On the other hand, although few if any readers of *Wuthering Heights* can identify totally with Mr Lockwood, he is consistently portrayed, and so we feel more and more confident in assessing his opinions in the light of our view of his personality and character.

In addition to choosing a narrator and (perhaps) an implied narrative medium, the novelist has to select a *form of address* for his narrator. In so doing, he or she normally helps to define what has been termed a *narratee*: the person to whom the narrative is addressed (see the Glossary). Note that the narratee may be the actual reader, but is not necessarily so. The narrative can, for instance, be directly addressed to the 'Dear Reader', or it can be spoken or written to another intradiegetic (or 'intra-fictional') target or destination, or it can be projected into a void. In *Tom Jones*, Henry Fielding uses 'interchapters' in which the reader is addressed directly, while the remainder of the novel is less overtly pointed at any reader or listener.

What, for example, do we make of the opening lines of Albert Camus's *The Outsider* (1942)? 'Mother died today. Or, maybe, yesterday; I can't be sure. The telegram from the Home says: *Your mother passed away. Funeral tomorrow. Deep sympathy*. Which leaves the matter doubtful: it could have been yesterday.' In a previous edition of this book I wrote of this passage: 'Clearly this could be addressed to someone (would there be any sense in saying it to oneself?), but the narrative might represent a state of mind and a sequence of events which the reader is not meant to think are actually aimed at any recipient in particular.' A correspondent has suggested that this could indeed be Meursault talking or thinking to himself. I had assumed that the passage gives the reader the *expression* of Meursault's thoughts or state of mind, whereas I concede that it can equally well be read as the *depiction* of these. A general problem here is that because our mental statements or questions to ourselves are not necessarily verbalized, or at least not rendered in formally correct sentences, when such processes are depicted in fiction the writer has the choice either to help the reader and use formally correct sentences (thus making the processes appear unrealistic), or to try to capture the nature of non-linguistic or semi-linguistic thoughts in unconventional language (thus risking losing the reader). My correspondent also pointed out that the importance of existentialist ideas to Camus needs to be taken into account, and it is certainly true that Camus may well be trying to capture Meursault's state of 'being in the world', and focussing on the tension between the unchangeable facts of the world and his own more fluid reactions to these facts.

As this suggests, the same fictional character can be both narrator and narratee. In the final section of James Joyce's *Ulysses*, Molly Bloom is both narrator and narratee. Part of the narrative complexity of *The Turn of the Screw* comes from the fact that there are different narratees for different levels of James's narrative (see the discussion on p. 190).

Recent writers associated with *rhetorical narratology* (see Chapter 9) have stressed the importance of the *occasion* on which a narrative is delivered. Is the narrator at ease, or under pressure? Has he or she one narratee or many? Is the narrative delivered long after the events it recounts took place, or a few days later? Such elements of the narrative situation are used by readers to interpret the significance of what they read.

Complicity and intrusion

Narratives can also involve such elements as *complicity*, *intrusion* and *intimacy* – all of which are normally instantly recognized by readers while remaining tricky to analyse.

Take for example the following brief extract from Chapter 3 of E.M. Forster's *Howards End* (1910), in which Mrs Munt is talking at cross purposes to Charles Wilcox, believing him to be engaged to her niece Helen:

> 'This is very good of you,' said Mrs Munt, as she settled into a
> luxurious cavern of red leather, and suffered her person to be padded
> with rugs and shawls. She was more civil than she had intended, but
> really this young man was very kind. Moreover, she was a little afraid
> of him: his self-possession was extraordinary. 'Very good indeed,' she
> repeated, adding: 'It is just what I should have wished.'
>   'Very good of you to say so,' he replied, with a slight look of surprise,
> which, like most slight looks, escaped Mrs Munt's attention.

That final narrative comment is the culminating stroke in a process whereby the reader is sucked into complicity with the narrator. We are amused with the narrator at Mrs Munt's obtuseness and self-importance, and as a result of such passages we are likely to be far more malleable in the hands of the narrator, far more willing to accept his value judgements and assessments of characters. It should perhaps be added that at this and other points many readers feel that it is the author himself with whom we become complicit, and although this view has become unfashionable in recent decades, it should not be dismissed. (It is perhaps for this reason that it seems natural to refer to this narrator as 'he'.)

The line between complicity and intrusion can be difficult to draw. For many readers, the last paragraph of Thomas Hardy's *Tess of the d'Urbervilles* (1891) starts with an annoyingly intrusive and heavy-handed comment from the narrator, a comment which such readers feel detracts from the power of the scene depicted at this point of the novel: 'Justice was done, and the President of the Immortals, in Aeschylean phrase, had ended his sport with Tess.' In contrast, at the end of the first chapter of Jane Austen's *Mansfield Park* (1814), we find this concluding sentence about Mrs Price (Fanny's mother): 'Poor woman! she probably thought change of air might agree with many of her children.' Although technically intrusive, this seems less to break in upon an established tone or perspective than does Hardy's comment, and so seems to have offended fewer readers than has that final paragraph of *Tess of the d'Urbervilles*.

A narrative can be either *recollective* or *dramatic*. Of course, *any* narrative involves recollection; to be told a story is to be informed of something which has already happened, something which is being *re*membered, *re*counted. We should probably except those rare examples of future narrative, although even here, because we are given the impression that the narrative *knows* what events are to happen, in a sense they exist already in completed form – have already taken place and are being recollected. In Margaret Atwood's short story 'Weight' (1991), for example, the present-tense, first-person narrative gives way in the four final paragraphs to the future tense. In these paragraphs the speaker is thinking about what she will do the next day and what will happen then, and so the emphasis is still on the present thinking rather than the future happening.

Present-tense narrative is more problematic, but it can be argued that this technique at least implies a gap between the happening and the recounting, although in English the use of the present continuous can give a sense of immediacy. Thus on the penultimate page of Atwood's 'Weight' we can read the following paragraph:

> Charles is walking me to the door, past white tablecloth after white tablecloth, each one held in place by at least four pin-striped elbows. It's like the *Titanic* just before the iceberg: power and influence disporting themselves, not a care in the world. What do they know about the serfs down in steerage? Piss all, and pass the port. (Atwood, 1991, 192)

There is no doubt that the reader is given a sense of being present as things happen here, although I think that probably this is the female narrator's retrospective imagining-what-it-was-like-when-it-took-place: the things that have happened unfold in her head as she remembers the events in the restaurant. What is narrated is the retrospective unfolding in the head rather than the actual events.

Intimacy and involvement

Such subtleties and marginal cases should not obscure what every sensitive reader of fiction knows: some ways of telling a story can have far more dramatic effect than others (as is clear from Samuel Richardson's comment on his epistolary technique, quoted on p. 231). Note how in the following passage Jean Rhys changes tense in order to create dramatic immediacy in her novel *Good Morning, Midnight* (1939):

> The lavatory at the station – that was the next time I cried. I had just been sick. I was so afraid I might be going to have a baby. ...
> Although I have been so sick, I don't feel any better. I lean up against the wall, icy cold and sweating. Someone tries the door, and I pull myself together, stop crying and powder my face. (Rhys, 1969, 101; ellipsis in original)

Compare a passage from a much-quoted scene in Chapter 4 of Charles Dickens's *Great Expectations*. The young Pip has robbed the pantry of food which he has given to the escaped convict, and is eating Christmas dinner with his family in fear and trembling:

> Among this good company I should have felt myself, even if I hadn't robbed the pantry, in a false position. Not because I was squeezed in at an acute angle of the table-cloth, with the table in my chest, and the Pumblechookian elbow in my eye, nor because I was not allowed to speak (I didn't want to speak), nor because I was regaled with the scaly tips of the drumsticks of the fowls, and with those obscure corners of pork of which the pig, when living, had had the least reason to be vain. No; I should not have minded that, if they would only have left me alone. But they wouldn't leave me alone.

Here the author does all in his power to reduce immediacy and emotionally to disengage the reader from Pip's experiences. In reading this passage although to some extent we do feel with the young Pip, we also watch amusedly with the older, narrating Pip. We observe from a distance, watching the young Pip from the perspective of his older self. Note how different this is from our intimate relationship with Joyce's Eveline (see p. 71). To indicate such variations in intimacy the term *distance* is used by narratologists and critics. Such narrative distancing does not necessarily prevent the reader from experiencing with a character; it can sometimes involve deliberate understatement which allows the reader to imagine for him- or herself what the experience involved must have been like. A novelist can control the extent to which a reader empathizes with a character by means of the manipulation of narrative distance. The more 'here and now' the narrative is – both spatially and temporally – the more likely the reader is to enter into the character's experiences.

Perspective and voice

A disadvantage with the traditional term 'point of view' is that it obscures what recent theorists have identified as an extremely important distinction, that between *perspective* and *voice*. We can sum up what these terms cover in two questions: 'Who speaks?' and 'Who sees?' In Katherine Mansfield's short story 'The Voyage' (1922), for instance, the voice is essentially that of a third-person narrator who is extradiegetic or 'outside the story'. The reader is, nevertheless, encouraged to see everything through the consciousness of the main character of the story, the little girl Fenella. We experience through her senses, even though what we know of these experiences comes to us via a third-person narrative. Hers is the only consciousness we enter. (It is always worth asking to whose thoughts we are made privy in a novel or a short story, as the answer gives us significant information about the author's focus of concern.) In 'The Voyage', then, the *voice* is that of a semi-omniscient third-person narrator, but the *perspective* is Fenella's.

We should also get used to asking whether the view of characters and events which is given by the narrative is a recognizably human one. In other words, does it resemble that which a real human being might actually have experienced; were the characters and events real? In the case of Conrad's Marlow, Defoe's Moll Flanders, Dickens's Pip or Jean Rhys's Sasha Jansen, we can say that a real human being might share such a relationship to the events depicted as they enjoy (which is not to say that such a real human being would *tell* his or her story as they do – or even at all). In contrast, no human being in real life would know what the narrator of George Eliot's *Middlemarch* knows about the characters and events that are depicted in that work. (Compare the claim I cite from Dorrit Cohn on p. 3, that only in fiction can a narrative enter into a consciousness other than that of the narrator.)

What difference does this make? Well, a good way to demonstrate this is by means of what we can call the *transposition test*: transposing a novel (in one's imagination) from one 'camera angle' to another. Imagine *Middlemarch* told in the first person by Dorothea, or by Dorothea and Lydgate in successive sections. What would *Wuthering Heights* be like as an epistolary novel, with Isabella's letter about her marriage to Heathcliff as only one of a whole sequence of letters describing the events and developments of the work? Or with the events of the novel seen exclusively through Heathcliff's eyes? It can be an extremely revealing exercise to take a brief passage from a novel and to rewrite it in this manner.

Thus it is interesting to know that Franz Kafka started his novel *The Castle* (1926) in the first person, and that the manuscript of the novel has 'I', crossed out and replaced by 'K', throughout the early part of the work. If you have read this work you will appreciate how very differently it reads with 'I' rather than 'K'; the reader's whole relationship with the main character is quite different. Like Jean Rhys (see p. 117), Kafka clearly found the right voice and perspective for his novel only after having started writing the work – when he could perhaps more easily put himself into the position of a potential reader.

One term which has, I think, a useful summarizing function here is *narrative situation*. We can indicate what this term covers by asking about the relationship between *the telling* and *what is told*. Is the narrator personified? If so, is he/she a character involved in the action of the work? Is the narrative dramatic and immediate or distanced? – and so on. Narrative situation thus includes both perspective and voice, and also a range of other matters such as tone and frequency (see below for discussion of these terms, and also the separate Glossary entries).

Narrative technique and history

The craft of the novelist has its history, and different narrative techniques emerge at different times in response to changes in the way people live and think. Thus the rise of the epistolary novel (see the Glossary) in the eighteenth century, for example, cannot be understood apart from the great importance of letter-writing at that time, while the emergence of the stream of consciousness novel in the twentieth century has to be related to the development of modern psychology and the increasing interest in mental operations that accompanies it. The following factors are all important in assessing the significance of a particular narrative technique.

↦ Changes in the dominant modes of human communication (think of the substantial effect that the telephone had on human communication during the first three-quarters of the twentieth century, and of the enormous reverberations of the computer revolution – including those of the internet – since the late 1980s).

↦ The effect of different world views, philosophies and ideologies (there is clearly a parallel between a belief in a God who sees everything, and novelists' use of omniscient narrators – witness Jean Rhys's phrase 'told in the third person with the writer as the Almighty' [p. 117]. The weakening of a universal belief in such a God seems to have been parallelled by a disenchantment with the possibilities of narrative omniscience).

↔ Changes in readership patterns and habits (it is perhaps harder to feel intimate with a larger, more amorphous and anonymous set of readers, but, paradoxically, it may be easier to be open with such readers).

↔ Larger changes in human life and modes of consciousness (think of the growth of urban living, of mass communication, of modern science and politics).

Such factors do not necessarily lead to immediate or substantial differences in the craft of the novel, and it can be hard to link one or more of them to a specific revolution in the novel. George Butte has commented on one such revolution that occurred at the close of the eighteenth century.

> A sea change in the representation of consciousness in narratives in English becomes visible in the time of Jane Austen. It is a change so subtle and fundamental that it has been difficult to conceive and describe. … One aspect of the change has received careful attention in recent years: the move into the interior of the self. (Butte, 2004, 25)

What causes such a change? A neat, all-embracing response to such a question is unlikely ever to be forthcoming, but it seems highly unlikely that the revolution was utterly unconnected to changes in the world at large – social, intellectual and ideological.

Stream of consciousness and interior monologue

Let me at this point say a few words about *stream of consciousness* technique and the *internal* (or *interior*) *monologue* (terms also defined in the Glossary). The two need carefully to be distinguished. Strictly speaking, an internal monologue implies the use of *language*, and if an individual is 'talking to himself or herself', then that in turn presupposes a certain amount of consciousness of what is going on in that person's mind. Milan Kundera, talking about 'the fantastic espionage of interior monologue', claims that James Joyce set a microphone within his character Leopold Bloom's head (Kundera, 1988, 28). The famous closing section of James Joyce's *Ulysses* gives us, essentially, the stream of Molly Bloom's consciousness, but in internal monologue; she is (I think) thinking to herself in words and is conscious of what she is thinking. I say 'I think' because novelists can transpose unverbalized thoughts and sensations into verbal statements which are attributed to the character in question, and it is possible that at least part of this chapter should be read in this way. The chapter opens:

> Yes because he never did a thing like that before as ask to get his breakfast in bed with a couple of eggs since the City Arms hotel when he used to be pretending to be laid up with a sick voice …

It is possible that the reader is meant to imagine Molly experiencing a primarily sensuous (visual/tactile) memory of the previous recumbent breakfast, and that the words we read are to be taken as a token of this set of sensuous, non-verbal memories. This seems unlikely though – first because the chapter in spite of its lack of punctuation has a logical structure and presents us with Molly's *arguments*, and it is difficult if not impossible to argue non-verbally, and second because Joyce typically presents thought processes as verbalized.

Now consider the following passage – the first two paragraphs of D.H. Lawrence's short story 'Fanny and Annie' (1922):

> Flame lurid his face as he turned among the throng of flame-lit and dark faces upon the platform. In the light of the furnace she caught sight of his drifting countenance, like a piece of floating fire. And the nostalgia, the doom of homecoming went through her veins like a drug. His eternal face, flame-lit now! The pulse and darkness of red fire from the furnace towers in the sky, lighting the desultory, industrial crowd on the wayside station, lit him and went out.
>
> Of course he did not see her. Flame-lit and unseeing! Always the same, with his meeting eyebrows, his common cap, and his red-and-black scarf knotted round his throat. Not even a collar to meet her! The flames had sunk, there was shadow.

The passage is extremely complex, in part because it mixes what the narrator tells us and what Fanny is thinking, so that at several points it is hard if not impossible to tell whether what we are reading represents a narrative comment or Fanny's thoughts. I would like to draw attention to the fourth sentence ('His eternal face, flame-lit now!') and the whole of the second paragraph down to the end of the penultimate sentence quoted ('… to meet her!'). It seems to me highly likely that these sentences represent Fanny's stream of consciousness rather than the narrator's commentary, although some parts could be both or either. However, what seems almost certain is that Fanny is not thinking by means of the actual words we are given. She is not thinking to herself 'His eternal face, flame-lit now! Of course he does not see me, flame-lit and unseeing! Always the same, with his meeting eyebrows, his common cap, and his red-and-black scarf knotted round his throat. Not even a collar to meet me!', although she may verbalize *some* of these thoughts by means of the words we read. What Lawrence's words do is to give us Fanny's stream of consciousness rather than her internal monologue. We can summarize and say that an internal monologue gives us a character's stream of consciousness (or at least part of it, if we imagine images accompanying words), but not every stream of consciousness is an internal monologue.

Free Indirect Discourse

The difficulty I mentioned above of distinguishing between what a narrator says and what a character thinks or verbalizes may become particularly acute with the use of a technique which is known by a number of different terms: 'Free Indirect Discourse (or Speech)', 'represented speech and thought', 'narrated monologue', or the German and French terms *erlebte Rede* and *style indirect libre*. The complications of terminology are worth wading through, for the technique itself is arguably one of the most important in the novel since Jane Austen. Indeed, the 'sea change in the representation of consciousness in narratives in English' that George Butte dates to the time of Jane Austen (see above, p. 124), a change that he claims allowed access to characters' inner lives without risking solipsism (or imprisonment in the self), seems to have involved a much greater, and more sophisticated, use of this technique.

Look again at the opening of 'Fanny and Annie'. Who is it who says 'Of course he did not see her'? The grammatical structure of the sentence, with Fanny referred to as 'her', might suggest that it is the narrator (it cannot be Harry, the man, precisely because he has not seen her). Is it not rather odd for the narrator to utter this comment, as if Harry's behaviour were expected but nonetheless irritating, and as if the reader knew enough about Harry to legitimize that 'of course'? The same can be said of 'Always the same, with his meeting eyebrows, his common cap, and his red-and-black scarf knotted round his throat. Not even a collar to meet her!' Is it not odd for the narrator to say this, first because we do not expect an omniscient narrator to get so quickly irritated by a character, and second because the statement assumes that whoever hears this comment will be familiar with poor Harry's shortcomings? How do we know that Harry is always the same? This is the first time that we have encountered him!

In fact, as most readers have no difficulty in working out, it is not Lawrence's narrator, but Fanny, whose irritation at Harry's familiar inadequacies is thereby expressed. Typical of Free Indirect Discourse – to use what is now generally accepted as the best term in English to describe this technique – is the use of the grammar of third-person utterance (with certain modifications) to present us with a character's speech or (verbal or non-verbal) thoughts. (As will be understood, terms such as Free Indirect Speech, represented speech and represented thought have a more limited application than does the blanket term Free Indirect Discourse.)

The traditional way of defining what we can refer to as FID makes use of grammatical or linguistic evidence. This involves seeing FID as a midway point between Direct and Indirect (or Reported) Discourse (DD and ID), or as a combination of the two which blends their grammatical characteristics in a distinctive mix. Thus we can use the following simple illustration, in which one can note that the third example retains the third-person 'he' and past tense from ID, but in its truncation resembles the words in inverted commas in the DD example.

DD: He said, 'I love her'
ID: He said that he loved her
FID: He loved her
          (example from Rimmon-Kenan, 1983, 111)

What should strike us immediately about the third example ('He loved her') is that, in common with the sentences in the passage from 'Fanny and Annie' at which we have already looked, in the context of a passage from a novel it could be ambiguous. It could either give us the consciousness of the 'he' referred to, his realization that he loves a woman, or it could give the reader a statement by a narrator about a character (who might not even realize, yet, that he loves the person concerned). This ambiguity is exploited by the most skilled writers of prose fiction, and very often allows them to move backwards and forwards between narrative comment and character consciousness, often with no apparent seams. Look once again at the opening of Lawrence's story. It clearly gives us both (i) comment that comes from a narrator or source outside the depicted characters and events, and (ii) what Fanny is thinking. It is nevertheless impossible to make a sharp distinction between the two such that one ends up with two neat piles, one labelled 'narrator's comment' and the other 'Fanny's thoughts'. This, I would argue, is a strength rather than a weakness of the passage; if you disagree, try rewriting it so as to exclude any ambiguity as to whom statements should be attributed.

Another example, this time another passage from Katherine Mansfield's 'The Voyage':

> 'How long am I going to stay?' she whispered anxiously. He wouldn't look at her. He shook her off gently, and gently said, 'We'll see about that. Here! Where's your hand?' He pressed something into her palm. 'Here's a shilling in case you should need it.'
>   A shilling! She must be going away for ever! 'Father!' cried Fenella.

The part of this passage to which I want to draw your attention is 'A shilling! She must be going away for ever!' Now you will note that (as with 'He loved her') these two utterances are ostensibly in the third person; Fenella is described as 'she' and quotation marks are not used. Even so, it is clear that it is Fenella's thoughts that are being given here as neither the narrator nor her father would be so surprised at her being given a shilling. In this passage the use of FID allows Mansfield to distinguish between what Fenella says (given in quotation marks), and what she thinks (given without the use of quotation marks).

Let me return to the issue of the ambiguity associated with the technique, an ambiguity which sometimes makes it impossible definitively to attribute a statement to either narrator or character. Take this extract from Virginia Woolf's *Mrs Dalloway*:

> Elizabeth rather wondered whether Miss Kilman could be hungry. It was her way of eating, eating with intensity, then looking, again and again, at a plate of sugared cakes on the table next them; then, when a lady and a child sat down and the child took the cake, could Miss Kilman really mind it? Yes, Miss Kilman did mind it. She had wanted that cake – the pink one. The pleasure of eating was almost the only pure pleasure left her, and then to be baffled even in that!

Whose consciousness is represented in the last three sentences? Is it (1) narrator, (2) narrator, (3) narrator? Or (1) narrator, (2) narrator, (3) Miss Kilman? Or (1) narrator, (2) Miss Kilman, (3) Miss Kilman? It is even possible that these sentences give us Elizabeth's thoughts as she imagines what Miss Kilman is thinking. As with the opening of 'Fanny and Annie', these ambiguities do not constitute a flaw in the passage but quite the reverse: we know what Miss Kilman is thinking and we understand the narrator's attitude towards her and her desires without having to attribute a form of words either to the narrator or to the character. Note that a 'principle of inertia' operates in our response to such passages: unless we are given good reason for changing the way we attribute statements to a particular source or consciousness, we tend to go on attributing them to the one already established as the operative one. The technical term for this 'principle of inertia' in narrative theory is *obstination* (see also the Glossary).

Another short story by Katherine Mansfield, 'The Daughters of the Late Colonel', includes a striking exploitation of the possibilities of FID. The two daughters of the title, Josephine and Constantia, have lived in the shadow of their tyrannical father all their lives, and are extremely close. In the immediate aftermath of his death, they find themselves in a strange and unfamiliar world. A visiting clergyman suggests that he could arrange a communion for them at home.

> But the idea of a little Communion terrified them. What! In the drawing-room by themselves – with no – no altar or anything! The piano would be much too high, thought Constantia, and Mr. Farolles could not possibly lean over it with the chalice. And Kate would be sure to come bursting in and interrupt them, thought Josephine. And supposing the bell rang in the middle? It might be somebody important – about their mourning. Would they get up reverently and go out, or would they have to wait … in torture? (Ellipsis in original)

If we follow these sentences in order, we see that (1) describes their reaction from a perspective detached from both of them, (2) gives their shared response in FID, (3) gives Constantia's thoughts in indirect or reported speech, while

(4) seems to show Josephine responding mentally to what her sister has thought, again using indirect or reported speech. But (5), (6) and (7) give us the shared thoughts of the two sisters, using FID. Thus the passage leaves open the possibility that the sisters can read each others' minds, but without actually stating this unambiguously. This is the achievement of the revolution of which George Butte speaks – giving us access to the inwardness of (in this case two) characters, while retaining an external, distanced perspective on them.

Yet another technique, one which has something in common with Free Indirect Discourse without having quite the grammatical specificity of this technique, is that of *coloured* discourse or narrative. This involves the 'colouring' of a piece of (normally but not necessarily) third-person narrative with words, phrases, expressions which the reader associates with the verbal habits of a particular character. The technique is closely related to techniques used to mock, mimic or satirize others in speech. The fiction of Dickens contains innumerable examples of it, from which the following (the opening of Chapter 25, 'Book the Second', of *Little Dorrit* [1857–8]) will serve as illustration:

> The dinner-party was at the great Physician's. Bar was there, and in full force. Ferdinand Barnacle was there, and in his most engaging state. Few ways of life were hidden from Physician, and he was oftener in its darkest places than even Bishop. There were brilliant Ladies about London who perfectly doted on him, my dear, as the most charming creature and the most delightful person …

The whole of this chapter is characterized by bitter and ironic mockery of the pretensions of those involved, but in this passage we see Dickens actually incorporating a verbal 'signature' from those he is mocking; 'my dear' is, we take it, the sort of frequent hypocrisy to be found in the conversation of the ladies being ridiculed, and its inclusion colours the narrative around it. Richard Walsh has suggested that '[m]imicry is a reasonably good model for how FID works' (2007, 97); here we see mimicry providing the model for coloured discourse (see also the entry for colouring in the Glossary).

Tone

Mimicry carries with it the idea of *tone*, or the way in which a particular utterance is coded to communicate a particular attitude on the part of the speaker with regard either to what is being spoken about, or to whoever is addressed. One fails to understand *Gulliver's Travels*, for example, if one does not perceive the satirical tone that pervades the whole work. In like manner, although it is true that a work like Kafka's *The Castle* suggests that life is meaningless and that effective communication between human beings is impossible, this aspect of the work has to be seen in consort with the tone of deep pity and sympathy for humanity which pervades the novel.

Character

Character and individuality

I suggested in Chapter 2 that it was a moot point whether much fiction from before the time of the modern novel could be said to contain characters as we understand the word. For us, 'character' is intimately bound up with individualism: a character is unique, not just the property of a person but somehow simultaneously both the person and the sign or token of the person. (See my comments in Chapter 2, p. 14, on the etymological connection with 'character' meaning 'handwriting'.) According to Clemens Lugowski, so long as human existence is dominated by myth (which is timeless and collective) rather than by history, 'there can be no individual characters', for instead of being autonomous individuals 'they are no more than components of a whole' (Lugowski, 1990, 83). Myth takes, typically, an oral form, whereas the novel, as I have argued in my opening chapter, has an intimate relationship with writing and printing. No literary or artistic form has a closer relationship to what we now know and understand as character than does the novel.

If we can conceive of a time during which characters as we know them, both in life and in fiction, did not exist, then it will be easier for us to consider a number of other possibilities. First, that how human individuals are represented in books has some connection with how they are conceived by themselves and by others in real life. Second, that as our view of human individuality in the real world changes, so too may our view of fictional character. Third, that just as there are conventions that govern (or at least influence) how speech is represented in the novel (see the end of this chapter, p. 154), so too there are comparable and changing conventions that govern the depiction of character in the novel. Finally, that if there was a time in which human beings saw themselves in ways untouched by the individualism which forms an important component in the developing concept of fictional character, then there might just be such a time again one day, so that those elements which may strike us as strange and unnatural in the way in which individuals are represented in modernist and postmodernist fiction *may* be prophetic of some such change.

We should certainly not assume that because we can respond so fully to characters in the fiction of past ages there is, therefore, no change in fictional characterization from age to age. Not only are there technical changes in the way novelists learn to create and reveal characters, but also changes in human beings outside literature (or at least the belief that such changes have taken place) often inspire novelists to use new methods to produce a new sort of character.

In her famous essay 'Mr Bennett and Mrs Brown' (1924), Virginia Woolf states her belief that:

> all novels ... deal with character, and that it is to express character – not to preach doctrines, sing songs, or celebrate the glories of the British

Empire, that the form of the novel, so clumsy, verbose, and undramatic, so rich, elastic, and alive, has been evolved. (Woolf, 1966a, 324)

This does not, however, mean that she sets up 'character' as a sort of human universal, or that she claims that the characters we find in books or in real life are always the same. Indeed, earlier on in the same essay she has already made the remark (doubtless part tongue-in-cheek) that 'in or about December, 1910, human character changed' (320). Woolf is of course exaggerating for humorous and other purposes, but it is clear that she is serious in the main point that she makes in the essay, that changes in human beings have taken place, and thus changes in the ways novelists represent human beings must also occur.

My earlier discussion of modernism and postmodernism should have suggested that recent fiction to which the labels 'modernist' or 'postmodernist' can be attached will be likely to portray the human individual in ways different from those to be found in the classic-realist fiction of the previous century. This is indeed the case. What often seem to disappear in the characters we find in modernist fiction are individual consistency and even coherence, comprehensive self-knowledge and autonomy. Virginia Woolf's *The Waves* is a textbook example of this sort of change. Her character Bernard repeatedly utters statements such as 'I am not one and simple, but complex and many'; 'I am more selves than Neville thinks'; 'We exist not only separately but in undifferentiated blobs of matter.' Not surprisingly, Bernard repeatedly asks 'Who am I?', and even describes himself as a man without a self. It needs to be said that *The Waves* does not attempt to universalize Bernard's view of himself: other characters in the novel *do* have a sense of their coherent and autonomous selves. Nonetheless, the novel opens up the possibility that the classic-realist view of character is either inadequate or historically limited – perhaps culture-specific. Other modernist novelists have also portrayed character as complex and problematic rather than simple and self-evident. Think of Klamm in Kafka's *The Castle*, who appears to be different to everyone who sees him and each time that he is seen. It seems clear that Kafka is concerned to open up certain conventional views of human individuality to renewed scrutiny by means of his character Klamm, both as these views operate in fiction and as they are circulated more widely in the world at large.

Postmodernist fiction generally takes this disintegration of character a stage further, playing with the conventions governing the representation of character in works of fiction so as to expose these to the reader's scrutiny. Thus a *cancelled character* (sometimes called an *erased character*) is a character in a postmodernist work who (or which) is introduced in order to make the reader accept him or her as a human individual, but who is later cancelled or erased and revealed to be only the creation of the novelist, a construct who (or, again, which!) has existence only in the pages of the work. Such a refusal to abide by established conventions has to be seen as comparable to the way in which modernist art frustrated realist expectations by perverting those conventions governing the representation of depth in pictures – perspective. The aim is also to make the reader or viewer think about the way in which these conventions govern our understanding both in literature and in the extra-literary world.

Cyberfiction takes some of these elements even further, imagining futures in which the grafting together of organic and non-organic materials is able to produce cyborgs, beings part-human and part-machine (see p. 228).

Types of literary character

These rather extended introductory comments seem to me to be necessary because 'character' may well appear to be one of the least problematic terms with which you have to deal in studying the novel. The proper names we encounter in a novel – Tom Jones, Anna Karenina, Daisy Miller, Huck Finn, Yossarian – seem very much like the proper names we meet in everyday life and by which we designate individual human beings.

Yet even if we stop at names we may realize that characters in novels are not quite like real people. In everyday life we sometimes meet a person with an unusually appropriate name: the very tall person called Long, for example. In novels it is different. The peculiar appropriateness of a name such as Heath-cliff is surely hardly ever met with in real life. What about Dickens's Esther Summerson – who acts like a 'summer sun' in *Bleak House*, dispelling the shad-ows with which the work is, initially, filled? Even 'Tom Jones' with its resolute lack of connotations or associations seems extraordinarily appropriate a name for the non-aristocratic, normally healthy hero of Fielding's novel.

'Tom Jones' is a rather different name from 'M'Choakunchild' – the name given by Dickens to one of his characters – however, and this reminds us of an important point: there are different *sorts* of literary character. Of course there are different sorts of people in ordinary life, but it is not this sort of variation that I have in mind. Think of Meursault in Albert Camus's *The Outsider* and Mr Guppy in Charles Dickens's *Bleak House*. Both are young men who have problems communicating with others and who have an odd relation to their mothers. There are also important differences between them, however, and if we were asked to explain these differences we would have to talk about them not just as if they were ordinary human beings but also in a way that recognizes that they are different *types* of literary character, existing within very unlike sorts of novel, very varied *narrative situations*.

A good test here is to ask to what extent a character from one literary work could be transplanted to another. We have little difficulty in imagining a meet-ing between, for example, the title character from Jane Austen's *Emma* (1816) and Mr Darcy from her *Pride and Prejudice* (1813, but written 1796/7). This is because the fictional worlds of these two novels are so similar that such a meet-ing, which is as much a meeting of fictional worlds as it is of characters, does not seem absurd. That is why we have films with titles like *Godzilla Meets King Kong*, but not, outside the realms of parody, with titles such as *Bambi Meets Godzilla*.

(There is actually a very short film with this title – you can find it through a Google search on the internet – but even without watching it you will be able to guess that it has to be a parody!)

If we go back to *The Outsider* and compare the narrator with Mr Guppy from Charles Dickens's *Bleak House*, we realize that Mr Guppy could not be transported to the fictional world of *The Outsider*; he could not survive in that novel as we know him in *Bleak House*. My concept of 'fictional world' is not just a matter of setting (about which I talk below). After all, the settings of *Moll Flanders* and *Robinson Crusoe* are very different, but there is a sense in which their fictional worlds are much less so. The concept refers, in other words, not just to the real-world elements (places, events, history) contained in the works, but also to the representational conventions governing the depiction of these and other things. *Bleak House* and *The Outsider* are held together in part by philosophical and ideological elements: views of the nature of the world which enter into the very fabric and texture of the novels.

Meursault lives in a world defined by the preoccupations of existentialist philosophy, a world from which Mr Guppy is very far removed. (Note that the important thing is not whether the *individual character* has certain philosophical or other concerns but whether their *fictional presentation* accords with these concerns.)

Subsequent to my writing the previous paragraph I discovered Christine Brooke-Rose's novel *Textermination* (1991), in which a conference of characters out of the great works of literature is convened at the San Francisco Hilton, to pray for their continual survival in readers' minds. It is not exactly *Bambi Meets Godzilla*, but it does have Emma Bovary sharing a carriage with Jane Austen's Mr Elton. Of course, the characters' knowledge of themselves as literary characters gives them something in common and something which their originals lack; thus the fictional world of *Textermination* is one coloured and formed by the post-structuralist interests of its author. It is not in any way a simple mixing of the fictional worlds of the different characters – and nor could it be.

Let us try to explore some of the differences that exist between literary characters. We have some well-established terms to draw on initially: major and minor characters, flat and round characters, stock characters, 'types' and so on.

We can sum up one important distinction that has a bearing upon all of the above terms: is the writer primarily interested in developing a character so as to *represent something*, or in order to present a *particular individuality*? The distinction is related to that between novels of 'life' and novels of 'pattern' to which I referred much earlier, for it is in novels of pattern that one is likely to find characters who stand for something (a giveaway feature is often the names) and in the novel of life that one finds characters possessed of a distinctive, idiosyncratic and unique individuality. However, even in the latter case we have to face the paradox that a highly individualized character may also stand for something: Mr Toots in Dickens's *Dombey and Son* and Prince Myshkin in Dostoyevsky's

The Idiot (1869) are 'originals', yet they also stand for certain valuable qualities which contribute importantly to the themes of the two novels mentioned. Moreover, just because a character is a recognizable *type* (another of Dickens's grotesques, one of Dostoyevsky's eccentrics) does not necessarily mean that he or she cannot also be a realized individual personality in the work.

In his book *Aspects of the Novel* (1927), E.M. Forster uses Dickens's Mrs Micawber (from *David Copperfield*) as an example of what he calls a 'flat character': 'The really flat character can be expressed in one sentence such as "I never will desert Mr Micawber." There is Mrs Micawber – she says she won't desert Mr Micawber; she doesn't, and there she is.' Mrs Micawber does not change because she is not allowed genuine *interaction* with other people and situations; even though she has, as it were, dealings with them, she is independent of them.

We have now suggested three different ways in which a fictional character can be unlike a real person: first, by being defined by the philosophical or ideological underpinnings of their fictional presentation; second, by being limited to one essential characteristic; and, third, by being possessed of a constituting individuality that is unshakeable by events.

In his book *Narrative as Rhetoric: Technique, Audiences, Ethics, Ideology* (1996), James Phelan refers to the model that he has developed for analysing character, and comments:

> (1) Character consists of three components – the mimetic (character as person), the thematic (character as idea), and the synthetic (character as artificial construct). (2) The relationship between these components varies from narrative to narrative. (Phelan, 1996, 29)

Phelan's division is on a more general and abstract level than my own, and it indicates components into which *any* literary character can be divided. But the two tripartite distinctions do overlap, and both I think draw attention to the ways in which a literary character is both like and unlike a real person.

The term *synonymous character* has been applied to recent, especially experimental, novels; synonymous characters are those which are possessed of essentially the same characteristics and functions in a piece of prose fiction, and are thus to all intents interchangeable. The term is very close to the more old-fashioned 'stock character'.

Functions and types

The word 'function' also deserves some attention at this stage. Its literary-critical usage is most associated with the analyses of folktales carried out by the Russian Vladimir Propp, who argued that all folktales consist of a selection from a finite number of functions, a function being 'an act of a character, defined from the point of view of its significance for the course of the action' (Propp, 1968, 21). Not all the available functions would be selected by the creator of the tale, but those which were selected had to appear in the tale in a strict order. Such a description seems foreign to those of us more familiar with the novel than with the sort of work with which Propp was concerned. However, just as I argued earlier that romance-like elements can be found in the novel, so too it is worth remembering that although the modern novel is to be distinguished from the folktale in terms of – among other things – its individual and individualized characters, nonetheless modern novelists are still capable of using characters as a means whereby an 'act significant for the course of the action' can be achieved. In other words, some characters are there to do things; they are primarily *vehicles*, and their significance relates less to what they *are* and more to what they *do*.

Thus although *in general terms* we can distinguish the novel from other fictional forms which represent human individuals but are less interested in their particularity and individuality than in what they do or stand for (the type-characters of the fable or parable, for example), we should recall that even those novelists most renowned and admired for their creation of living characters utilize recognizable types: think of the characters created by Jane Austen and Charles Dickens. Indeed, because in real life we classify people ('a typical schoolmaster'), we should not automatically assume that depictions of realistic characters cannot also be representations of human types, or of characteristics typical of particular groups of human beings.

In recent years a number of critics have developed the concept of *projection characters*, that is characters into whom the novelist projects aspects of him- or herself – often aspects which cannot be acknowledged either to others or to the author him- or herself. (Psychoanalytic theories of projection lie behind the term, the idea being that what we cannot accept in ourselves we often project onto others.) In Charles Dickens's *Great Expectations*, for example, the character Orlick is like a dark shadow of the hero Pip, and seems almost a personification of Pip's repressed desires. He stands up to Mrs Joe (who treats Pip so unfeelingly) and eventually strikes her down, and he openly lusts after Biddy, for whom Pip eventually acknowledges his own desire. In a late, climactic scene he announces his intention of murdering Pip himself, thus dramatizing what otherwise would be a purely internal struggle in Pip. If we take into account the considerable extent to which Pip's portrayal (like that of David Copperfield) is modelled by Dickens on his own character and experiences, then we can understand that Orlick can be described as a projection character: whereas the similarities between Dickens and Pip are open and overt, those between Orlick and Dickens are concealed and even denied. (For a comparable application of the concept of the 'projection character' to another novel by Dickens – *David Copperfield* – see Roger Sell [1983].)

'Telling' and 'showing'

A classic but still useful distinction between two fundamental ways of creating (or 'revealing') character is one that we owe to Percy Lubbock's *The Craft of*

Fiction (1921). Lubbock's distinction between 'telling' and 'showing' (a distinction he probably owed to Henry James) is very similar to that which Georg Lukács makes between 'narration' and 'description' in a famous essay entitled 'Narrate or Describe' (1936). (In neither case, it should be said, is the critic talking exclusively about characterization.) When Jane Austen opens her novel *Emma* in the following way, she is *telling* (or in Lukács's terminology describing) rather than showing us what Emma is like:

> Emma Woodhouse, handsome, clever, and rich, with a comfortable home and happy disposition, seemed to unite some of the best blessings of existence; and had lived nearly twenty-one years in the world with very little to distress or vex her.

Later on in the novel, however, when we witness the conversation between Emma and Mr Knightley in which he criticizes her rudeness to Miss Bates, we are *shown* an aspect of Emma's personality through her behaviour and her responses to him. It may be worth adding that Austen's use of the word 'seemed' in the above passage encourages the alert reader to wonder whether Emma's happy situation may turn out to contain some less positive elements.

Since Lubbock, critics have generally privileged 'showing' over 'telling' as a method of revealing character, believing that this method unlocks the life in characters rather than treating them (as Lukács puts it) as inanimate objects. We feel that *we* decide what a character is like when we observe him or her behaving in front of us; we can use our critical intelligence and our knowledge of human beings to reach an assessment of them, whereas when we are *told* something we can only take it or leave it. This is why, in real life, we prefer to make up our minds about people through personal acquaintance and observation rather than on the basis of others' assessments.

If we think of the most memorable literary characters we probably find that we remember them doing or saying things; we do not so much remember being told things about them. Where a narrative comment on a character does stick in our minds it is probably as a result of something other than characterization: the narrator's use of irony, moral discrimination or whatever.

So far as the creation of lifelike characters is concerned, it is very often the interplay between 'shown' and 'told' attributes that makes them fascinating. Think of Heathcliff in *Wuthering Heights*; we partly understand why he is as he is because we have witnessed key elements of his upbringing. However, some of his attributes seem to be beyond such an explanation; they are presented as givens rather than as effects or results.

I repeat, however, that creating a lifelike character may not always be what a novelist is aiming at – even in pre-modernist or pre-postmodernist fiction. It is not lifelike for Gulliver to be so acute and humane at one part of *Gulliver's Travels* and so obtuse and unconcerned about talk of human suffering at others. It seems apparent that Swift's primary aim here is not the creation of a consistent and lifelike character so much as the creation of a character whose alternating qualities and abilities will allow him to explore different aspects of that 'human race' that is perhaps the real subject of *Gulliver's Travels*.

Methods of characterization

What are the most important methods of characterization available to the novelist? I would suggest four that are worth thinking about. First is *description* or *report*. In Conrad's *Heart of Darkness*, we know a very large amount about Mr Kurtz before ever he appears before us; other characters in the novella have talked about him so much, reporting his actions and beliefs, that we feel almost as if we had met him ourselves.

The description of physical characteristics – and especially of physiognomy – is a very traditional means whereby the writer can suggest what sort of character we are encountering. Here is a description taken from the second paragraph of Philip Larkin's novel *Jill* (1946). The novel's main male character, John Kemp, is travelling by train to Oxford:

> It looked cold and deserted. The windows of the carriages were bluish
> with the swirls of the cleaner's leather still showing on the glass, and
> he confined his eyes to the compartment. It was a third-class carriage,
> and the crimson seats smelt of dust and engines and tobacco, but the
> air was warm. Pictures of Dartmouth Castle and Portmadoc looked at
> him from the opposite wall. He was an undersized boy, eighteen years
> old, with a pale face and soft pale hair brushed childishly from left to
> right. Lying back against the seat, he stretched his legs out and pushed
> his hands to the bottom of the pockets of his cheap blue overcoat. The
> lapels of it curled outwards and creases dragged from the buttons. His
> face was thin, and perhaps strained; the expression round his mouth
> was ready to become taut, and a small frown lingered on his forehead.
> His whole appearance lacked luxuriance. Only his silky hair, as soft as
> seeding thistle, gave him an air of beauty.

Just imagine that you have met someone on a train, and when discussing this meeting with someone you know, later on, you start to describe him. You would, I venture to suggest, hardly come out with something along the lines of the above paragraph. If you did, it would probably be because you were a student of literature indulging in a little parodic behaviour. To put the matter another way, we can say that Larkin's description of John Kemp depends upon certain fictional conventions which regulate the depiction of character, conventions that require that physical characteristics be seen to have a much more reliable function as indicators of non-physical qualities (and even, perhaps, of past or future events and experiences) than they do in real life. (This is not to deny that the *sort* of observations we are presented with in this passage and the *sort* of deductions implied by these observations are closely related to those observations and deductions we make in real life. Railway journeys seem to encourage this sort of speculation about other people: Virginia Woolf makes this the basis of her essay 'Mr Bennett and Mrs Brown'.)

Thus from this passage we can detect that John Kemp is not rich, and is not a thrusting, self-confident youth ready and eager for heroic exploits. We assume that the journey he is making has not been made by him before, otherwise he would not notice so many details about his surroundings. (We are not told that it is he who sees and smells these details, but we are encouraged to assume this.) We deduce too that behind his lack of position and self-confidence there reside qualities which now are apparent only to the discriminating and which will allow him to deal well (finally, perhaps) with whatever trials he has to face. It is almost unthinkable that this is a description of a man who will turn into a pompous and conforming hypocrite, who the reader will end up hating. Behind his portrayal we may, even at this stage, recognize what can be called a mythic element: the unregarded person who has a potentiality that, when revealed, may surprise those who take him at face value. That silky hair of John Kemp's, along with the expression round the mouth and the frown on his forehead, betoken much more on the first page of a novel than they would in real life: they stand for that unregarded quality or virtue which exists only *in potentia*, whose emergence the novel will trace. As the description also insists on the shabby cheapness of Kemp's clothes and of the third-class compartment, we can feel reasonably confident, too, that the novel will pay particular attention to the problems raised by his background and by issues of social class – especially as the first paragraph of the novel has informed us that the train he is on is heading for Oxford. Notice how much we know of Kemp and how much we are already expecting – and he has said nothing and done nothing so far!

Second, character can be established by *action*; when Insarov in Turgenev's *On the Eve* (1859) throws the insolent German into the water – an action of which his effete Russian companions are palpably incapable – then we learn something about him which pages of description could not give us.

Third, through a character's *thought* or *conversation*. Dialogue in particular is a wonderful way of revealing character: think how much we learn about Miss Bates in Emma merely through her conversation – so much so that comment from Austen's narrator is really not needed. Modern novelists have shown how much we can learn about a character merely by following his or her thoughts; in Virginia Woolf's *Mrs Dalloway* (1925), Clarissa Dalloway and Peter Walsh actually *do* very little, but by the end of the novel we feel that we know them quite well just by having followed so many of their thoughts (and through their thoughts Woolf is able to retrieve actions and encounters from their pasts, shared and private).

In the third paragraph of Chapter 2 of Jane Austen's *Sense and Sensibility* (1811), we learn as much as we feel we need to learn about Mrs John Dashwood through a report of her comments on her husband's intended generosity to his two sisters. Austen here uses that variant of Free Indirect Discourse known as represented speech (see p. 126), and as this is frequently used for ironic purposes, we are alert to the hints concerning the narrator's disapproval without their ever becoming overt and intruding directly. The paragraph reads:

> Mrs John Dashwood did not at all approve of what her husband intended to do for his sisters. To take three thousand pounds from the fortune of their dear little boy, would be impoverishing him to the most dreadful degree. She begged him to think again on the subject. How could he answer it to himself to rob his child, and his only child too, of so large a sum? And what possible claim could the Miss Dashwoods, who were related to him only by half blood, which she considered as no relationship at all, have on his generosity to so large an amount. It was very well known that no affection was ever supposed to exist between the children of any man by different marriages; and why was he to ruin himself, and their poor little Harry, by giving away all his money to his half sisters?

The pleasure we get from this passage is related to the fact that although we do not feel that we are being told how to regard Mrs John Dashwood and coerced into a particular attitude towards her, we sense that our amused disapproval of the character is shared by Jane Austen (through her narrative voice). The very omission of comment on Mrs John Dashwood's more outrageous statements indicates a narrative opinion that they *are* so outrageous as to require no comment.

Finally, the novelist can use *symbol* or *image* to reveal and develop a character. In Jean Rhys's novel *After Leaving Mr Mackenzie* (1930), the heroine, Julia, has just been to see a Mr James, shortly after visiting her dying mother and her spinsterish sister Norah:

> She wanted to cry as he went down the stairs with her. She thought: 'That wasn't what I wanted.' She had hoped that he would say something or look something that would make her feel less lonely.
>
> There was a vase of flame-coloured tulips in the hall – surely the most graceful of flowers. Some thrust their heads forward like snakes, and some were very erect, stiff, virginal, rather prim. Some were dying, with curved grace in their death. (Rhys, 1971, 84)

The tulips present us symbolically with the varied fates of the different women in the novel: snake-like cunning and self-interested behaviour; prim and virginal lifelessness (like Norah); and death – like Julia's mother. Such a passage contributes to our knowledge of and attitudes to characters in the novel even though nothing is said directly about any character.

Plot

Let us start with a definition: a plot is an ordered, organized sequence of events and actions. Plots in this sense are found in novels rather than in ordinary life; life has stories, but novels have plots and stories (see the earlier comments on the double chronology of literary fiction on p. 6). E.M. Forster claimed that a story was a narrative of events arranged in their time sequence, whereas a plot was a narrative of events with the emphasis falling on causality. Not all commentators would agree that causality is the distinguishing feature, but all would agree that there is a necessary distinction to be made between the incidents about which we are told in a novel in their chronological order, and the actual narrating of these events in perhaps quite a different order. I prefer the terms 'story' and 'plot' to make this distinction, but some critics use terms created by a group of theorists known as the Russian Formalists (see p. 206), the terms *sjužet* (plot) and *fabula* (story).

Narratologists (see p. 198) have performed a useful function in providing terms and concepts such that we can more accurately analyse how and why the plot of a novel deviates from strict and simple chronological progression. We owe many of the terms I discuss below to structuralist narratologists, especially Gérard Genette.

Order

First of all are a number of terms connected to what is termed *order*. The plot of a novel may move backwards and forwards in time, instead of proceeding steadily forward in chronological order. If life always goes ABCDE, novels often go DEACB. Any deviation from such strict chronological progression is termed an *anachrony*, and there are a large number of such deviations possible. The most frequent are *analepsis* (or flashback) and *prolepsis* (or flashforward). The italicized terms are perhaps to be preferred, as 'flash' suggests a rather short movement backwards or forwards in time whereas an analepsis or a prolepsis may be of very considerable duration.

Ellipses

Second, a novel's plot may include gaps, omissions, absences. These can be referred to collectively as *ellipses* – the same term as is used to refer to the succession of dots in a text that indicates that something has been left out. Thus in *Wuthering Heights* we never get to know what Heathcliff does after his sudden disappearance and up to the time of his reappearance. This is what can be termed a (relatively) *unmarked* ellipsis – in other words, the text does not ostentatiously display the fact that something is not there. But when in Charles Dickens's *Bleak House* Esther Summerson seeks to explain why she finds Mrs Woodcourt irksome, and breaks off with the words, 'I don't know what it was. Or at least if I do, now, I thought I did not then. Or at least – but it don't matter', then we have a clearly *marked* (or explicit) ellipsis: the reader's attention is drawn to the fact that something that is known to the narrator is being withheld. A novelist typically uses a marked ellipsis to get the reader's imagination working: what has happened here? Why are we not told? An unmarked ellipsis may turn out to be of great importance later on – especially in sub-genres such as the detective story.

Duration

Third, the element of duration is also of great significance. Nearly all works of prose fiction vary the relationship between narrating and narrated time (The term *tense* is sometimes used to refer to this relationship, although this usage – taken from structuralist narratology – has not achieved general acceptance among Anglo-American critics.)

Whatever term we use, the essential characteristic involved is crucial to how novels work. A novelist can spend fifty pages to tell us about one day in the life of a heroine and then ten further pages to cover fifty years. Such extremes are sometimes referred by means of the linked terms *scene* (a passage in which there is a sort of equivalence between narrated and narrating time – for example a dialogue in which all the words exchanged are given) and *summary* (where it is clear that the narrative presents the reader with a descriptive outline of what he or she is encouraged to imagine actually involved more than is detailed). Within a single novel the ratio of narrated to narrating time can alter very substantially, and it is worth paying careful attention to such shifts.

In *Tristram Shandy*, for example, Laurence Sterne makes frequent jokes about the relationship between narrated and narrating time. At the start of Chapter 21 the text breaks off into a digression in the middle of a sentence uttered by uncle Toby, to utter which he has had to take his pipe out of his mouth. The digression finished, the text continues: 'But I forget my uncle Toby, whom all this while we have left knocking the ashes out of his tobacco pipe.' The suggestion that narrated and narrating time are coterminous is a joke, we know, because in many novels the narrator can leap over enormous gaps of time. Think how few pages are devoted to the period of Cathy's married life prior to the return of Heathcliff in *Wuthering Heights*.

Frequency

Fourth, narrative theorists also isolate the important topic of *frequency*, and note the following fundamental possibilities:

(i)   one event narrated once (*singulative frequency*)
(ii) a repeated event narrated the same number of times that it occurs (*multiple frequency*)

(iii)   one event narrated many times (*repetitive frequency*)
(iv)   many events narrated once (*iterative frequency*)

Probably the most usual of these is (i): many unique events that are depicted in a novel are recounted to the reader only once. The same event can, however, be recounted many times, as in (iii). Sometimes this has the effect of sharpening our understanding: the detective novel typically recounts the same events more than once, so that what was unclear the first time becomes comprehensible in the detective's final version. In Joseph Heller's novel *Catch-22* (1961), as Snowden's death in the bombing raid is as it were 'replayed' repetitively through the anti-hero Yossarian's consciousness while the novel unfolds, the reader is reminded of a psychoanalytic patient recalling more and more of a repressed event. As the reader gradually comes to learn what happened, the repetition conveys the traumatic effect that the event has had on Yossarian. Sometimes clarity is not the intended result: the repeated but different depictions of the same events in Alain Robbe-Grillet's *The Voyeur* (1955) lead the reader to lose confidence in the existence of a single, isolable series of events.

Many similar events may, as in (iv), be recounted as one. In Conrad's *Lord Jim*, Marlow's narrative is introduced as an iterative narrative – in other words, we are told that what we are about to read is an account that has been given many times. (The word 'would' often confirms that the account is an iterative one, as can be seen in the extract below from Guy de Maupassant's novel *Bel-Ami*.) By the time Marlow's account ends it has become a single, particular act of recounting. In the same novelist's *Nostromo*, the shifts between the singulative and iterative modes are technically contradictory, but they draw attention to important thematic concerns about the uniqueness of events and the repetitions of history. Conrad deliberately and repetitively frustrates his readers' expectations: passages change unexpectedly from singulative to iterative mode, and from iterative to singulative mode (I have written more on this elsewhere: see Hawthorn, 1998).

Gérard Genette has isolated a variation on the above alternatives which he calls the 'pseudo-iterative'. According to his definition, the pseudo-iterative occurs when 'scenes presented, particularly by their wording in the imperfect, as iterative', are possessed of a 'richness and precision of detail [which] ensure that no reader can seriously believe they occur and reoccur in that manner, several times, without any variation' (Genette, 1980, 121). Consider the following passage from Guy de Maupassant's novel *Bel-Ami*:

> So they would go into low dives and sit down at the end of the squalid murky room on rickety chairs at decrepit wooden tables. An acrid cloud of smoke and the smell of fried fish filled the room; men in their working clothes were shouting at each other as they downed their glasses of raw spirits; and the waiter would stare at the strange couple as he put the two cherries-in-brandy down in front of them.

Scared and trembling, but blissfully happy, she would begin sipping the red fruity liquid, looking around her, bright-eyed but uneasy: each time she swallowed a cherry she felt she was doing something wrong, every drop of the spicy, burning liquid that slipped down her throat gave her a sharp pleasure, the pleasure of forbidden fruit, of being naughty.

Then she would whisper: 'Let's go.' And so they would leave. She slipped away hastily, tripping along and holding her head down, like an actress leaving the stage, between the drinkers sitting with their elbows on the table, who looked up with a suspicious, surly air as she went by. And when she was through the door, she gave a big gasp as if she had just escaped from some terrible danger.

Sometimes, with a shudder, she asked Duroy:

'What would you do if they insulted me in a place like that?'

He said airily:

'Defend you, of course!' (Maupassant, 1975, 124–5)

It seems clear that the detailed dialogue provided here is not fully reconcilable with the suggestion that it represents what was said again and again on different occasions. Maupassant wants to give the reader a sense of repeated – even obsessively repeated – actions, while giving them enough individualized flavour to dramatize them and to prevent the reader from getting bored. Note that technically there is a change of frequency at the end of this passage from 'Sometimes ... she asked Duroy' (*iterative* – she asked more than once) to 'He said' (*singulative* – he replied only once; we are not told 'he would say'). This oscillation between the iterative and singulative modes is often a sign of the pseudo-iterative.

Chronology and coherence

If a novelist abandons strict chronology, how else can he or she retain coherence, make the novel hang together? Well, as Forster points out, *causality* is one important possible way: even if we know *what* happened, we read on to discover *why*.

Another technique is for a novelist to draw *parallels* and *resemblances* between characters, situations and events such that the novel has coherence even if it plots neither chronological sequences nor causal relationships. It is only to a limited degree that we believe that the experiences of the second-generation characters in *Wuthering Heights* are actually caused by the lives and actions of the first-generation characters. Even so, the parallels (with variations) and resemblances between the younger Cathy, Linton Heathcliff and Hareton Earnshaw and their parents suggest that this latter part of the novel continues themes and enquiries from the first part of the novel. It is important for the reader first to encounter the mature and embittered Heathcliff; this means that we see the young Heathcliff in the context of what we know he will later become, and thus our attention is focussed in very particular ways as Nelly Dean starts to tell Lockwood of the childhood and young adulthood of Heathcliff and Catherine.

Alternatively, a novel can be held together by a common character or event. The picaresque novel and the *Bildungsroman* (see the Glossary), for instance, are held together by the personality of the central figure. The extent to which this provides a sophisticated or a crude unity depends to a certain degree upon the complexity of the central character. The work of major modernist and post-modernist writers has led many to question whether it is desirable that a novel should compose a unity: in her essay 'Modern Fiction' (1919), Virginia Woolf represented the traditional, well-structured, realist plot as one of a number of distorting conventions in need of being discarded.

Types of plot

We can categorize plots in two ways: either in terms of the dominant human activities which form the motivating principle in them or which are induced in the reader by them, or in more technical ways. In the first category we can include plots structured around *conflict* as in many ways the plot of *Nostromo* is; around *mystery* as are many of Dickens's novels; around *pursuit* or *search* as is *The Castle*; around a journey as is *Gulliver's Travels*; or, finally, around a test as is Joseph Conrad's *The Shadow-Line*. Now of course these are very simplistic descriptions and we would want to say that all of these novels engage with far more complex issues than the single topics mentioned. Even so, it is worthwhile remembering that a novel is often given force and coherence by a dominating element such as one of these plot types provides. *The Shadow-Line* is structured around a journey as well as a test, but the theme of the test is a sort of archetypal bedrock within the organizing logic of the plot.

A more technical classification of plots will provide us with terms such as 'picaresque/episodic'; 'well-made' (the traditional nineteenth-century realist plot); 'multiple' (many novels have two or more lines of plot, sometimes inter-connecting and sometimes not). It is very often important to be able to single out a *main plot* from its attendant *subplot(s)* for the purpose of analysis.

You may recall that much earlier on in this book I quoted Johnson's remark that if one were to read Richardson 'for the story', one would be so fretted one would hang oneself (p. 33). Plot and story fulfil different sorts of functions in different novels. According to Johnson, the story in a novel by Richardson is there only to give occasion to the sentiment; in other novels the tension and suspense relative to our desire to know 'what happens next' are an integral part of the appeal of the work. When the 'outer' or 'frame' narrator of *Heart of Darkness* warns us (indirectly) that we are about to hear 'about one of Marlow's inconclusive experiences', we may feel encouraged to adjust our expectations with regard to the plot of the novella. Modernist works of fiction very often have inconclusive endings, endings which leave the reader perhaps puzzled and unsatisfied, but puzzled and unsatisfied in ways that are productive of further thought. You should, again, remember that such matters go beyond the merely technical. Novels without omniscient narrators and with inconclusive endings are perhaps less likely to betoken a conventionally Christian world view in which everything is concluded in the manner in which God wishes; a novelist whose novels all have happy endings is unlikely to suffer from very much existential doubt. (See the entry for closure in the Glossary.)

Structure

Structure and plot are closely related to each other, and it might have made sense to include this section as a sub-section of 'Plot'. However, critics often use 'structure' in a rather wider sense than such treatment might suggest. If we can think of the plot of a novel as the way in which its story is arranged, its structure involves more than its story, encompassing the work's total organiza- tion as a piece of literature, a work of art. Nor are the terms 'structure' and 'form' to be confused; the latter does not normally include thematic elements in the work (see my comments concerning theme later in this chapter), whereas such thematic elements are involved in a novel's structure. Structure involves plot, thematics and form: it refers to our sense of a novel's overall organization and patterning, the way in which its component parts fit together to produce a totality, a satisfying whole – or, of course, the way in which they fail to do so.

Let us start by observing that different novels have very different sorts of structure. We feel, for example, that some parts of *Moll Flanders* or *Huckleberry Finn* (1884) could be shifted around in position without making too great a difference to the works in question: how many readers of the former work remember clearly whether Moll robbed the little girl of her necklace before or after she robbed the drunken man in the coach? But to shuffle around the parts of *Wuthering Heights*, or of Henry James's *What Maisie Knew* (1897), would, we feel, seriously damage the works in question. Clearly the fact that a novel has an *episodic* structure has an important bearing upon such issues; if a work is structured around a series of relatively self-contained episodes, then these can be assembled in different orders without making too much difference – just as on a modular degree scheme with self-contained modules one can often take different courses in any order one chooses.

The matter goes beyond plot, as I have suggested. In *Moll Flanders* there is very little alteration in Moll's character, or in the values the narrative under- writes, or in the symbolic meanings contained in the work (if there are any worth noting in this novel!). In short, *Moll Flanders* is consistently structured on the principle of 'repetition-with-slight-variation'. There is somewhat more develop- ment and change in *Huckleberry Finn* – in the characters and relationship of

Huck and Jim, in the general tone of the novel before and after the return of Huck and Jim to 'civilization', and so on. Thus, although some of the scenes in this novel might be switched around without too much effect, such alteration would have to be more limited than with *Moll Flanders* if we wished to avoid damaging the work. The intricate patterning of a novel such as *What Maisie Knew* would, surely, be completely destroyed if we started to move sections of it from place to place.

Very often the *chapter* and *section* divisions made by the author impose a structure upon a work – or bring out one that is implicit but not overt in it already. (My earlier comments on *paratextual* elements in a novel are relevant here: see p. 78.) It is interesting to read Conrad's *The Shadow-Line* in his manuscript version, in which there are no section divisions, and then to see how differently the published text of the novel reads with these divisions included (there is evidence that Conrad himself was not responsible for introducing the divisions, as he criticized the way the work was divided for periodical publication).

Very often such divisions perform the useful function of telling the reader when he or she can pause and put the book down for a bit, and, as it is at these points of time that we think backwards over what we have read and forwards to what we hope for or expect, such divisions can be very significant. It is doubtless for such reasons that Virginia Woolf (in her essay 'Modern Fiction') disapproved of the 'ill-fitting vestments' of the 'two and thirty chapters' of what she called the materialist novel. If clothes or vestments 'make the man' (or woman), then the wrong chapter divisions may make the novel something other than its author wants.

Order and *chronology* – issues upon which we touched when talking of plot – can be crucial to the matter of structure. The difference between a novel's 'story' and its 'plot' can tell us much about its structure. It is often an interesting exercise to map out a novel's story and plot in note form one above the other – as I did when discussing Conan Doyle's story 'Silver Blaze' on p. 53.

As I have argued, structure involves thematic elements too. Note how the repetition of thematic elements in Charles Dickens's *Bleak House* helps to structure that work. To take one example: Esther Summerson, like her mother Lady Dedlock, has to choose between two suitors: a rich, older, 'safe' one and a younger, less wealthy, more 'risky' match with more passionate potential. Whereas Lady Dedlock makes what we are led to see as the wrong choice in marrying the older man, Esther – after an initial false decision – makes what is clearly the right decision for her. Now this produces an element of *pattern* in the work which contributes to our sense of its structure, a pattern which blends in with other things in *Bleak House* to produce a satisfying work of art.

Consider a different example. In Katherine Mansfield's short story 'The Voyage' we have a very simple story: a little girl leaves her father at a New Zealand port and travels by boat with her grandmother to the south island of New Zealand, to her grandparents' home. In the course of the voyage we discover that her mother has died, and the reader comes to understand what Fenella – the girl – has not yet realized: that henceforth she is to be brought up by her grandparents. What is striking about the story is that, whereas images of darkness and cold dominate the opening of the story, these gradually give way to images of light and warmth which (especially the images of light) dominate the close of the story. Now clearly this shift of images contributes to the structure of the story: without actually being told it directly we realize that Fenella is moving out of an unhappy period of her life into a potentially much happier one. The physical voyage is from one *place* to another, but this is complemented structurally by travel from one *emotional state* to another.

Structure involves ideas and sensations of some sort of pattern: *completion, reiteration, contrast, repetition, complementarity* – all of these and others can be invoked by a work's structure. We should note too that the *frame* of a narrative – what constitutes its outer limits – can contribute importantly to our sense of structure. Consider the narrative framing of the 'tale within a tale' of *Heart of Darkness* and *The Turn of the Screw*. Think of the importance of the fact that the events recounted in James Joyce's *Ulysses* and Virginia Woolf's *Mrs Dalloway* take place within twenty-four hours. Note the thematic framing effect of our being told in E.M. Forster's novel *Howards End* that the work will not be concerned with the very poor, who are 'unthinkable'. In each case our view of what is 'in' the novel is given structure by our sense of what is excluded from it.

Setting

'Setting' is one of those terms about which recent literary critics tend to feel a little uneasy. Does the term not suggest a perhaps too-simple relationship between characters and action on the one hand, and the context within which these take place on the other? Does it not sound rather unsatisfactory to talk about the Nottinghamshire 'setting' of D.H. Lawrence's *Sons and Lovers* or the Yorkshire 'setting' of *Wuthering Heights*, as if the same actions might conceivably have taken place elsewhere – in Tunbridge Wells or Minnesota? The fact that so many characters in Emily Brontë's novel have names that are also the place names of towns and villages around her native Haworth suggests a relationship between character and environment too organic, we feel, to be described with the term 'setting'.

There may well be other reasons why this has become a relatively unfashionable term of late. Much twentieth-century fiction, especially that which we can term modernist or postmodernist, presents a view of human beings as symbolically homeless, deracinated, alienated from their environment. That close bond between individual and place that is celebrated in the regional novel (see the Glossary) is harder to find in our own time than it was in the nineteenth century. As a result, many novelists present the reader with settings whose unfamiliarity and unwelcoming aspect are frequently generalized or universalized. If all large towns are unwelcoming and dehumanizing, then does it matter which large town one is in? It is surely an essential part of the force of Franz Kafka's *The Trial* (1925) that the setting is not specified in real-world or real-time terms. The point is that in our age the events depicted could take place in many different locations: our time is the time of universal human experiences.

Yet even today it is important to be aware of the context within which the action of a novel takes place – and this does not just mean its geographical setting; social and historical factors are also important. It is just as important to ask why the author has chosen the setting he has chosen when it is generalized (as in the case of *The Trial*) as when it is highly specific (as with, say, Walter Greenwood's *Love on the Dole* [1933]).

To start with we need to distinguish between realistic and conventional or stylized settings. The famous country house of the classic detective story is obviously a highly *conventional* setting; we are not interested in the particularity of such country houses and their environments – they serve, rather, the function of providing a stylized and familiar setting within which a conventional set of happenings can unfold. Many detective stories actually choose relatively artificial settings that have the function of isolating the characters (or suspects) from the outside world: the closed world of Agatha Christie's Orient Express stuck in the snow is a paradigm case.

At the other extreme we can cite highly realistic settings like that of the tuberculosis sanatorium that dominates Thomas Mann's *The Magic Mountain* (1924). Here, however, we need to tread carefully, for although this may be a realistic setting, it is a very *symbolic* one as well. It is not hard to see the sanatorium full of sick people as representative of pre-First-World-War Europe with its sicknesses and fatal illnesses. Authors are very often quite conscious of such symbolic meanings; in his essay 'Well Done' (1918), Joseph Conrad refers to 'the ship' as 'the moral symbol of our life', and clearly we need to take such a statement into account when looking at those of his works which are set on board ship.

Sometimes the choice of a suitable setting helps an author to avoid the need to write about things that he or she is not good at, or interested in, writing about. A setting in the historical past can often help an author to avoid contemporary issues about which he or she feels confused; the setting that E.M. Forster chose for *Howards End* enabled him to avoid writing about the very poor. It is generally agreed that Jane Austen chose settings for her novels which allowed her to exercise her strengths and conceal her weaknesses so far as her knowledge of different sorts of people and of human experiences was concerned.

Dickens's frequent choice of London as the setting for his novels was convenient in other ways: the mass of concealed relationships, indirect forms of human communication and innumerable secrets to be found in London offered a perfect opportunity to a novelist whose plots contain all of these elements in abundance. (See also my comments on the four passages detailing a character's movement through London streets on p. 31.)

Just as there are conventions relating to the description of individual human appearance (see the earlier section on character), so too descriptions of places and environments are conventionally seen to denote something about the people associated with them. Think of the symbolic force of the descriptions of Wuthering Heights and Thrushcross Grange in *Wuthering Heights*, or between Mansfield Park and the Portsmouth home in Jane Austen's novel.

A setting can also be a crucial factor in the creation of *mood* or *moral environment*. If we think of *The Great Gatsby* we can see, I think, how a setting can make an essential contribution to a work's mood. This example reminds us that theme and subject and setting can be inextricably intertwined: you could no more set *The Great Gatsby* in the England of the 1930s than you could set *Love on the Dole* anywhere else.

Remember that there is a difference, in this context, between 'mood' and 'tone': the latter term involves narrative *attitudes towards* what is recounted and described. A setting may help to create a particular *mood* in a story, but only the narrative treatment can confirm a certain *tone*.

Theme

'Theme' is a much-used word in the literary criticism of the novel, and a favourite word for use by lecturers and teachers in essay and examination questions. 'Discuss the treatment of the theme of evil in *Crime and Punishment*'; 'Write about the theme of escape in *Huckleberry Finn*'; 'Examine the theme of alienation in *The Castle*' and so on. A fundamental distinction used in literary criticism is that between the *formal* and the *thematic*. 'Sin and Retribution in *Bleak House*' clearly indicates an interest in one of the novel's supposed themes, whereas 'The Unreliable Narrator of *The Good Soldier*' promises the reader a more formal or technical reading of the novel in question. In practice, of course, it is hard to write about themes without taking account of formal matters, and although it may be easier to write about formal issues without confronting thematic questions, few studies of the novel are flushed clean of all interest in matters thematic. Nonetheless, the distinction is a useful one.

So what exactly is a theme? Well, the confusing answer to this question is that the term is used in a number of different ways.

Theme and thesis

Some critics find it useful to distinguish between theme and thesis. The simple distinction here is that although both pose questions, a thesis also suggests or argues for answers. A theme, in contrast, can involve establishing a set of issues, problems or questions without any attempt to provide a rationale or answer to satisfy the demands these make of the reader. Traditionally, novels dominated by a thesis have been valued less highly than those in which certain themes are raised or treated: in contrast to earlier generations of readers perhaps, some recent critics have preferred our novels not to be overtly didactic, to be open-ended rather than pointed towards solutions at which the author has already arrived. We should ask whether such an attitude is always justified; novels that are fired with their creators' crusading zeal or commitment to a belief or a cause constitute a very substantial part of the body of fiction, and since its birth the modern novel has had a significant commitment to didacticism.

One problem with distinguishing between theme and thesis is that for some commentators 'theme' is something of an umbrella concept and includes what we have just termed 'thesis'. If we define theme in the former, weaker sense (distinguishing it from thesis) then we will not be surprised to discover that a large and complex novel can have a range of varied themes attributed to it. Charles Dickens's *Bleak House*, for instance, has been variously interpreted as containing the themes of 'parental responsibility', 'the heartlessness of the law', 'the evil of "causes"', 'the destructiveness of choosing money and position rather than love', 'the centrality of writing to Victorian society' – and many more. It needs to be remembered that a complex novel is likely to be susceptible to analysis in terms of numerous different – perhaps interlocking – themes.

Overt and covert themes

A theme may be overt or covert. That is to say it can be either consciously intended and indicated as such by the author or, alternatively, discovered by the reader/critic as an element in the novel of which perhaps even the author was unaware. (If we retain the distinction between theme and thesis then it will be understood that a thesis is much more likely to be consciously intended than a theme.) Thus although we can be pretty certain that Saul Bellow had the *carpe diem* theme ('Live today, while you can') consciously in mind in his novella *Seize the Day* (1956) – because the title makes this much clear – we cannot be so sure that Alan Sillitoe had the theme of working-class socialization equally in mind with regard to the writing of his *Saturday Night and Sunday Morning* (1958). (We should also bear in mind the possibility that Bellow recognized his theme and chose his title after he had completed his story.)

Symbol and image

Symbol

In E.M. Forster's *Howards End* the motor-car plays an important role. 'Not surprising', someone might comment, 'the car had not been around for very long at the time that the novel was written, and Forster was merely incorporating a piece of contemporary reality into his novel for the purpose of increased veri-similitude.'

Few readers of the work would find this an adequate response. The motor-car in *Howards End* clearly *stands for* or *represents* something; it is not merely a means of transport but a *symbol* in the novel. By this we mean that it carries with it various ideas, associations, forms of significance that in ordinary life it might not have in people's minds: 'innovation and the destruction of tradition'; 'the mechanical as against the organic'; 'unfeeling social change'; 'violence and death'; 'the selfish pursuit of personal comfort by the rich' – and so on.

Notice that I have not suggested that the car in *Howards End* stands for just one, fixed thing; it is characteristic of symbols that they do not have a simple one-to-one relationship with what they stand for or suggest. In this respect a symbol can clearly be distinguished from an *allegory*, the secondary meaning of which is usually single and distinct. Thus the allegorical meaning of Bunyan's *Pilgrim's Progress* (1676) is that life as a Christian brings problems comparable to those experienced by Bunyan's pilgrim. In contrast to such a one-to-one rela-tionship, the lighthouse in Virginia Woolf's *To the Lighthouse* (1927) has obvious symbolic force in the novel, but it would be an unwise critic who stated defini-tively the one thing that it stood for. Perhaps the lighthouse does stand for the unfulfilled dreams of youth, or masculine aggressiveness – but part of its power comes from its multiple suggestiveness and indirect significance. Note that Forster's car and Woolf's lighthouse can be said to exist on two planes: on the realistic level they are what they are in the real world – a car and a lighthouse – while on the symbolic level they have meanings that cars and lighthouses do not necessarily have outside of fiction.

Symbols are not limited to literature and art: they are central to all known human cultures. When a woman gets married in white she makes use of the symbolic force of that colour of dress within our culture – a symbolic force that has existed for an extremely long time. Any writer who incorporated this convention in a novel would be taking what we can call a public symbol and adapting it for use within his or her work – just as a film-maker who produced a Western with a hero dressed in black would be challenging another (rather stale) convention.

Thus in James Joyce's story 'The Dead', we feel that the repeated refer-ences to snow have a symbolic force. This is partly because snow is referred to so repetitively and suggestively that the reader of the story cannot but feel that there is something significant in the function that snow performs in the story. It is also, of course, because we naturally associate snow with some things rather than others – especially in countries like Britain and Ireland where extensive falls of snow are relatively rare. Put briefly, we can suggest that in 'The Dead' snow stands for or suggests *death*: it is cold, it covers the graveyard, it affects the whole country just as death comes to us all, and so on. Now the justification for this interpretation is partly that snow is naturally associated with death, because it is cold like a dead body and because people lost in snow die. Moreover, in 'The Dead' Joyce draws attention to certain of these qualities and associates them with other references in the story (not least with its title) so as to make these associations clear. If we think of the death of Gerald in the snow in D.H. Lawrence's *Women in Love* (1920) we will see, I think, that both Joyce and Lawrence are able to incorporate a public symbol into the private or internal world of meaning in their respective fictional works.

On occasions a writer will create a symbol that has the meaning and significance that it does have only in the context of one particular work. If we think of a green light, for instance, the natural symbolic associations that it has for most of us today are positive: advance, road clear, eco-friendliness – all of those extensions of meaning that have accrued from the greenness of nature and from our use of green lights in traffic regulation systems. It is arguable that none of these references or associations is active in our response to the repeated mention of the green light that marks out the quay by Daisy's house for Gatsby in Scott Fitzgerald's *The Great Gatsby*. What Fitzgerald succeeds in doing in this novel is to create a private symbol, something that has meaning only within the world of the novel.

A synonymous set of terms for public and private symbols is *motivated* and *unmotivated* symbols. In practice, of course, it is hard to find a completely public or a completely private symbol. I suggested, for example, that Forster's use of the motor-car in *Howards End* developed associations that 'motor-car' might not have in people's minds prior to their reading the novel. However, for some people the motor-car *might* have had these associations, and the symbolic force that the motor-car has in *Howards End* is, as it were, a potential force already implicit in the motor-car as it was experienced in Edwardian England. (Think of the role played by the motor-car in a work of fiction that is nearly contemporary to Forster's: Kenneth Grahame's *The Wind in the Willows* [1908]; Messrs Toad and Wilcox may belong to very different fictional worlds but they do have certain qualities in common.)

Before concluding, I should point out that, although I have chosen to discuss things or objects which have a symbolic force, actions and settings can be equally well-possessed of this. When Hester in Nathaniel Hawthorne's *The Scarlet Letter* (1850) undoes her hair and lets it fall free, the action has an enormous symbolic charge: in a novel so concerned with repression and concealment it suggests a breaking of bonds, a triumph of natural and healthy impulse over artificial and corrupt restraint. Similarly, innumerable novels also make use of another symbolic potentiality involved in this scene in *The Scarlet Letter*: the contrast between indoors (representing society, the artificial, restraint) and outdoors – especially in a wild or undomesticated setting (representing pre-social impulses, the natural, the outpouring of feeling). Think of the role performed by windows as the dividing line between these two sets of associations in both Brontë's *Wuthering Heights* and Joyce's 'The Dead'.

Image

I referred earlier to Katherine Mansfield's short story 'The Voyage', and commented upon the movement from dark and cold references at the start of the story to warm and – particularly – light images at the end. Let me quote a little from the close of the story:

> On the table a white cat, that had been folded up like a camel, rose, stretched itself, yawned, and then sprang on to the tips of its toes. Fenella buried one cold little hand in the white, warm fur, and smiled timidly while she stroked and listened to Grandma's gentle voice and the rolling tones of Grandpa.
>
> A door creaked. 'Come in, dear.' There, lying to one side of an immense bed, lay Grandpa. Just his head with a white tuft, and his rosy face and long silver beard showed over the quilt.

You will notice the recurrence of words that connote light and warmth here ('white', 'warm', 'silver', 'rosy'). These I would dub images rather than symbols. The distinction is not an easy one to explain, and there are differences of usage that complicate matters, but the following points are probably worth remembering.

- ↪ Images are usually characterized by their evocation of concrete qualities rather than abstract meanings; they normally have a more sensuous quality than symbols – calling the taste, smell, feel, sound or visual image of the referred-to object sharply to mind.
- ↪ Symbols, in contrast, because they stand for something other than themselves, bring to mind not their own concrete qualities so much as the idea or abstraction that is associated with them.

Thus in the extract from Katherine Mansfield the feel of the cat's fur, its whiteness and warmth, are brought sharply to our minds in *themselves*   we do not automatically wonder what they 'stand for' (note how this tactile sense is encouraged by the contrast with Fenella's cold hand). We do not experience sharp sensory responses to Gatsby's green light or Woolf's lighthouse: it is what these stand for or call to mind *apart from* themselves that is important. If we think of a continuum stretching from the sensuous to the intellectual, we can say that images are located towards the sensuous end while symbols are located towards the intellectual end.

With Joyce's snow and Forster's motor-car we may pause: in these cases we think both of what they stand for and of their individual sensory qualities. In these two cases, therefore, we may guess that the references have an imagistic function alongside their primary symbolic purpose.

This is not to say that images never contribute to thematic elements in a work. Although it is true that an image is distinguished by its concrete qualities in an immediate sense, it sets up waves of association in the mind that have other than a purely concrete significance. Thus, as I have already suggested, the images in Mansfield's 'The Voyage' contribute importantly to our sense of the multilevelled nature of Fenella's voyage, away from unhappiness and suffering and to the promise of something more cheerful and enjoyable.

Speech and dialogue

The voices of the novel

According to Mikhail Bakhtin, 'the decisive and distinctive importance of the novel as a genre [is that] the human being in the novel is first, foremost and always a speaking human being; the novel requires speaking persons bringing with them their own unique ideological discourse, their own language' (1981, 332). This does not, however, mean that people in novels speak the same way as do people in the everyday, extrafictional world. It does mean that novels tend to have not one centre of authority – the narrator's or author's voice – but many such centres, centres which typically are in conflict with one another. For Bakhtin, it will be perceived, a voice is not just a mechanical means whereby thoughts are broadcast; it has an ideological dimension. Different voices in the novel represent and disseminate different points of view, different perspectives. Moreover, for Bakhtin different voices can be isolated even in a narrator's or a single character's words: when we speak, our utterances contain a range of different voices, each of which carries its own values, such that an utterance can represent a veritable war of different viewpoints and perspectives. (When you telephone home to your parents you speak in a different way from the way you chat with friends.)

Speech in life and speech in fiction

In today's world we take the ability to record conversations for granted. We are thus able to study normal, unselfconscious conversation in a way that our ancestors could not – and can thereby discover that nobody actually talks quite as people are portrayed as talking in novels. The conventions that govern the speech that is represented in novels cover technical matters such as the syntax of the sentences that make up separate utterances. They also govern matters such as the sort of things that can be talked about and the sort of language that can be used in such discussions – which have, of course, a significant ideological dimension. There is an amusing exemplification of this point in Josef Skvorecky's novel *The Engineer of Human Souls* (first published in Czech in 1977) in which a character, Mrs Santner, tries to defend the 'bad' language used in a novel by referring to how people in real life would actually speak if in the same circumstances as the novel-character in question:

> 'You have to read it in context,' she explains. 'After all, those words
> are spoken by an anti-Nazi revolutionary who's afraid the Gestapo will
> catch him. When people are afraid, they use strong language. It's a
> well-known phenomenon.'
>
> Her defence is too scholarly for Mr Senka. 'But this is a book,
> madame,' he cries. 'A book.'
>
> This time it is Mrs Santner's turn not to understand. For her the
> word 'book' has none of the sanctimonious overtones it has for
> Mr Senka, for whom a book is a household object to be taken up
> only on very special occasions. Mrs Santner's husband leans over her
> shoulder and whispers, 'Now, Betty, don't let's get into an argument,'
> but this only goads her on.
>
> 'I can't help it. In context, language like that has a valid function.
> That's the way people actually talk in situations like that.'
>
> 'But they don't talk like that in *books*.'
>
> Each is partly right, according to his experience. (Skvorecky, 1985,
> 158–9)

This is the sort of conflict towards which the realist imperative almost inevitably impels novelists and their readers. We want the novel to give us our recognizable, everyday world, warts and all: but that world includes taboos, prescriptions, repressions to which the novel is not immune.

In his book *Art and Illusion* (1960), Ernst Gombrich has explored at length the paradox that the world does not look like a picture, but a picture can look like the world. In like manner, we do not talk like people in books, but the dialogues in books seem to us to be like the conversations we have in real life. People in novels tend, unlike real people, to talk in complete sentences, with few indicated hesitations, mistakes of grammar, 'ums' and 'ers', and so on. As Skvorecky's narrator notes, perceptively, both Mr and Mrs Santner are partly right. Why is this? The answer has to be that the novelist follows conventions in the representation of speech and dialogue with which we are so familiar that we are unaware of any conventionality. (Just as individuals from Britain or the United States are unaware that they follow conventions governing the nodding and the shaking of heads to mean 'yes' and 'no' – until they travel to a country like Turkey or Bulgaria where these conventions are reversed.)

The novelist has to convey exclusively in words what in ordinary conversation we convey by words, tone of voice, hesitations, facial expression, gesture, bodily posture – and by other means. Learning how to do so was not accomplished overnight, and we can note a great difference between the way novelists in most of the eighteenth century represented dialogue and the way later novelists have done so. If, for example, you open Henry Fielding's novel *Joseph Andrews* (1742) at Chapter 5, which is the chapter directly parodying Richardson's *Pamela* in which Lady Booby attempts to seduce her servant Joseph much as Mr B in Richardson's novel had attempted to seduce Pamela, then you will notice something odd about the layout of the page. Although conversation takes place all through this short chapter, the prose is set out in one continuous unparagraphed stream. Thus Fielding has to keep including 'tag-phrases' such as 'he said' and 'she replied'. The result is not just that reading the chapter is rather hard work, but that the guiding presence of the narrator keeps intruding: we have narrative tag-phrases in addition to the actual words spoken by the characters.

By the time Jane Austen's *Pride and Prejudice* is published, a little over half a century later, we see a very different picture. Dialogue is presented in a recognizably modern form, with each new utterance by a different character given a new paragraph. Here the narrator may intrude or remain hidden at will. If necessary the characters can be left to speak for themselves with no interruption from anyone. This certainly increases the *dramatic* effectiveness of scenes involving dialogue; we feel that we are actually witnessing conversations taking place rather than being instructed by an intrusive stage manager who keeps pointing out what we have to notice. Take the conversation between Mr Bennet and his wife that opens *Pride and Prejudice*:

> 'My dear Mr Bennet,' said his lady to him one day, 'have you heard that Netherfield Park is let at last?'
>
> Mr Bennet replied that he had not.
>
> 'But it is,' returned she; 'for Mrs Long has just been here, and she told me all about it.'
>
> Mr Bennet made no answer.
>
> 'Do not you want to know who has taken it?' cried his wife impatiently.
>
> 'You want to tell me, and I have no objection to hearing it.'
>
> This was invitation enough.

Note how Jane Austen wrings so much significance out of her use of Direct and Indirect Speech here. 'Mr Bennet replied that he had not' must be one of the most economically sarcastic lines in English literature: the shift to Indirect Speech somehow conjures up Mr Bennet's weary, long-suffering response to his wife's importuning. Even so, our sense of a narrator who shares Mr Bennet's weariness does not intrude on our impression that we are witnessing a real conversation. We are aware of the presence of an ironically observing narrator, but she is in the background with as it were a faint smile on her face. In the foreground are Mr and Mrs Bennet, who we observe directly.

Ivy Compton-Burnett's *A Family and a Fortune* (1939) shows what is perhaps near to the maximal role that dialogue can play in a novel. At a rough estimate, 75 per cent of the novel consists of dialogue, and this dialogue performs a crucial narrative function in the work. The novel's heavy reliance upon dialogue is fascinating and revealing, but the final impression is of a writer rather straitjacketed by her narrative technique.

Representing speech or reproducing speech

Recent narrative theorists have pointed out that the writer of fiction has at his or her disposal a range of more or less distanced means whereby characters' speech can be rendered. In her *Narrative Fiction: Contemporary Poetics*, Shlomith Rimmon-Kenan reproduces a useful seven-element survey of the full continuum of possibilities open to the writer of narrative fiction.

At one extreme we have what she calls *diegetic summary* (in her usage 'diegetic' means loosely 'of or within the story'). This is where the reader is given the 'bare report that a speech act has occurred, without any specification of what was said or how it was said'. Second there is *summary, less purely diegetic*, which 'to some degree represents, not merely mentions, a speech event in that it names the topics of conversation'. Third is *indirect content paraphrase* (or: *indirect discourse*), 'a paraphrase of the content of the speech event, ignoring the style or form of the supposed "original" utterance'. Fourth is *indirect discourse, mimetic to some degree*, which is a 'form of indirect discourse which creates the illusion of "preserving" or "reproducing" aspects of the style of an utterance'. Fifth comes *Free Indirect Discourse*, which I have already discussed on p. 126 (and which, we should remember, can be used to represent thought as well as speech). Sixth is *direct discourse*, in which the actual words spoken are 'quoted', although, as Rimmon-Kenan points out, always with some degree of stylization. Finally there is *free direct discourse*, which is 'direct discourse shorn of its conventional orthographic cues', a good example of which would be first-person interior monologue.

If these descriptions are hard to follow, the examples provided by Rimmon-Kenan may make the distinctions easier to comprehend. All are taken from John Dos Passos's trilogy *U.S.A.* (1938):

1. When Charley got a little gin inside him he started telling war yarns for the first time in his life.
2. He stayed late in the evening telling them about miraculous conversions of unbelievers, extreme unction on the firing line, a vision of the young Christ he'd seen walking among the wounded in a dressingstation during a gas attack.
3. The waiter told him that Carranza's troops had lost Torréon and that Villa and Zapata were closing in on the Federal District.
4. When they came out Charley said by heck he thought he wanted to go up to Canada and enlist and go over and see the Great War.
5. Why the hell shouldn't they know, weren't they better off'n her and out to see the goddam town and he'd better come along.
6. Fred Summers said, 'Fellers, this war's the most gigantic cockeyed graft of the century and me for it and the cross red nurses.'
7. Fainy's head suddenly got very light. Bright boy, that's me, ambition and literary taste. ... Gee, I must finish *Looking Backward* ... and jez,

I like reading fine, an' I could run a linotype or set up print if anybody'd
let me. Fifteen bucks a week … pretty soft, ten dollars' raise.

(Rimmon-Kenan, 1983, 109–10; her examples are taken from
McHale, 1978, 249–87)

Earlier I used the word 'continuum', and it is worth stressing the fact that,
although many theorists quantify the possible variations according to grammatical distinctions, the novelist has a wide sweep of alternative possibilities
from which to choose, ranging from a summary by the narrator which merely
reproduces the gist of what a character has said (and not how it has been said),
at one extreme, to a rendering which appears to have no narrator involvement
and maximal mirroring of the character's speech in terms of both content and
delivery, at the other extreme.

As to *why* a novelist should choose to render speech at one point along this
continuum rather than at another, a number of different explanations are possible. In one sense we are back to life and pattern; at the number 7 end of the
continuum we have maximum life, we are close to the actuality of a character's
living use of language. At the number 1 end we have at least maximum potentiality for pattern: the novelist can choose what lessons to draw, what moral to
underline, as the character's speech is summarized. Here the novelist's or the
narrator's view of the character predominates over the character's actual speech.
You can probably think of many other reasons why a novelist may or may not
wish to render a given character's use of slang, colloquialism or dialect. These
evoke ways of life, values, cultural specifics which may or may not be what the
novelist wants to bring to mind at a given stage of a narrative.

As Mikhail Bakhtin has pointed out, a voice is not just a 'medium' or a channel of communication; it involves complex ideological elements as well. Take
the following passage from Lewis Grassic Gibbon's *Grey Granite* (1934), the
final part of the trilogy *A Scots Quair*. Ewan Tavendale is talking to a number of
other apprentices, and one of them, Norman, reveals that, while he can never
be bothered to go to a trades-union meeting, his father has a more positive
attitude:

And he looked a bit shamed, He's Labour, you see.
    Tavendale said There are lots of chaps that, my stepfather was,
and you all cheered up, sitting on buckets in the furnace room, a slack
hour, and having a bit of a jaw, you were none of you Labour and knew
nothing about politics, but all of you had thought that the Bulgars
of toffs were aye Tory or Liberal or this National dirt. And somehow
when a chap knew another had a father who'd been Labour you could
speak to him plainer, like, say what you thought, not that you thought
much, you wanted a job when apprenticeship was over and a decent
bit time and maybe now and then a spare bob or so to take your quean
to the Talkies – och, you spoke a lot of stite like the others did, about

the queans that you'd like to lie with, and the booze you'd drink, what
a devil you were, but if you got half a chance what you wanted was
marriage and a house and a wife and a lum of your own. ...

Now it hardly needs saying that on a simple level the use of elements from Scots
dialect gives this passage added verisimilitude. If we are not Scottish then we
may be sent to a specialist dictionary to discover the meaning of some of the
dialect terms in the passage, but most of us can probably guess at their meaning without too much difficulty, and British readers will probably work out that
'Bulgar' is a euphemism for 'Bugger' – a term that Gibbon's publisher would
certainly have bridled at in 1934.

Beyond vocabulary, the language of the passage is crucial to certain other
effects. We can say that it mimics the speech and thought patterns of a working
man of the period, especially one talking among a group of his peers. The use of
'you' is especially interesting. On the one hand it represents an accurate piece of
observation on Gibbon's part; in Britain men of this background will use 'you'
as a generalizer where a person from a middle-class background would use 'one'
(as Virginia Woolf does throughout her writing, and the British royal family do
throughout their speech). On the other hand it involves the reader in a process
of collective sharing of attitudes: we feel as we read that we are part of the group
that is thinking out its beliefs; it is as if these beliefs come out of a group to which
we belong. We thus experience the ideology of the group from the inside while
having it displayed in a manner that allows us to look at it more objectively. The
natural form of the work-group conversation conceals what is actually quite an
unnatural process – whereby a group is made to speak those taken-for-granted
items of ideological positioning that, just because they *are* taken for granted, are
normally not spoken. Virginia Woolf does something rather similar in *The Waves*,
although revealingly the statements in this work are more individual and even
individualistic; the class with which she is concerned lacks the collective voice and
consciousness that Gibbon wishes to display. (Compare my comments on p. 42
about the ways in which in Ngũgĩ's *Weep Not Child* the narrative has to combine
the consciousness of a character and the collective consciousness of a people.)

There is, in other words, a sort of sleight of hand in the above passage.
Gibbon is actually in one sense telling us something about the working class
from a vantage point outside of its typical self-knowledge. Because he dramatizes this telling in the form of a discourse that belongs to the class, however,
the reader is given the impression that as we experience the ideology with the
collectivity, so too we are simultaneously detached from it and allowed to look
at it through its members' self-aware analysis of themselves. (One of the things
that is being mimicked here is the style of a working-class anecdote. It is as if
the reader is being addressed in an intimate way by the collective voice that is
thus personified through the language that it speaks.) Gibbon could not have
achieved such a complicated effect without having borrowed the language and

habits of expression of the group, even if he uses these in a way that members of the group would not have done.

We should, in other words, be very suspicious of views which look upon the language that a novelist uses to represent speech and dialogue (or thought, or an unexpressed sense of identity even) as merely a *medium*. A medium is relatively untouched by what it transmits. Bakhtin has argued that 'the language of a novel is the system of its "languages"' (1981, 262) – in other words, that the action that takes place on the surface of a novel is only one level of the total action to be found within its pages. Below the level of literal event is the level of ideological action, an action in which the participants are not characters but positions encapsulated in language. For Bakhtin:

> The word in language is half someone else's. It becomes 'one's own' only when the speaker populates it with his own intention, his own accent, when he appropriates the word, adapting it to his own semantic and expressive intention. Prior to this moment of appropriation, the word does not exist in a neutral and impersonal language (it is not, after all, out of a dictionary that the speaker gets his words!), but rather it exists in other people's mouths, in other people's contexts, serving other people's intentions: it is from there that one must take the word, and make it one's own. (293)

This, surely, is what we see in the passage from Gibbon: men using other people's words, words which contain opinions that are not their own but which they are led to believe *are* their own, while they begin to discover their own views and interests, and begin to appropriate the word for their own uses.

Topics for discussion

↪ Do you prefer a novel to be told by an 'anonymous voice' or an identified character? Why?

↪ Take one or more novels you know, and imagine them as told in different ways by different narrators. Discuss the gains and losses of such changes.

↪ Why on earth should a novelist choose to use an unreliable narrator?

↪ Find examples of 'flat' and 'round' characters. Discuss their use.

↪ Find examples of 'showing' and 'telling'; is showing always preferable?

↪ 'The essence of telling a story is to keep some information from the reader.' Is it?

↪ List the themes of a favourite novel. Are you sure that they were all intended by the novelist? Does it matter?

↪ Find examples of symbols and images in a work of fiction. How do they differ?

Chapter 7
Studying the novel

Preview

This chapter deals with:

↬ how to preserve your fleeting responses to a novel
↬ how to take notes and what to note
↬ how to choose critics; how to assess the significance of their affiliations
↬ using libraries and using computers
↬ writing essays: analysing topics, planning your response
↬ preparing for examinations and taking them

Reader and critic

Given that studying literature involves being conscious of many of those aspects of a literary work that operate on the 'common reader' without their being conscious of the fact, there is always an element of tension and even incompatibility between the activities of reading for pleasure and reading for study. Moreover, because the novel is often read by those interested in 'losing themselves' in its pages – and some commentators have argued that the genre invites readers to read in this manner – maintaining an attitude of distanced observance of formal and technical issues can present greater problems to the novel reader than to the reader of poetry.

Wordsworth's aphorism that 'we murder to dissect' has in some ways a greater force when applied to prose fiction than when applied to poetry. On the other hand, most students of literature find that, after a period of awkwardness, practice in analysing technical issues can lead to an enrichment of their reading pleasures. Being made aware of, for example, complex shifts in the manipulation of point of view in a novel can increase a reader's appreciation of a writer's skill without lessening those pleasures experienced by the common reader.

However, if the student of the novel must learn to combine a more detached appreciation of the skills of the novelist with an experience of those pleasures that do after all constitute the reason for finding the novel worth studying in the first place, he or she must also learn how to convince the teacher or lecturer responsible for grading essays or examinations that this state of grace has been achieved. Just as learning to pass the driving test involves not just looking in the mirror, but letting the examiner know that you are looking in the mirror, so too you need to be able to write essays and examinations in such a way that your skills of reading, analysis and discussion are displayed to the person with the red pen. It is with the successful mastery of these three stages – attentive reading, controlled analysis and intelligent discussion – that this chapter is concerned.

Response: retaining the ephemeral

We may read a shortish novel in one sitting, while anything up to twenty or more sessions will be required for a long and complex novel such as Tolstoy's *War and Peace*. For those readers who read Victorian novels when they were first published in serial form there was no choice: they *had* to stop and wait at certain stages in their reading. When we pause in our reading of a novel we go over what we have read and we think forward to what we guess will happen or what we would like to happen. Frequently we will imagine ourselves in situations described in the novel; perhaps we will hold imaginary conversations with characters, or wonder what we might have done in their positions.

In other words, expectation, surprise, disappointment, foreboding, tension, suspense, imagination and fantasy all form part of our reading of a novel. To read a novel is to be involved in a *cumulative process*.

The problem which this raises for the study of the novel is that there are certain experiences in us, and certain events in the novel, which lodge far more permanently in the mind than do others. Indeed, it is part of the way that a novel works upon us – part of its power as a source of enjoyment – that some aspects of our reading experience should fade more quickly than others. Moreover, our memory may play tricks with us once we have finished a novel. If it is some time since you read *Wuthering Heights* then try this test on yourself: at what stage in the novel does the older Catherine die? I suspect that unless you are an unusually retentive and conscientious reader you are likely to place this event far later in the novel than it actually occurs.

The issue is complicated by the fact that we often read a novel more than once. On a subsequent reading we are normally less preoccupied with what will happen and so are able to read more carefully and notice many details that slipped our attention on first reading. To retain such details we need to take notes. Taking notes is actually a skilled operation and one that requires practice. It takes time to develop one's skill to the point at which it does not interfere with pleasurable reading.

How to take notes

Notes can be written either in the novel itself or in a separate notebook. The advantage of the former method is that it does not disturb one's reading too much; the disadvantages are that it spoils a book, it affects one's second reading, there is not always sufficient room for notes on the page and *retrieval* of the notes afterwards for purposes of study is difficult. One way round these problems is to write very brief notes in pencil in a novel as you are reading, and then to copy these up and expand them in a separate notebook or folder later on. This also allows you to copy out brief extracts from the novel which strike you as important, and it means that you file for future reference only notes about which you have thought a second time after having finished reading the novel. Pencil marks can be erased once they have served their purpose.

If something in the text strikes you as important or significant but you do not want to puzzle over why, lest you break your train of thought, then mark or underline the passage in question, note the page reference on the inside back cover of the book, and come back to ponder the point once you have finished the novel.

What to note

Learning what is of significance in a novel, and in your response to it, is a matter of practice. Teachers and lecturers often ask for analyses of selected passages from novels, and undertaking such analyses is an excellent way of sharpening your eye for important detail in the reading of fiction. Such close reading is, however, only part of what constitutes a full critical reading of a novel. In addition to responding to significant detail in the prose of a work of fiction, you need also to be able to perceive larger patterns and movements in the work as a whole, as well as connections to other works. The list that follows is intended to serve a double purpose. On the one hand, I hope that it will be useful to work from when you are engaged in the analysis of a particular passage from a novel or a short story. In addition, however, I hope that its perusal will serve as a reminder of the sort of points that can be noted in the process of reading or re-reading a work of fiction. The golden rule here is: if in doubt, then make a note.

Checklist

Narrative technique All information relating to the manipulation of narrative in the work: clues about the values or personality of the narrator; voice and perspective; what the narrator does not know; changes of narrator or narrative perspective; narrative intrusion or comment. 'Telling' and 'showing'.

Story and plot Sketch out what happens (i) in chronological order and (ii) as it is told. What differences are there? What is added, missed out, repeated?

Action Any information that advances the plot, gives significant new developments in human relationships or new events.

Tone Is it familiar or formal, intimate or impersonal? Who (if anyone) is apparently being addressed? Do the vocabulary or syntax suggest a particular style of delivery?

Characterization Information about how we learn about characters; any indication that characters are changing or developing; significant new information about a character; views as to what the writer is trying to achieve in the presentation of character.

Speech and dialogue Use of Direct, Indirect or Free Indirect Discourse. Do characters speak for themselves or does the narrator intrude, comment or direct? Is the dialogue realistic or conventional? What functions does it perform? (Development of character, of plot, introduction of dramatic element, discussion of theme[s].)

Thoughts/mental processes Do we 'get inside characters' heads'? If so, which heads, when and how?

Dramatic involvement Is the reader drawn into events as they happen, or rather encouraged to observe them dispassionately? How is this achieved? (Manipulation of distance.)

Setting and description What is significant about where the action takes place, and about descriptions of people and places?

Symbol or image Anything apparently significant should be noted. Do symbols/images relate to others used elsewhere in the work?

Theme(s) Any development of themes dealt with elsewhere in the work; introduction of new thematic elements. Moral problems/issues raised for the characters or for the reader.

Your own response Strong personal preferences/responses the work evokes in you – or dislikes/disapproval. Strong identification with a character – or the opposite. Tension, desire to know what happens. Particular expectations (especially at the end of chapters/sections, or when a mystery or problem is presented). Any experience of bafflement or surprise; and points where you feel you disagree with or react against a narrative opinion (or the opinion of a character).

Using critics

In the previous edition of this book I opened this sub-section as follows: 'A glance at the library shelves may convince you that you will never even scratch the surface of what might be read: even for a single major novelist it seems that a good library can provide weeks or even months of reading. How should you proceed?' Even in the short five years since I wrote those words, the digital revolution has continued to accelerate. The student essays that I look at today generally contain many more references to material accessed electronically than to material pulled off the shelf of a library ('What's a library?', as one of my students joked). So that the problem my opening sentence confronted has become even more acute for the poor student. How are you to select what to read from the enormous amount of available and potentially relevant material?

The first thing to do is to heed the advice of your lecturers. Syllabuses and booklists generally contain advice on 'secondary reading', and this advice is based upon your lecturers' knowledge of the set texts and of your needs and capacities. Lecturers rarely expect you just to plough through everything on such a list: you have to be selective. Remember that it is possible to talk to even busy lecturers, and to ask them about the secondary reading that they have (and have not) recommended. Explain what your interests are, describe the essay you want to write, and ask for suggestions.

Any good academic library should subscribe to certain journals that are particularly concerned with the novel. Titles such as *Novel: A Forum on Fiction* or *Eighteenth-century Fiction* speak for themselves. You will probably not find many of these on shelves nowadays, as it is more and more common for library subscriptions to be to electronic editions. Such subscriptions allow for electronic downloading, and it is also possible legally to download other articles that are 'open access' (see below). Of course many important essays on the novel are published in periodicals with a less focussed concern, and here electronic searches (again, see below) can be invaluable.

If you are not looking for help with a particular essay, but feel that you want to read some criticism on a novel or a novelist, then again it will probably be worth spending a bit of time planning. Remember that different 'secondary works' will be concerned with very different aspects of a writer or a text. In Chapter 9 you will find a discussion of critical approaches to fiction, and this should help you to categorize the books and articles on your library shelves in a general way. A biography of Henry James might help you with material for your essay on *The Turn of the Screw*, but this material is likely to be very different from a recent psychoanalytic reading of James's novella, and both will differ from a New Critical essay on the tale written in the 1950s.

If you look at a scholarly edition of a novel, such as the highly respected ones published by Norton, you will note that normally the text of the novel comes right at the beginning of the book, preceded only in certain series by a brief note on the text. Material on 'backgrounds', contemporary responses, critical essays and debates – all these come after the text of the novel. This order is chosen because almost every authority believes that a relatively open-minded reading of the actual text should come before the reading of biographical, contextual or critical material. My strong advice, then, is that you divide your search for secondary works up into two stages, following your reading of the 'primary text' – the literary work itself.

So, you have read the novel. What next? *Stage 1* of your search for secondary material should involve two things: first, a listing of all the questions that your reading of the novel has raised, and, second, a general survey of the matters discussed and debated by critics. If as I have recommended, you have taken notes while reading the novel, you should have a basis for constructing a list of issues arising from your own reading, especially those concerned with *problems* or *puzzles* – questions that you want answers to. Here for example are the issues about which I felt I wanted to read more when I had finished a first reading of Ford Madox Ford's novel *The Good Soldier* (1915). The points are adapted from notes I found scribbled in my copy of the work, and are listed in the order in which I found them.

↦ The narrator Dowell: how much are his shortcomings recognized or shared by Ford? How much does Ford expect the reader to be critical of him and his values (his leading the life of the idle rich), his violence (two physical assaults on others), his report (that 'This is the saddest story I have ever heard')?

↦ Ditto the characters: I am not positively inclined towards any of them. Is that a comment on me, or is Ford writing a sort of social satire that requires the reader to be distanced from the characters being satirized?

↦ Religion: clearly crucial for certain characters (Catholicism and Protestantism). Is the reader free to situate him- or herself with regard to religious/spiritual issues, or does the novel adopt a standpoint and impose this on the reader?

↦ Novel published at the start of the First World War. Easy to see it in terms of Ford's portrayal of a way of life that is now threatened or destroyed – but is this the effect of hindsight?

↦ Lots of references to 'hearts' – thematic importance?

↦ American/English contrasts: Ford writing in the shadow of Henry James?

Now you may well not have read Ford's novel, but even so I think that you should be able to recognize that the issues raised for me by a first reading of this novel are of very different *sorts*. Some are what we can term *textual* or *interpretative* – for example the issue of 'hearts'. In this case I would be likely to receive help from more interpretative or analytical studies of the novel that pay detailed attention to elements in it that may well have thematic or symbolic significance (see the previous chapter).

My puzzlement concerning Ford's narrator is also in part a textual matter, but we can term it as much *technical* as thematic, and a study of Ford's *narrative technique* is likely to be of use to me here.

So far as the issue of religion is concerned, a good biography of Ford is likely to let me know what Ford's own religious position was when he wrote the novel, although this may not help to isolate the function that religion plays in the novel. A good biography may also help to fix Ford's attitude to the lives of the idle rich, and it may tell me something of the effect of the war on the novel's composition, although again this may not answer all the questions raised for the reader by these matters. (In Chapter 9 you can read about some of the problems of using biographical information to illuminate a literary work; see p. 211.)

If biographical information has its limitations, it can be supplemented and often corrected by more interpretative or analytical studies of a work that attempt to isolate themes and patterns of meaning. Thematic studies of *The Good Soldier* are thus likely to have much to say about the importance of religion in the novel – and about the significance of the fact that the novel defines characters not just in terms of their religion but also in terms of their nationality, their wealth and their cultural traditions.

If you look at a modern scholarly edition of *The Good Soldier*, such as the Norton Critical Edition edited by Martin Stannard (1995), you will find, in addition to the text of the novel and commentary on textual issues, sections containing contemporary reviews of the work, a long section on literary impressionism and a section containing biographical and critical commentary. My questions concerning the narrator and Ford's narrative are the easiest to find answers to: other readers of the novel have needed to investigate Ford's use of – and attitude towards – Dowell, and their discussion helps me to explore this matter. I also find discussion of the issue of 'hearts', and some concern with issues of religion – although not as much as I feel the need for.

Surveying relevant criticism

Let us leave my reading at this stage, and ask how you can start to get a sense of the tradition of critical discussion associated with a particular novel. After you have looked at the titles of essays reprinted in scholarly editions such as the Norton or the Bedford ones, pull a few books off the shelf of the library or search for criticism of the novel in a database such as Literature Online (see below). Look at the titles, chapter titles and (if you are looking at books) index entries in a range of critical works. Consult works such as *The Year's Work in English Studies*, which give useful summaries of critical responses to particular works. Electronic bibliographies and databases now offer continually updated material that can be accessed speedily online. See the sub-section on using computers below.

Now you can move to *stage 2*. You have your two lists; compare them. To what extent will some of the sequences and traditions of critical discussion that you have uncovered help you with the questions that your own reading has thrown up? You are now better able to start looking for particular essays or books that you can use to deepen your involvement in the novel you have just finished reading. You should find that a brief survey of the critical debate around a particular writer or work will actually open your eyes to issues of which you have been unaware, issues which do not feature on the list you compiled on the basis of your reading notes, but which you recognize to be important once your attention is drawn to them.

Thus when I started to look at critical responses to Ford's *The Good Soldier*, I found discussion of some issues that my own reading of the novel had not raised for me: Ford as impressionist writer, for example, and articles which see *The Good Soldier* as comedy (in one case) and tragedy (in another). These articles sent me back to the novel to reconsider my reading, to look at certain scenes and passages again – and generated a checklist of issues to consider on a re-reading of the work. Critics do not just provide answers to questions; they also provide questions for you to answer.

If you have been given an essay topic and a deadline for submitting the finished essay then you may be under more pressure. But you should not just rush to the library with a list of words from the essay topic that you then attempt to find in the table of contents or the index of a succession of critical works. Spend some time *analysing* your essay topic: this will help you in your literature search.

At the end of stage 2, you should have a shortlist of books and articles that you can now proceed to read. Remember that you may not be able to obtain all of them in time (inter-library loan can take many weeks if an article is not in or accessible through your library, and you may have to pay a fee). Remember too that as you read criticism you will refine your shortlist: some new references that you may want to consult are likely to be thrown up, and you may also be sent back to re-read parts of the literary text with which you started.

Using computers

If more and more is available on the internet, not all of it is free. Some of the most useful tools – for example databases like Literature Online, produced by Chadwyck Healey – are expensive to subscribe to and generally beyond the pockets of individual student subscribers. All university libraries are far from having subscriptions to all such commercial databases, and indeed the rocketing cost of scientific and technological periodical subscriptions is, as the fashionable euphemism has it, 'impacting negatively' on library spending on the humanities.

Your first step should be to find out exactly what your college or university library (and also your public library, if you live in a large town or city) does subscribe to. But if you can access a database like Literature Online, it is worth learning how to exploit what it has to offer; there is no doubt that such tools, sensibly used, are enormously useful.

Many of the electronic services that are aimed at individual student subscribers need to be either avoided completely or treated with great circumspection. In the 'not to be touched at any cost' category are the straightforwardly dishonest – companies that sell either pre-written or written-to-order essays for cash. Your institution will almost certainly have a regulation concerning plagiarism and using such companies will risk contravening this regulation. Remember that academics and university administrators are getting clever at detecting web plagiarism and cheating, and there are now programs that will help your teachers to find out if you have cheated.

Then there are those companies that, for a few pounds (or, more usually, dollars), will sell you a text that gives you a plot summary of a novel, with commentary on characters, narrative technique, historical background and so on. If you do not actually reproduce material in unacknowledged form from these you may escape being accused of cheating, but it is clear that such material is designed to enable you to avoid reading and thinking about the text in question, so that not only will use of it diminish your teachers' opinion of you, it will also deny you the ability to develop the skills that your course is designed to foster.

There is, however, much that can be accessed via a PC and an internet connection that can be very useful to you in your studies and that can quite legitimately be used in writing an assignment if properly acknowledged. Remember that it is always better to err on the side of caution and to be as open and comprehensive as possible in your acknowledgements. And if you are in any doubt, talk to your lecturer in person.

I list below some of the different ways in which you can use your PC as a study tool. All of these require an internet connection, although after you have downloaded material you can then use it on a PC without such a connection.

1. Many of the novels and short stories you study can be downloaded as complete texts and saved on the hard disk of your own computer. A simple web search along the lines of <nostromo + electronic> will soon establish whether there is an available and downloadable electronic text of Conrad's novel (there is). Remember that if the work was first published, or its author died, fewer than seventy years ago, then the work will probably be in copyright and you will be unlikely to be able legally to download a free electronic text of it.

    If you call up the text of all or part of a novel into even a standard word-processing program, it will allow you to do such things as find all examples of a particular word or phrase, or to compare – say – the average sentence length in two short stories by the same or two different authors. Because novels are generally longer than poems or plays, this facility is particularly useful for the student of the novel.

If for example you think that you remember (as I once did) that Chablis wine is described as 'straw-coloured' in Henry James's *The Ambassadors*, then the computer will locate the reference in seconds (I had searched for hours in the printed text, but had been looking in the wrong place). Remember that not all electronic texts are reliable, and even a reliable text may be based on a different edition from the one on your syllabus (see the discussion of different versions of the same work on p. 180).

Imagine that you are struck by the phrase 'paradise of snakes' in Joseph Conrad's *Nostromo*. Does this betoken a concern to link the development of the silver mine in that novel with the expulsion of Adam and Eve from the Garden of Eden? In a matter of a very few minutes you can electronically search through the text looking for words such as 'Eden', 'fall', 'snake', 'serpent', 'Adam', 'Eve', 'Satan', 'Devil', 'tree', 'forbidden', 'fruit' and so on. Whatever you do, don't think that you can just list the results of such searches in an essay! You need to think about what such searches uncover, and relate the results to your reading of the work as a whole and to what critics have written about it. You can count how many times a word or phrase occurs in a text just by using search-and-replace for the same word or phrase; the program will tell you how many replacements it has made. Why bother? Well, Joseph Conrad's novel *Under Western Eyes* is a novel that foregrounds a concern with speech and language. But by means of such simple searches in an electronic text of the novel I discovered that although the words 'language' and 'languages' occur only thirteen times, cognates of the word 'word' occur an impressive 165 times. That forced me to consider what particular perspective on language Conrad has in this novel.

When I was a student in the 1960s we used to joke that our final degree qualification should be written 'B.A. (Penguin)'. Today perhaps it would be 'B.A. (Google)'. Jokes aside, Google provides some very useful additions to its basic search engine. Google Books (http://books.google.com) allows you to enter a word or phrase and find a page reference to where this word or phrase appears in an edition that Google has scanned. This is a useful tool in the case of texts which cannot be downloaded electronically. Google Scholar (http://scholar.google.co.uk – substitute '.com' to access the American site) allows you to search through published scholarly material. Both of these resources should be used as stepping stones: they indicate where you will find fuller and more contextualized information.

2. I mentioned above the Chadwyck Healey Literature Online database. This is mostly what is known as a full-text database, meaning that it will allow you to search – for instance – for examples of the word 'photo-graph' in a very large number of – again, for instance – nineteenth-century poems. Its coverage of fiction is at present less comprehensive, but it is a very good place to start looking for criticism. When I searched

for 'author: Fielding' and 'keyword: picaresque', it threw up a list of sixteen articles, six of which could be downloaded in full-text format. With a more open search you can get a good sense of the critical issues associated with a particular text. Thus a search for 'author: Ford, Ford Madox' and 'keyword: good soldier' threw up the titles of 316 items ranging from reviews through articles to books. Just looking at the titles of these items will give you a sense of the different emphases in criticism of this novel over the past four decades, and many of the articles listed can again be immediately downloaded free in full-text form. (As a sign of how fast things are changing, when I did these searches in 2004 I got four hits for the Fielding search and 112 for the Ford one.)

More specialist databases are available. To take a representative example, ECCO – Eighteenth Century Collections Online – offers at present '26 million pages of text from more than 138,000 titles (155,000 volumes)' with 'full-search capabilities'. (Again: in 2004 I reported: 'full-text searchable facsimile page displays of approximately 24,000 books published in Britain and its colonies during the eighteenth century', with the long-term aim of raising the number of books covered to 150,000. In five years a 'long-term aim' has been exceeded.)

The British Modern Humanities Research Association (MHRA) publishes a range of specialist bibliographies and also ABELL: *The Annual Bibliography of English Language & Literature*, published annually in electronic and printed form, which 'aims to list annually all scholarly articles, books and reviews concerning English language and literature and related topics published anywhere in the world, and in any language'. The American Modern Library Association (MLA) also produces an authoritative annual bibliography. Most academic libraries should be able to provide access to these databases – either online or on CD-Rom.

I should stress that any material you obtain from any of these databases is just as respectable as it would be had you obtained it in hard-copy form, and you need in no way feel that you have to conceal the fact that you obtained it online. Literature Online gives you two ways of downloading texts: either as 'full text' or as 'page image'. The latter option gives you an article paginated exactly as it is in the printed version, so references can be given precisely as they would for an article consulted in a printed journal. 'Full-text' downloads enable you to quote accurately, but you need to reference the fact that the pagination quoted is for an electronic download.

3. One of the commonest questions I get from fellow lecturers, it seems, is 'What do you do about Wikipedia?' What lies behind this question is a concern that accessing information from Wikipedia is so quick, so easy (and so free!) that students are losing the habit of looking for less accessible and, the argument runs, more reliable or respectable sources of information. My own view is that like fire, Wikipedia is a good servant but

a bad master. I use it myself very often when I want a quick information fix. It certainly has the merit of allowing for extremely fast updating, and doubtful or controversial material can be marked as such very quickly.

This said, it is also the case that although on occasions an entry may be written by a (or even the) world expert on a subject, you are very likely to get a more profound, reliable and nuanced account of a topic in a specialist book or journal that has been subjected to what is called peer review: reported on by (normally two) anonymous experts.

So if you are sitting at your PC writing an essay and you want quickly to confirm that you have remembered the year in which *The Good Soldier* was published correctly, by all means zip over to Wikipedia. And if you want an initial overview of the work of – say – Gérard Genette, then by all means read what Wikipedia has to say. But my strong advice would be to move then to a source that includes more conventionally peer-reviewed material – an academic book published by a respectable academic publisher, or a good academic journal. The best entries in Wikipedia contain information about such sources. An essay that ends with a bibliography citing only entries in Wikipedia is not likely to impress your lecturer.

4. Electronic discussion groups on e-mail or (more usually nowadays) the internet allow you to follow debates between other students all over the world about a particular novel. You can also submit questions to such discussion groups, although, if participants think that you are trying to get them to do your work for you, you will get the cold shoulder. Specialist questions can often get useful replies: if you want tips on essays dealing with a relatively specialist topic, sometimes a discussion group can help where a scholarly bibliography cannot.

5. Even the general 'search' function in an internet search engine (such as Yahoo or Google) can throw up useful leads. One Sunday, when my academic library was closed, I found very useful scholarly material on Thomas Hardy's short story 'An Imaginative Woman' merely by searching for 'Hardy + Imaginative' on my PC. Often lecturers put out material on their departmental or university web page which is well worth consulting. You may well be able to access useful material put out for students in other universities. It is absolutely acceptable to use such material in an essay *provided you acknowledge where you got it from and furnish a web-page reference.*

If you want more detailed information about using the internet which covers such topics as the different ways to refine web searches, how to assess the academic reliability of web pages and how to reference web material, you can consult the second section of Paul Goring, Jeremy Hawthorn and Domhnall Mitchell, *Studying Literature: The Essential Companion* (2001) entitled 'Guide to the Use of Electronic Media'.

Revision

'Revision' is what American readers will know as 'review', but in spite of the difference in terminology the activity is prompted by the same need to refresh one's memory of what may have been studied months earlier. You may take an examination requiring knowledge of a number of novels up to a year after you have read some of them. Full re-reading is impossible, and some elements will certainly have slipped your memory. Do not try to skip-read the whole work again, but concentrate upon reading selected passages with care. These should always include the opening and closing pages of the work – beginnings and endings of novels are invariably revealing. Is the opening dramatic or descriptive? Does it plunge the reader into the middle of things, or carefully establish a scene? Does it set a dominant tone, and establish the narrative perspective or personality of the narrator? Is the reader addressed directly, and are we given an indication of what sort of reader (or reading) the narrative invites or appears to assume? Is the ending happy or sad? Why does the author choose to make it so? Does it tie up all the loose ends or leave many questions unanswered? With what effect?

Apart from opening and closing pages, you should pick some key passages – either those that have seemed important to you, or those that critics have found of great interest. Pick a couple of passages at random, preferably ones that seem unfamiliar on leafing through the work. Analyse these in detail.

If it makes you feel easier, construct a list of character names (just the main characters) for each work prior to an examination. If you forget a name in an examination do not panic, just leave a blank and go on writing. If the name does not come to you by the end of the examination then asterisk the gap and write in a footnote explaining that you have forgotten the character name and indicating who the character is by other means such as relationships to other characters.

So far as critics are concerned, it is useful to be able to situate their arguments and positions – both in the context of critical debate about the work in question, and also in the context of the critic's own principles and theoretical allegiances (see my comments on p. 196).

Essays and examinations

Some rules concerning the writing of essays are not specific to study of the novel. There are a number of textbooks that will advise you on such matters, and you should find out which if any of these your lecturers recommend. But the best way to learn how to write an essay is to read articles in respected academic journals and note the conventions that they follow. The tips below are not specific to essays or examination answers on the novel, and you may find them irritatingly basic. But if you have not previously been aware of their importance you should pay careful attention to them.

- ↔ If you are using a computer you should *never* submit an essay without spell-checking it. It takes very little time, and reduces the risk that an irritated teacher will mark you down for careless spelling. But remember that spellcheckers can make mistakes: an essay that I set included a passage from Joyce that contained the word 'sottish'. Those that spell-checked their essays in Word were recommended to replace this with 'Scottish'. And remember that if you use British English but quote passages written in American English (or vice versa), then unless you mark such quotations as in another language variant then the spellchecker will pick up non-existing errors.
- ↔ I am much less enthusiastic about the grammar-checkers contained in basic word-processing programs. But if you know that you regularly make basic grammatical mistakes, then the grammar-check facility can help you to guard against them. But *never* accept every recommendation that such a program makes without thinking about it.
- ↔ I am a strong believer in the use of sub-headings. This is partly because they help whoever reads your work to find his or her way through your argument, and partly because they may reveal to you that a particular section or paragraph in an essay would be better placed in another position. Similarly, remember to use paragraphs sensibly. If you are not sure about the conventions governing paragraphing, consult a more specialist book on the writing of essays.
- ↔ Try to use an appealing layout. Heed your teachers' advice on such things as line-spacing, reference systems, bibliographies.
- ↔ Always start your essay or examination answer by making it clear which question or topic you are addressing (but you do not need to copy the whole question out on the first page).

When it comes to writing essays and examination answers there is no substitute for practice: the more that you write, and have your writing commented upon, the more clearly and easily you will come to write. The following advice picks up what in my own experience are the most common sorts of weakness in essays and examination answers dealing with the novel, but it is important to listen to the advice of your teachers.

Be relevant

You will be responding to a specific question or topic. Do not just pick out a couple of words from it and proceed to write all you know about the text(s) mentioned. (Remember that an essay or answer is like a meal: selection, preparation and order are necessary if the result is to be pleasing.) Use coloured pens and underline key words in the question. If the question has several points then *number* these. After every second page you write, look back to make sure that what you are writing is of relevance to the topic or question.

Argue a case

A question requires an answer, not just a response. You will be expected to take up a position in relation to what has been asked, and to argue your position as logically as possible. Do not be afraid to express a personal opinion, but, if you do, say that it is a personal opinion and justify it (see below). If you refer to the opinion of others (critics, for example), say whether or not you agree with them, and why. If the question or topic includes a quotation, remember that you may disagree with the opinion of the person quoted. (Very often the person who has written the question expects you to do this.) Remember, however, that if you are to argue successfully, you need to ...

Plan your answer

If you only have a very short amount of time, you may have to restrict this to a five-minute sketch of what you intend to say, but if you are writing an essay in your own time then you should plan more carefully. With an essay, you can afford to restructure what you have written for its final presentation, such that the introduction and conclusion can be added on at the end in case your argument has become modified or more complex in the course of writing. Because essays are now usually written on a PC you may get used to moving material around on screen. Remember that you cannot do this in a time-test examination, which means that examination answers need to be more carefully planned. In an examination you may find as you write that your answer is moving in a rather different way from that laid out in your introductory paragraph. If so, the best thing is to admit to this change of direction, and even to explain why.

A good essay or examination answer should have an introduction which explains what attitude you are taking to the question asked, and how you are going to answer it. This need only be half a page long at most. You should then provide, in as ordered a way as possible, evidence to substantiate the position you have taken up. At any stage in an essay or examination answer, the person reading it should know (i) what you are trying to argue, and (ii) how this argument fits into your general thesis or response to the question. Anyone who has marked examinations knows that a sure sign that there is something wrong is when you have to flip back to page 1 to check exactly which question the script is supposed to be answering. See below for some further suggestions on how to make a positive impression with the opening sentences of your essay or answer.

Back up your arguments with evidence

There are different sorts of evidence that can be adduced in an essay or an examination answer. Unless the question specifically focuses upon extratextual matters, the most important evidence that you can bring forward is likely to be *textual*. The general rule about textual evidence is that it should be *detailed* and it should be *analytical*. In an essay you should quote enough to make your point, and you should *never* assume that a quotation speaks for itself. Every time you quote from a novel or a short story in an essay you should explain what it is in the quotation that is important – pointing to *particular* words, *particular* phrases, *particular* techniques (such as those outlined in my suggested checklist on p. 164).

Examinations may present a different problem. Generally speaking, examinations have to be written without access to the novel or short-story texts on which they are based. I do not recommend that you spend hours learning selected passages by heart. Not only is this extremely time-consuming, but there is also a tendency for those who have shed blood learning long quotations to insist on demonstrating the fact in the examination room, and the quotations that have been learned may well not be relevant to the question asked. Even if you cannot quote at length from a novel, though, you can still be detailed in your reference to it. Refer to particular *scenes*, isolate the operative *events*, *actions* and *utterances* (you do not have to quote to do this), draw attention to relevant aspects of *narrative technique* and comment upon such things as *symbolism* and *imagery* if they play a significant role. If you can refer to particular words and phrases used, all the better.

In addition to textual evidence, there are various forms of extratextual evidence that can be incorporated in an answer: comments and opinions from critics, statements from or about the work's author, parallels with other works either by the same author or by others, information of the sort mentioned in my brief discussion of 'the sociology of literature' (p. 209), information about relevant social, historical and cultural events or states of affairs. In all of these, two issues should be borne in mind: *influence* and *relevance*. You may reproduce a lot of accurate facts, but did they have any influence on the writing (or do they have any influence on the reading) of the work? Are they relevant to the question asked?

Do not tell the story

I suppose I ought to concede here that it is possible that one day you might encounter an essay topic or examination question which starts, 'Tell the story of *Wuthering Heights* and then proceed to comment on ...', but 99.9 per cent of essay topics and essay questions do not require you to open with an obligatory three-page précis of what happens in the novel in question. You have to assume that the person marking the essay or answer has read the work and knows what happens: he or she will be irritated, and not impressed, by such a plot summary.

Remember that the characters are not 'real people'

Although it is quite legitimate at times to discuss the characters and actions in a novel as we discuss the people we know in real life (almost all critics do this at some time or another), you should also indicate clearly that you are aware that what we read are words that have been created and crafted by an author. Peter Lamarque has suggested that the reader of fiction needs to be able to combine the imaginative involvement of an internal perspective with the awareness of artifice of an external perspective (1996, 14), and you should make sure that the person reading your essay knows you are aware of this difference.

Arouse your reader's curiosity

Compare the following selection of opening passages for an essay on Virginia Woolf's novel *Mrs Dalloway*.

1. Virginia Woolf was born Virginia Stephen in 1882. Her father was Sir Leslie Stephen, famous for his work on *The Dictionary of National Biography*. She had periods of mental disturbance all her life, the first in 1913 and the final one associated with her suicide in 1941. She was a member of the so-called Bloomsbury Group, and is credited with being one of the most important forces behind the modernist novel in England.

2. Towards the end of Virginia Woolf's novel *Mrs Dalloway* we follow Clarissa Dalloway's thoughts as she considers Sir William Bradshaw, 'a great doctor, but to her obscurely evil, without sex or lust, extremely polite to women, but capable of some indescribable outrage – forcing your soul, that was it …' The words take the reader aback: it is as if being without lust is presented as a negative quality. What lies behind this attitude?

3. The very brief opening scene of Marleen Gorris's 1998 film of *Mrs Dalloway* shows Septimus on the battlefield in Italy in 1918. He shouts 'Evans! Don't jump!', but a massive explosion and his look of horror reveal that he has shouted in vain. The scene is not to be found in Virginia Woolf's novel, which opens with the words, 'Mrs Dalloway said that she would buy the flowers herself' in the novel's 'present' of June 1923. The film-maker's instinct that in Woolf's novel the past is always there, influencing the present, is, however, perceptive.

4. *Mrs Dalloway* is the first novel by Virginia Woolf that I have read. I had been looking forward to reading this novel because I had heard that Woolf was a fighter for women's rights and a major influence on feminist thinkers during the twentieth century. My first reading of the novel came as something of a shock: how could feminists respect a writer capable of producing such a negative, stereotyped portrayal of a lesbian character as Woolf does with Miss Kilman?

I venture to suggest that any teacher who has pulled the first of thirty (or 130) essays off a pile to be marked and has read opening number 1 will feel his or her heart dropping. This is not because there is anything wrong about the information it contains, but because it suggests very strongly that it has been copied straight out of a reference book by someone who does not have a burning desire to propose an original response to whatever question has been asked. Anyone marking a large number of essays on *Mrs Dalloway* is likely to encounter more than a few that begin much like this, and he or she is unlikely to be positively disposed to them.

In contrast to opening number 1, openings 2, 3 and 4 all suggest that the writer does have something interesting and original to say. Moreover, they all raise issues, problems, questions that stimulate the reader's curiosity. We want to read on to find out how the writer deals with the problem that he or she has outlined. We are hooked. Consider the different techniques involved: raising a textual or interpretive problem (2); using a film adaptation of a work to illuminate aspects of the original (3); starting with a report of a strong personal reaction that you then use to lead into an issue relating to the text or its critical history (4).

Now care is needed here, because if there is one standard failing for which essays and examination answers are marked down in literary studies, it is that of failing to answer the question. So that immediately after an opening along the lines of alternatives 2 to 4 the writer needs to establish that he or she is indeed going to tie in a resolution of the problem raised with a relevant response to the chosen question.

Topics for discussion

- ↪ 'Lecturers say they want our personal responses, but then they tell us our personal responses are wrong.' Is there such a thing as a 'wrong' response to a novel?
- ↪ What is the best way to revise a long novel that was read six months ago?
- ↪ How does writing an essay with access to text and notes help prepare us to write exams with access to neither?
- ↪ Is it useful to 'learn quotes'?
- ↪ What is the best way to prevent 'exam panic'?

Chapter 8
Versions and adaptations

Preview

This chapter deals with:

→ the difference between a version and an adaptation of a novel
→ different types of adaptation
→ gains and losses in film and television adaptations

Versions

We generally refer to novels and short stories by means of their titles — *Bleak House*, or *Ulysses*, or *Lucky Jim*, or *Do Androids Dream of Electric Sheep?* For convenience we often abbreviate the titles under which novels were first published, so that we talk not of *The Personal History, Adventures, Experience, & Observation of David Copperfield the Younger of Blunderstone Rookery (Which He never meant to be Published on any Account)* but more manageably of just *David Copperfield*. Abbreviated or not, however, our use of such titles betrays a confidence that novels have a fixed identity that is not eroded or confused by many printings and editions. It is true that sometimes our attention is drawn to the fact that there are textual issues associated with novels: recent editions of Charles Dickens's *Great Expectations* generally print both of the endings that Dickens wrote for this novel, and the influential *Norton Anthology of American Literature* has included quite significantly different versions of Mark Twain's

'The Celebrated Jumping Frog of Calaveras County' in successive editions. Generally speaking, though, we discuss novels and short stories as if their titles denoted unambiguously single texts. But the reality is rather more complex than this, and I would like to illustrate this by means of a representative example.

In September 1907 the first English book edition of Joseph Conrad's novel *The Secret Agent* was published. If you study this novel you will probably read it in a modern paperback that is based upon this edition. Critical essays concerned with this novel will also almost certainly be based on an edition that descends in one way or another from the first English book edition. But behind this seeming unanimity a much more complex reality can be revealed. It is as if this single text is the visible part of a verbal iceberg, one that has a massive hidden presence extending backwards and forwards in time rather than in space.

If you consult the scholarly 'critical' edition of *The Secret Agent* published by Cambridge University Press in 1990, you will find in it a dense ninety-two-page discussion of the novel's textual history. From this you can determine not only that the novel was first published in a considerably shorter periodical version, in instalments, but also that it was published in separate book editions in Britain and America. Behind these published editions a web of manuscripts, typescripts and copy edited proofs has been uncovered by the editors of this edition, a web so complex that it is represented in their discussion by a sequence of graphic representations resembling a map of the London underground system. Establishing who made changes to these various texts, and when, is often difficult, as later printings of the first edition seem on occasions to reintroduce earlier formulations that Conrad had altered.

In November 1922, just over fifteen years after *The Secret Agent* was first published in book form, an adaptation of the novel for the stage opened in London at the Ambassador's Theatre. The adaptation had been written by Conrad himself. Not only did this dramatization remove many scenes present in the novel, in transforming the work from a *printed narrative intended to be read silently* to a *play written for performance*, it also completely removed the non-character narrator along with his ironic perspective on the events recounted – perhaps the most radical change that transformation from printed novel to performed play entailed. It also changed some aspects of the story, so that the character Winnie Verloc does not commit suicide but instead goes mad at the end of the work.

The play was not a great success, and ran for only a week. But in the audience for one of the few performances sat a young man named Alfred Hitchcock, who was shortly to begin a career in the film industry (see Spoto, 1983, 62). Fourteen years later, after having directed a film entitled *The Secret Agent* that had nothing to do with Conrad, Hitchcock directed a film entitled *Sabotage* that included the acknowledgement 'From the novel "The Secret Agent" by Joseph Conrad' in the opening credits, but that transposed the action to the present day and made very significant alterations to the setting and story of both Conrad's novel and his stage adaptation. Sixty years after Hitchcock's film was first shown, a new film entitled *The Secret Agent*, written and directed by Christopher Hampton and starring Bob Hoskins and Patricia Arquette, was released in the United States. Both Conrad's own dramatization of his novel and Hampton's screenplay have been published and can be consulted.

Instead of a single text, then, we now have a bewildering succession of texts, not all of which have survived. How should the poor student of the novel cope with this diversity?

By convention these different texts are divided into separate categories. All of the variants and versions associated with Conrad's writing of the novel are usually deemed to be the preserve of the textual editor. Unless you are writing an advanced thesis on *The Secret Agent*, you will not be expected to pore over periodical and book versions of the novel in their British and American editions, nor to sit in front of a microfilm reader or PC deciphering the handwriting of Conrad's manuscript. Nor is it likely that you will be expected to read the novel in a full critical edition such as the Cambridge edition mentioned above. But you may – and in my opinion should – be expected to read the novel in a modern edition with a text based upon the results of recent scholarship. Such an edition will draw your attention to substantial variations in the text of the novel, and it should also allow you to ponder the significance of some of Conrad's own textual revisions. Recent editions of classic novels published by reputable imprints such as Norton, Penguin and Oxford World's Classics will almost certainly be reliable – that is to say they will not give you texts that repeat mistakes or changes unauthorized by the writer after these have been pointed out by scholars, and they will contain information about the textual history of the work and about important textual variants.

Adaptations

But what about those later versions that we generally refer to as adaptations? And what is the difference between a version and an adaptation? Although the two terms overlap, generally speaking we call a rewriting of a novel or short story an adaptation when it does not seek to *replace* a known work ('known', typically, because it has been published or performed), but to be treated as a new work, one that it is hoped will have a life of its own *alongside* that of the work of which it is an adaptation. It is usual for an adaptation to involve some generic change – from prose fiction to play or film, for example – so that we may find that a play that is based on another play is termed 'a modern-dress version' rather than 'a modern-dress adaptation'. Conrad, like most novelists, was very keen to establish just one authoritative text of his novels, but he did not want people to stop reading *The Secret Agent* once he had dramatized it, and neither we assume did Alfred Hitchcock after he had made his film *Sabotage*.

Some introductory questions

There are many different ways in which a short story or a novel can be adapted.
Let me try to list some key general issues here.

1. *How great an involvement in the adaptation does the author or the source text
    have?*
    If for example the author writes a one-person monologue based on a
    short story and then directs him- or herself in a performance of this
    monologue, the involvement is very considerable. If the adaptation is
    written and performed after the author's death by someone with only the
    original story or novel as basis, there is no such involvement.

2. *How different are the medium and genre for which the adaptation is produced
    from those of the source text?*
    Although a play is written to be performed, its reliance upon language
    is generally greater than is the case for a film. And the collective nature
    of film production inevitably reduces the importance of the writer's
    role when set against the writer's dominating importance for a novel.
    Remember that a basic issue such as the length of time available for a
    dramatization will vary between a film and a television series. Adapting
    John Galsworthy's *The Forsyte Saga* for a two-hour film would be a very
    different task from adapting it for a television series of many instalments.
    See below for more detailed comments on such issues.

3. *How long a time is there between the writing and publication of the source
    text and the writing and publication or performing of the adaptation?*
    A director who wishes to film *Hamlet* today must contend with issues
    of cultural change that do not arise in the case of the filming of a Harry
    Potter novel. A similar point applies to the production of an adaptation
    in a different culture from the one to which the source text belongs,
    even if there is a small gap in time between the writing of source and of
    adaptation. *The Seven Samurai* and *The Magnificent Seven* are not so far
    removed in time or in medium and genre, but the cultures within which
    these two films were produced, and the cultures that they depict, are
    radically different. The term 'reculturation' has been applied to such
    adaptations. Remember that this issue arises even if an author adapts his
    own work: *The Secret Agent* was performed as a play sixteen years after
    Conrad's novel was published, in a very different England and world
    from those in which the novel was written and first read.

4. *How well known is the source text?*
    Anyone adapting *Hamlet* for a new film cannot ignore the fact that almost
    everyone who sees the film will have *some* idea of what Shakespeare's
    play is about. But many films based on relatively unknown literary works
    can be made on the assumption that most of those who see the film will
    not have read the source text beforehand and will probably not read

it afterwards either. A director may choose to satisfy or challenge an audience's expectations but he or she cannot ignore them completely. No director could make a film of Tolstoy's *Anna Karenina* which ended with Anna marrying Vronsky and settling down to a blissful married life without taking into account that a very significant number of those who saw the film would be aware that this ending is quite different from the ending of Tolstoy's novel. But when Conrad changed the ending of *The Secret Agent* in adapting it for the stage, he may well have assumed that the plot of his novel would not be familiar to many in his London theatre audience. And when Beeban Kidron filmed Conrad's much less well-known short story 'Amy Foster' as *Swept from the Sea* in 1997, she almost certainly assumed that only a very few members of her film's audience would know anything of the source text.

5. *Does the adaptation display or conceal its relationship with the source text?*
   Clearly the starting point here is the title, followed shortly afterwards by character names. A change of title (from *The Turn of the Screw* to *The Innocents*, for example) may signal a desire on the part of writer, director or producer to establish greater distance between the film and Henry James's novella than might have been implied by retaining his title for the film adaptation.

6. *What sort of adaptation are we dealing with?*
   There are many ways of categorizing adaptations; one of the most influential has been Dudley Andrew's distinction between adaptations that 'borrow', 'intersect' with and 'transform' their sources (see Andrew, 1992, 422–3). Andrew glosses these terms as follows.
   Borrowing: Andrew describes this as 'the most frequent mode of adaptation. 'Here the artist employs ... the material, idea, or form of an earlier, generally successful text.' Citing Richard Strauss's *Don Quixote*, Andrew comments that there is 'no question of replication of the original', but instead 'the audience is expected to enjoy basking in a certain pre-established presence and to call up new or especially powerful aspects of a cherished work'.
   Intersecting: Andrew notes that 'here the uniqueness of the original text is preserved to such an extent that it is intentionally left unassimilated in adaptation'. An adaptation in the intersecting mode tends to 'present the otherness and distinctiveness of the original text', thus initiating a dialectical interplay of literary and cinematic forms. An example of this ambitious form of adaptation is Francis Ford Coppola's *Apocalypse Now*, although as Jakob Lothe points out, this film – which did not on first release acknowledge its debt to Joseph Conrad's *Heart of Darkness* – 'could be seen as an example of borrowing as well as intersecting' (Lothe, 2000, 88).
   Transformation: 'Here it is assumed that the task of adaptation is the reproduction in cinema of something essential about an original text.'

Andrew finds that as transformations tend to be faithful to the literary text, they may 'become a scenario written in typical scenario form'. Yet it does not follow that this kind of adaptation is artistically inferior to the two other variants. An example of a generally successful adaptation in the fidelity and transformation mode is John Huston's 1987 film *The Dead*, which closely follows the plot of James Joyce's short story.

The economy of Andrew's tripartite distinction stands in sharp contrast to Robert Stam's mention of 'a well-stocked archive of tropes and concepts to account for the mutation of forms across media: adaptation as reading, rewriting, critique, translation, transmutation, metamorphosis, recreation, transvocalization, signifying, performance, dialogization, cannibalization, reinvisioning, incarnation, or reaccentuation' (Stam, 2005, 25). Indeed, in his concluding comments, Stam adds yet more terms when he proposes that 'source-novel hypotexts are transformed by a complex series of operations: selection, amplification, concretization, actualization, critique, extrapolation, popularization, reaccentuation, transculturization' (2005, 45). ('Hypotext' in this context means the underlying, or foundational text that is the basis for later adaptations or transformations.) If the issue of fidelity, of how much of the source text the adaptor wishes to preserve – ranging from 'little' through 'to some extent' to 'something essential' – is central to Andrew's tripartite distinction, a much greater range of other issues is introduced by Stam's extended lists.

A good starting point is to ask very generally what has been omitted, added and 'concretized' in the transition from novel to film. The most obvious omissions will probably relate to excisions from the plot and from the cast of characters – especially if we are dealing with a narrative film that is based on a longish novel. By convention, films are not normally more than about three hours long, and even adaptations for television have less space for long complex plots and large character casts than do novels. While noting this fact it might be worth pausing a moment to ask why this is so. Why are we prepared to extend our reading of a long novel over several weeks if necessary, while anything over three hours in a cinema feels excessive? A simple answer to this involves the fundamental point that we have control over our private reading of a book in a way that we do not have over a film: we can pause, flick back to refresh our memory of earlier scenes, increase or decrease the speed of our reading – or even stop and think about what we have read or talk about it with a friend – so that we can pace ourselves as we read and adjust our reading to our mental state. But this is only part of the story, since electronic versions of films and television adaptations have enabled us to do much the same with a film, although with somewhat less ease than we do with a printed source. It is of course possible that as more and more people have access to films on DVD players then films may start to extend in length and to take as long to watch as it takes to read a novel; but I rather doubt this – not least because films are expensive things to create, and making them very much longer will increase their cost dramatically. Even long television adaptations are typically shown in instalments rather than in, say, a continuous six-hour session, and this suggests that there is something fundamentally different in the way that we experience a silently read novel and a dramatization or a performance, and that this is one of the factors that lies behind the issue of length.

Whatever the reason, a filmed or televised version of a novel is likely to involve very significant abridgement, and a first point of interest in the study of adaptation has to be: 'What has been cut?' Why has the screenwriter or director chosen to cut this rather than that scene, this rather than that character? What effect do such cuts have?

Abridgement need not involve elements of the plot or characters – it can involve aspects of a novel that are integral to its narrative. In discussing Free Indirect Discourse, for example, I noted how the examples I chose (from Katherine Mansfield's 'The Voyage', Virginia Woolf's *Mrs Dalloway* and D.H. Lawrence's 'Fanny and Annie') managed to present a particular scene in such a way as to combine what a narrator tells us and what a character is thinking. Turn back to p. 125 and read once again the first two paragraphs of Lawrence's short story 'Fanny and Annie' (1922) that I quote there.

How could one film this scene? Clearly a skilled film-maker could depict Fanny's irritation as Harry fails to see her, and could reproduce some of the effects of flame and shadow that the passage presents. But how could a filmed adaptation of this scene convey the fact that 'the nostalgia, the doom of home-coming went through her veins like a drug', when we are not even sure that Fanny herself is aware of what is happening to her? How could the film-maker convey her sense of his unchangingness ('His eternal face'; 'Always the same') without the crudity of a voice-over? In his introduction to *Aren't You Rather Young to be Writing Your Memoirs?* (1973), the novelist B.S. Johnson has commented with regard to film that it 'is an excellent medium for showing things, but it is very poor at taking an audience inside characters' minds, at telling it what people are thinking' (Bradbury, 1990, 166).

What about additions? Some of these may well be straightforward: added scenes or new characters. But some additional elements can be the result of the inevitable 'concretization' that film involves. Here is critic Robert Stam again, considering exactly this issue in a discussion of John Ford's adaptation of Steinbeck's novel *The Grapes of Wrath*, which was released in 1940, the year after the novel was published. Stam comments in detail on a passage in which the character Ma Joad contemplates her memorabilia just before leaving her Oklahoma home for California. The passage in Steinbeck's novel reads as follows:

> She sat down and opened the box. Inside were letters, clippings, photographs, a pair of earrings, a little gold signet ring, and a watch chain braided of hair and tipped with gold swivels. She touched the letters with her fingers, touched them lightly, and she smoothed a newspaper clipping on which there was an account of Tom's trial.

Stam comments as follows.

> In the film version of this passage we do indeed see Ma Joad sit down,
> open the box, and look at letters, clippings, photographs, and so forth.
> But even here the 'cinematization' generates an inevitable supplement.
> Where Steinbeck writes 'photographs,' Ford has to choose specific
> photographs. The mention of 'earrings' in the novel, does not dictate
> Ford's choice of having Ma Joad try them on. The newspaper account
> of Tom's trial requires the choice of a specific newspaper, specific
> headlines, illustrations, fonts, none of which is spelled out in the
> original. (Stam, 2005, 18)

Let us pause at this point just to absorb the force of some of Stam's discussion.
We may be tempted to suggest that it is almost as if with Steinbeck's text we
have a 'script' on the basis of which the reader can mentally perform the scene in
question, whereas with Ford's film we have a single performance of the scene.

I would not want to reject such a view entirely, but what is questionable about
it is the assumption that every detail that is concretized in the film is also given
a sort of mental concretization in the mind of the reader as he or she reads the
scene in Steinbeck's novel – and this seems to me unlikely. Imagine reading the
passage from Steinbeck's novel, then having someone snatch the book away and
demand: 'Describe the earrings!' I suggest that we would not be able to do so
if asked, and neither would we have imagined the wording of the newspaper
clippings. The filmed version of this scene *has* to add detail that is not present
in the written text and is not even 'performed in' by a reader. Concretization
requires addition. One of the important things to note here is that the writer
of prose fiction can ensure that only that which is relevant to his or her artistic
intention is conveyed to the reader. The writer can state: 'He sat down.' But the
film-maker has to decide on what sort of chair, with what sort of movement he
sat down. The economy of prose fiction contributes fundamentally to its artistic
focus.

Stam also reminds us that there are other necessary additions in any filmed
version of this scene.

> Thus nothing in the novel prepares us for the idea that Ma Joad will
> look at the memorabilia by the light of a fire, the reflections of which
> will flicker over her face. Nothing dictates the point-of-view editing
> which alternates close shots of Ma Joad's face with what she sees, within
> a contemplative rhythm of shot/reverse shot. Nor does the Steinbeck
> passage mention music, yet the Ford version features a melancholy
> accordion version of the song 'Red River Valley.' Even if the text *had*
> mentioned 'Red River Valley' that would still have been quite different
> from our actually hearing it performed. And even if the passage *had*
> mentioned both the music and the firelight, and the light's flickering

over Ma Joad's face, that would still not have been anything like our
seeing her face and hearing the music *at the same time*. (18)

Stam notes that although critics writing about adaptation from novel to film tend
'to emphasize the cinema's impairments and disabilities vis-à-vis the novel ...
yet, on almost any plane one might mention, cinematic adaptation brings,
whether for good or ill, not an impoverishment but rather a *multiplication* of
registers' (20). We are used to metaphorical accounts of novels, or of our experience of them, as 'rich', of their 'complex texture', and so on. These metaphors
are not inaccurate, as we build up a sense of varied patterns and impressions in
the course of our reading, and these different elements do combine in rich and
complex ways. But if we exclude for the time being the issue of illustrations, the
traditional novel is 'single-track' in the sense that everything that we experience
in our reading of a novel comes from words and the arrangement of words. A
film, in contrast, has many 'tracks' – moving pictures, music, speech and noises,
for example.

A brief case study: Henry James's *The Turn of the Screw*

Henry James's *The Turn of the Screw* is a much-adapted work. In addition to
Benjamin Britten's opera and a number of less well-known adaptations for the
stage, there are at least ten film or television-film adaptations of the work. Not
all of these are readily available; among the lost adaptations is a 1959 live television play with Ingrid Bergman playing James's unnamed governess. Even so,
anyone prepared to scour libraries and retailers should be able to find five or six
adaptations of the tale on video or DVD, along with a 1972 'prequel' starring
Marlon Brando as the living Quint entitled *The Nightcomers*. Two adaptations of
the story have been released with different titles: *The Innocents* (1961) and *The
Haunting of Helen Walker* (1995).

The existence of so many film adaptations of the same story illustrates an
essential point. A single adaptation, like a dramatic performance, never exhausts
the dramatic potential of the original. Put another way: any adaptation is partial,
both in the sense that it has its own interpretive preferences, and in the sense that
it displays only a part of the complex richness of the original. This reminds us of
an important difference between narrative and performance to which attention
has already been drawn. Because a dramatic or film performance concretizes
characters, events and settings, it necessarily reduces the play of possible variety
that a written narrative possesses. A few lines above I noted that concretization
required addition; without wishing to confuse you, I must now add that it also
involves the exclusion of certain responses open to the reader of the printed text.
We may read one line of dialogue in our heads in a large number of ways, with
different emphasis, intonation and so on. But a line delivered in a film can be
said in only one way. When we read 'the coachman' in a story we can imagine the

individual in all sorts of ways; when we see him in a film he can look like only what he does look like.

Culture, convention and adaptation

In a straightforward sense a film adaptation can accommodate a story to a new culture by changing its setting. Thus Rusty Lemorande's 1992 version of *The Turn of the Screw*, which sets it in the 1960s and has a female narrator (played by Marianne Faithfull) tell her story to a woman's therapy group, clearly 'reculturizes' the story. But an adaptation does not have to change the setting of a story to reculturize it. Adaptations are like forgeries and translations: they always seem to bear traces of the cultures from which they have emerged. Unless it has been produced by a real master-forger, a sham Modigliani painting produced in the 1950s now strikes us as inescapably '1950s'. We see marks of the time of its production in it that were invisible to all but experts in the 1950s. Similarly, a translation of a Tolstoy novel dating from the 1920s will bear the marks of its translator's age and culture, which is why even the best of translations rarely lasts as long as the original. So far as James's novella is concerned, what seems in particular to have interested so many film-makers during the past four or five decades is its underlying suggestion of sexual corruption. It is hard to imagine that so many adaptations would have been made had the Freudian interpretations of the novella – which, broadly described, see the ghosts as hallucinations produced by a sexually frustrated governess – not drawn attention to hints not just of sexual frustration but also of paedophilia, homosexuality and extramarital sex in James's text. James's text is also full of religious elements and suggestions, and some adaptations do try to do justice to these, but the relative weight accorded to these two aspects of the novella in many recent adaptations reflects the cultures of the adapters rather than the cultures in which James lived and about which he wrote.

By common consent one of the best film adaptations of the novella is the 1961 *The Innocents*, directed by Jack Clayton. According to Lawrence Raw, 'The screen play for *The Innocents* went through several drafts, with many different people – including Archibald, Clayton, and the writers John Mortimer, Nigel Neill, Rhys Adrian, and Truman Capote – contributing to it' (Raw, 2006, 60), although not all of these are mentioned in the film's credits. In its own way the film is a splendid example of successful adaptation, and a number of the terms suggested by Robert Stam could be appropriated to describe it, including perhaps 'selection, amplification, concretization, actualization, critique, extrapolation, popularization, reaccentuation, transculturization'.

The Innocents stars Deborah Kerr as the governess, and (again by common consent) one of the most shocking moments in the film is when the young boy Miles kisses the governess goodnight on the lips, but extends the kiss in what is unambiguously a sexual manner. It seems clear that this is an element in the film that comes from the culture of the 1960s and not of 1898 when the novella was first published. It is not that the novella contains no hints that the young pre-adolescent children have had some sort of sexual relationship with adults, but that the way in which this element is presented in the film bears the mark of a culture later than James's. Lawrence Raw reminds of the importance of the film's 'conditions of production'.

> Much had changed in Hollywood in the decade separating *I'll Never Forget You* from *The Innocents*. Censorship had been relaxed; in December, 1956, the Production Code was rewritten to allow references to previously forbidden subjects such as drug addiction, abortion, prostitution, and miscegenation, although topics like sexual perversion were banned. (57)

Two other significant factors concerning the film – the age of the lead actress and the decision to use monochrome film – need also to be understood in the light of cultural attitudes in the Britain of the early 1960s.

At the time Deborah Kerr made the film she was about forty years old, whereas the governess in James's story is, we are told, twenty years old at the time of the events she reports in her narrative. Laurence Raw notes that it had become something of a tradition for the role of the governess to be played by older actresses. 'Beatrice Straight was thirty-four and Flora Robson was fifty when they starred in *The Innocents* on Broadway and in London; in two of the television adaptations, the leading role was played by Sarah Churchill (forty-three) and Ingrid Bergman (forty-four)' (59). Why should this be?

We may venture the guess that one of our culture's most lasting stereotypes during the time since James's story was published is that a 'frustrated, hysterical, unmarried governess' would be more likely to be older than just twenty years old. The one-sentence summary of the film given in the 1999 edition of Halliwell's *Film and Video Guide* reads: 'In Victorian times, a spinster governess in a lonely house finds her young charges possessed by evil demons of servants now dead.' The word 'spinster' is used neither in the film nor in James's tale. Laurence Raw suggests that director Jack Clayton wished 'to challenge the prevailing view of spinsters as witches or people suffering from mental problems' (63), and that this is why he contrived to make the governess remain something of an enigma. Assuming that Clayton did indeed have such an aim, it is a moot point whether or not he realized it in the film.

Filming *The Innocents* in black and white would have been more obviously a decision in 1961 than we might today assume. Films were still being made in black and white at this time, and *The Naked Edge* in which Kerr also starred in 1961 was also made in monochrome. But the five films in which Kerr starred before these two films were in colour, and by 1961 to make a film in black and white bespoke either a desire to save money or a decision that monochrome was somehow fitting. I suspect that the conventional associations of monochrome were deemed appropriate to the filming of a ghost story designed to scare the viewer: Alfred Hitchcock's *Psycho*, released a year earlier in 1960, was also filmed in monochrome.

Narrating vs enacting

The case of *The Turn of the Screw* is particularly useful in illustrating some of the crucial differences between a verbal narrative such as James's novella and a performance such as one of the film adaptations of the work. This is because the fact of narrative in *The Turn of the Screw* is so central to its artistic effect. In the opening pages of the novella an unnamed 'outer' narrator reports on a scene (set, we presume, in the present day of the time at which it was published – 1898) in which a group of adults exchange ghost stories on Christmas Eve. One of these adults, a man named Douglas, mentions a story concerning two children who witness some ghostly apparition. He agrees to tell the story, which he explains was told to him forty years earlier, by a woman who experienced these events and who was not just his own governess but the twenty-year-old governess of the story itself. Some days later her written account is delivered, and he reads this story over several evenings to those assembled. The frame narrator explains that what the reader will then be given is a transcription of the governess's written account which Douglas passed on to him, but this is preceded by the frame narrator's summary of Douglas's introductory comments, which describe a meeting in London between the governess and her employer-to-be, the uncle of the two children in the story.

It is worth pointing out that although earlier in this book (p. 114) I suggested that Douglas delivers the framed narrative, in strict point of fact he narrates the unnamed governess's story only to the extent that he reads her account to the assembled group. What the reader (as against the listeners) gets is not his reading, but a transcript of the governess's written account. His introductory comments may (half) frame the governess's comments for the reader, but not in the way that Marlow's account in Conrad's *Heart of Darkness* is framed by the outer narrator's comments.

The foregoing account may strike you as long-winded, but even it compresses and simplifies the chain of connections necessary for the narrative to be delivered to Douglas's listeners and to the reader of James's tale. What is interesting is that film adaptations of the story typically simplify or omit this chain of transmission. In *The Innocents*, for example, the Christmas Eve ghost-story session is missing completely – which means of course that the 'outer' narrator and Douglas, and their exchanges and comments, are also absent. The film's opening credits actually run alongside an image of a woman's hands clasped in prayer. After a while the hands are seen in a new shot to belong to the character who we later learn is the governess, played by Deborah Kerr. She changes the position of her hands from 'clasped in prayer' to 'clasped anxiously'. On the soundtrack a sort of sobbing, accompanied by birds twittering, can be heard. The shot changes from profile to full face, and the woman says: 'All I want to do is save the children, not destroy them. More than anything I love the children. More than anything.' The scene then fades into the governess's interview with the uncle. At the end of this interview the governess agrees to accept the position on the difficult conditions specified, and the film then moves to the governess's arrival at Bly, where the main action takes place.

What difference do these changes make? Perhaps their most important effect is, I think, to remove that combination of distance and claustrophobic imprisonment that James's original gives the reader. The distance comes from the fact that when we *read* the account of the governess's experiences we seem to be at the end of a long chain of narrative transmissions. The governess told her story – which took place forty years before the opening of the tale – to Douglas, who repeats it to the gathered guests after the governess's death. The frame narrator receives the governess's written account from Douglas shortly before the latter's death. We are cut off from the source of the narrative by time and death. We have only the words, written ostensibly by the governess. Neither she nor Douglas is alive to explicate them. In the first few pages of the novella the reader learns that the governess is dead; at the start of *The Innocents* she is very much alive, there, in front of us. In the film there is one 'present time'; in the novella there are many. In the novella, everything we read after the frame narrator's introductory pages comes from the governess, and is given in her words. We are imprisoned in her account, in her way of seeing things. We can no more see her from the outside than we can see ourselves.

In the film our sense that what we are seeing is *the governess's version* is more or less impossible to retain. Right from the start we look *at* as well as *with* her. The short opening scene of her praying and agonizing about the children raises an issue of which the first-time reader of James's novella becomes aware only towards the end of the tale: that in trying to protect the children she may actually destroy them. In the subsequent scene with the uncle there is no suggestion that what we see may not actually have occurred – there it is, taking place before our eyes. But in James's novella, we learn of this scene through Douglas's report and not as part of the governess's account, even though, logically, Douglas can have had his information only from the governess. What the reader gets is Douglas's report of what the governess must have remembered about her interview with the uncle and told him. What the film viewer gets is the interview itself. The tale gives us a report of a report, a version of a version, while the film gives us the scene itself, however much the use of camera angle, cutting and so on may encourage us to perceive the scene in a particular manner.

Because film *enacts* rather than *tells*, in other words, the governess is shown as a character along with other characters, and not as the source of all our knowledge about characters and events. It is true that by means of a variety of technical and artistic methods, a good film-maker can cause us to sympathize with the governess and to adopt her point of view, but we never actually see things through her eyes and understanding in the way that we do when reading James's story. (There is even a scene in the film in which we observe the governess while she is asleep.)

The director of *The Innocents* does manage to keep the viewer in a certain doubt as to whether the ghosts are really there or are a product of the governess's imagination. But it is much more difficult for a film-maker than for a writer to sow doubt as to whether something 'really happened'. Alfred Hitchcock has a nice comment in an interview in which he admits that in his film *Stage Fright* he made a mistake in putting in a flashback that was a lie. His comment draws attention to a key difference between films and written stories:

> Strangely enough, in movies, people never object if a man is shown telling a lie. And it's also acceptable, when a character tells a story about the past, for the flashback to show it as if it were taking place in the present. So why is it that we can't tell a lie through a flashback? (Truffaut, 1986, 275)

This brief comment isolates a crucial difference: a lie can be *told* but it is very difficult for it to be *shown*. When the real crime documentaries shown on Discovery Channel dramatize accounts told by suspects, they very often have the word 're-enactment' superimposed on the screen so as to prevent the viewer from making the automatic assumption that if we see it then it really happened. When we do see things happening on screen it is very hard, and often impossible, for us to perceive them as someone's report, or memory, or hallucination. Films concretize. Even in the age of digital image manipulation, our senses still tell us that the camera cannot lie.

In James's novella the reader learns that the previous governess, Miss Jessel, has died. The cause of her death is never given, even though – tantalizingly – when asked in the opening pages what she died of, Douglas replies: 'That will come out.' But it does not. In the course of her narrative, the governess (who has just learned that the housekeeper, Mrs Grose, does not share Douglas's view of the previous governess's respectability) asks the housekeeper about her death:

> 'Poor woman – she paid for it!'
>> 'Then you do know what she died of?' I asked.
>> 'No – I know nothing. I wanted not to know; I was glad enough I did n't; and I thanked heaven she was well out of this!'
>>> 'Yet you had then your idea –'
>>> 'Of her real reason for leaving? Oh yes – as to that. She could n't have stayed. Fancy it here – for a governess! And afterward I imagined – and I still imagine. And what I imagine is dreadful.'

'Not so dreadful as what *I* do,' I replied; on which I must have
shown her – as I was indeed but too conscious – a front of miserable
defeat.

What seems obvious here – and this is amply confirmed by Henry James's own
comments about his strategy in this tale (from which I quote briefly on p. 56) –
is that James's aim is to get the reader to *imagine* why the previous governess
had to leave and how she died. An unwanted pregnancy, suicide – these are
possibilities that inevitably spring to the reader's mind. But in James's text
these imaginings are never confirmed, and they have to be set against Douglas's
statement in the opening pages of the tale that Miss Jessel 'had done for them
[the children] quite beautifully – she was a most respectable person – till her
death …'. Note too that the reader has to guess not just what happened to
Miss Jessel, but also what both Mrs Grose and the governess *imagine* happened
to her.

In *The Innocents* all of this indeterminacy is lost. Mrs Grose tells the
governess: 'Miss Jessel put an end to herself; she was found in the lake.' In
the film Mrs Grose also tells the governess that after Peter Quint died, Miss
Jessel went into the blackest mourning, and that she 'died of a broken heart',
although in James's tale it is never made clear whether Quint or Jessel dies
first. A later film version of James's novella – Ben Bolt's 1999 television film
The Turn of the Screw – actually opens with a shot of Miss Jessel committing
suicide by jumping into water. Accordingly when we see the ghost of Miss
Jessel in this later adaptation we have already seen her in life. As the 'ghost' is
clearly the same as the person we saw committing suicide, a person who in life
has *not* been seen by the governess, the viewer must assume that there really is
a ghost and that it really is Miss Jessel.

My emphasis up to this point has been on what can be achieved in prose
fiction that is beyond the ordinary scope of film. Clearly there is another tale to
be told, and those interested in reading it will find an excellent starting point in
the article by Robert Stam from which I have quoted a number of comments in
this chapter. Film can do much – enormously much – that is beyond the scope
of the printed page. Just the ability to combine moving pictures, sound and
language opens up for complex effects of potentially great artistic significance.
The way in which the soundtrack at the start of *The Innocents* combines speech,
the sound of sobbing and the twittering of birds establishes complex associations
that are subtly developed as the film proceeds. We can see and hear Miles playing
the piano, and piano music can later be used to suggest his presence even when
he is off-screen. Film is certainly no less subtle a medium than prose fiction, but
its subtleties are of a different order. In comparing an adaptation such as *The
Innocents* with its source in a work of prose fiction we can learn to appreciate the
unique potentialities of two different media, two related but independent artistic
traditions.

Topics for discussion

↪ 'Short stories make better films than do novels.' Do they? If so, why?

↪ Should a film-maker try to be faithful to the novel he or she is adapting? Is it possible?

↪ Do you agree that the biggest problem a film-maker faces is that in a film private experience cannot be shown, and the public life cannot be hidden?

↪ 'In comparison to novels, films leave too little to the imagination.' Do they?

Chapter 9
Critical approaches to fiction

Preview

This chapter deals with:

↪ classifying criticism into schools and approaches
↪ structuralist and rhetorical narratology
↪ literary-critical traditions and approaches to the novel
↪ textual, contextual and ideological approaches

This chapter is not meant to substitute for a more detailed and comprehensive introduction to different literary theories and approaches. It is rather designed to help you to recognize these theories and approaches in the books and articles you consult, while at the same time providing some information concerning their particular relevance to the study of the novel and shorter fiction. It includes a more extended discussion of narratology in both its structuralist and its rhetorical variants. Literary criticism of prose fiction, and narratology, have increasingly fed off each others' insights and advances in the last two or three decades; as a result, studying prose fiction today requires some familiarity with narratology and its terminology.

Categorizing criticism

Critical books and essays, unlike chocolate bars, are not required by law to contain a list of ingredients. In some cases the titles chosen by critics are helpful: 'A Postcolonial Reading of *Jane Eyre*' or *Queer Henry James* leave little doubt as to the critical approach and theoretical allegiance of the writer (do not look for these in the library as I have invented them, but you will find many similar titles in bibliographies). If you are looking for criticism of *Jane Eyre* or of James's *The Turn of the Screw* that has a lot to say about narrative method then these titles are not too promising – although of course you cannot rule out stumbling across some striking insights about narrative technique in a book or an article with a similar title. A title such as 'The Personified Narrator in Charlotte Brontë and Henry James' is likely to indicate a work of much more use to you.

This much is relatively simple. If you can pull a book off the library or the bookshop shelf then a skim through the contents list, the index and a few pages will help you to decide if it is worth more serious reading. What students often find more difficult is the process of using a *categorization* of a particular critic's approach as a basis to *assess the force* of that critic's comments on a particular work.

Let me give a particular example. The second edition of the Norton Critical Edition of Joseph Conrad's novella *Heart of Darkness* included an extract from a book on Conrad by Robert F. Haugh to which the Norton editor gave the title '*Heart of Darkness*: Problem for Critics'. Haugh pours scorn on the argument that Conrad's novella is a critique of Belgian imperialism, suggesting that this reveals a superficial understanding of the work, and concludes by arguing that the Conradian hero (such as Kurtz in *Heart of Darkness*) 'in his remarkable actions ... defines the mortal condition, and in his last moment of vision ... sees all the scheme of the universe; and we share it in a moment of tragic exaltation' (Conrad, 1971, 167).

Let us imagine that you are writing an essay on *Heart of Darkness*, and in the course of your argument you state that Conrad's novella is not primarily a critique of imperialism – Belgian or otherwise – but rather represents a tragic view of the mortal condition, and you quote from Haugh's chapter to back up your argument. What is problematic about this is that it does not assess Haugh's contentions in context: his book was published in the United States at a time (1957) when, because of the dominance of New Critical ideas, it was extremely fashionable to play down the extent to which works of literature engaged with specific socio-political situations or events, but it was more common to argue that 'great' literature draws our attention rather to the human condition in general. This does not mean that we can just dismiss Haugh's arguments out of hand. It does, however, mean that they have to be assessed in the light of Haugh's apparent critical beliefs and of the time at which he wrote. If you want to strengthen the force of your argument that Conrad's novella is about the human condition in general rather than an attack on a specific phase of imperialism, then you need other substantiating material: the views of critics who have taken a different view of *Heart of Darkness*, quotations from Conrad himself and from contemporary responses to the work, and renewed analytical attention to the literary text itself.

Being able to categorize critical approaches should not mean that one prejudges the worth or the relevance of a book or an article, but it does help in assessing the force of a given critic's argument. However, before I outline the different critical approaches to prose fiction of which the student should be aware I would like briefly to go back to some of the fundamental categories that I have discussed early in this book, and consider their implications for criticism.

A return to some fundamental categories

The three categories that I want to focus on are the following:

- ↦ literature
- ↦ fiction
- ↦ narrative

If you are reading this book because it has been recommended by the lecturer responsible for a particular course, then it is likely that most of the syllabus texts that you will be expected to read for this course will belong to all of these categories: they will be literary texts, they will be works of fiction and they will be narratives (following the definition of narrative that I suggest on p. 6). I should note in passing that in different ways all of these terms have their blurred edges and contested usages; what constitutes a 'literary' text, for example, is by no means universally agreed; some works have a habit of drifting in and out of the literary canon from generation to generation, and 'the canon' itself is a contested term.

Now although these three terms can overlap, they may not. There are literary works that are neither works of fiction nor narratives (lyric poems in which the poet speaks in his or her own voice, for example). There are works of literature that are clearly in some sense fictional, but that are not narratives; one could argue that Jonathan Swift's 'A Modest Proposal' (1729) belongs to this category. Finding an example of a work of fiction that is not a narrative or a work of literature would lead us in the direction of such things as 'legal fictions' – assumptions that are not literally true but that are maintained for the sake of simplifying complex and contradictory states of affairs in the real world. There are narratives that are fictional but that do not merit the honorific title of 'literature' – jokes, and pornographic stories, for example. There are non-fictional narratives that have on occasions been granted admission to the literary canon: James Boswell's *The Life of Samuel Johnson LL.D* (1791), for example. And the world is full of narratives that are neither literary nor fictional: historical accounts, statements by legal witnesses, case histories of patients written by doctors, accident reports written by policemen and many others. We should moreover remember that narratives need not be written down: they can be spoken, or even delivered by means of a succession of graphic images in a comic book.

Now what this means is that there are different traditions of study and analysis that are associated with different sorts of text, traditions that are closely related and often overlapping, but are nonetheless distinct. For present purposes we can say that the most important of these are those of literary criticism and narratology – an ancient and a very young tradition. Both of these traditions have their splits and factions, their disagreements and their alternative attendant theories and analytical methods. And although these two activities or disciplines overlap, they do not share an identical focus of interest. Narratologists are typically interested in all narratives, and as we have seen, many narratives are neither fictional nor literary. Both narratologists and literary critics (and remember that a single individual can be both) may, for example, be interested in a novel by Virginia Woolf, but the literary critic will be interested in aspects of this work that are not necessarily of interest to the narratologist.

In introducing these two traditions I find it most straightforward to do this in reverse chronological direction, and to start with the newer development.

Narratology

Structuralist narratology

According to one account the term 'narratology' was coined as late as in 1969, and was subsequently popularized in the 1970s by *structuralist* writers, who applied the general principles of structuralist theory to the analysis of various examples of narrative. As I have noted, what distinguishes narratology as an academic discipline is that it has as its object of study *all* examples of narrative – those I list above and many more, including all examples of literary narrative and (in the work of some narratologists) 'film narrative' and 'theatrical narrative'.

Narratology as an area of study is so recent that although it is a recognized academic discipline its practitioners are not, generally, to be found in departments of narratology. Narratologists may be found in departments of English, Comparative Literature, Law, Linguistics, Medicine, Sociology and many others. However, because some of the most important and most highly valued narratives in our culture – and in other cultures – are works of literary prose fiction, narratologists have had much to say about novels, novellas and short stories. And such has been the impact and influence of narratology that a good many of the concepts and terms that its practitioners have developed have been imported into literary criticism and into the study of literary narratives. It is no exaggeration to say that the development of narratology has revolutionized the study of prose fiction, and it has done this in a remarkably short time. Several of the terms that I list in the glossary at the end of this book, for example, were coined by narratologists and adopted by literary critics in the course of a brief period of about a couple of decades. And behind the new terms were new concepts, or significant refinements of old concepts. Moreover, if literary criticism took much from narratology, it gave much too. The foundational work of modern narratology – Gérard Genette's *Narrative Discourse* (first published in

French as *Figures III* in 1972 and in English translation in 1980) – in its attempt to chart the system governing all narratives, pays detailed analytical attention to Marcel Proust's *A la recherche du temps perdu* (1913–27).

Narratology is a rapidly expanding and many faceted field of study, but in the course of its brief but influential life two distinct phases or types can be discerned: *structuralist narratology* and the more recent *rhetorical narratology*. The origins of structuralism as a body of theory are generally dated to Ferdinand de Saussure's *Course in General Linguistics* which was compiled by Saussure's students after his death from notes taken from his lectures, and first published in French in 1916. Saussure's most influential move in this work was to distinguish between what he terms 'static' and 'evolutionary' linguistics. Nowadays the terms 'synchronic' (or structuralist) linguistics, and 'diachronic' (or historical) linguistics are generally used to make the same distinction in English.

Saussure pointed out that language could either be studied in the way that, at the time he wrote, was traditional: by charting its development over time, or, alternatively, by looking at a given language as a functioning system at a particular moment of time without any concern for how it got to be that way. Saussure, incidentally, believed that these two approaches were complementary, although it is common to read claims that he wished to replace historical linguistics with synchronic linguistics. Those structuralists who used Saussure as their theoretical starting point adopted his synchronic approach to the study of language as a model (or 'paradigm' – hence 'the linguistic paradigm'), and they attempted to construct a 'grammar' of different systems of meaning in the way in which Saussure had written of the construction of a synchronic grammar of language.

It is for this reason that early structuralist narratologists adopted some of the terms used by structuralist linguisticians. In elucidating his use of the term 'mood', for example, Gérard Genette notes: 'one can tell *more* or tell *less* what one tells, and can tell it *according to one point of mood or another*; and this capacity, and the modalities of its use, are precisely what our category of *narrative mood* aims at' (1980, 161–2). Genette further uses the term 'voice' to designate the narrative situation or its instance (1980, 30–1). These and other terms are taken from the terminology applied by linguisticians to the grammar of verbs. In my discussion of rhetorical narratology below I will summarize some of the problems attached to such terms, and the reasons that may lie behind a stubborn Anglo-Saxon reluctance to adopt some of them. Certain of these terms have, however, indubitably caught on: for example, one of the most fruitful appropriations of a term and its related concept from structuralist grammar by narratologists involves the concept of 'frequency', which I discuss on p. 141.

Central to structuralist linguistics is a concern for an abstract form of analysis that is not concerned with the particular meaning of a single sentence, but in the underlying system that makes meaning possible – its *grammar*. Structuralist narratologists share a comparable concern, although they have differed as to whether they are looking for the grammar of a particular narrative text, a set of texts or of narrative in general. Thus the Russian folklorist Vladimir Propp (mentioned on p. 134) was interested not in any particular folktale, but in the underlying system or grammar that enabled the generation of a large number of seemingly different folktales. Just as one grammar allows the generation of an enormously large number of grammatical sentences in English so too, the argument goes, one 'grammar' of the folktale could be discerned behind any given folktale in a particular cultural or generic tradition.

Structuralist narratology in its purer form accordingly focuses far less on the detail of individual works than on the manner whereby they exemplify a set of possibilities open to the genre as a whole. Like the variant of linguistics upon which they are based, literary-critical structuralisms tend to be ahistorical, concentrating upon systems as they operate at a given moment of time rather than on their modification over time.

What structuralist narratology has given the student of the novel and of shorter prose fiction, then, is a set of concepts and their related terms that denote aspects of the underlying 'grammar' of narratives. In some cases this has involved refining and sharpening existing terms and concepts – thus the older term 'point of view' has been refined by modern narratologists so as to enable a distinction between 'perspective' and 'voice' (see p. 122). Another example involves a narratological appropriation of the terms 'diegesis' and 'mimesis', used in the third book of Plato's *Republic* to distinguish between cases where the poet himself is the speaker (diegesis) and cases where the poet creates the illusion that speeches should not be attributed to him personally (mimesis). Gerald Prince's *Dictionary of Narratology* (1988) defines 'diegesis' as either the fictional world in which events occur in a narrative, or 'telling' as against 'showing' (see p. 229).

Several other important contributions by structuralist narratologists to the analysis of literary narrative can be listed. Perhaps the most important of these has been the refinement of the distinction between 'story' and 'plot' (see p. 140). But many other theoretical advances in the study of literary narrative have been powered by the work of structuralist narratologists – important work on key techniques such as Free Indirect Discourse (see p. 126), for example. However, not all attempts to transpose concepts and terms from structuralist linguistics to structuralist narratology have been successful. Take the fundamental distinction between 'langue' and 'parole'. For Saussure this was the distinction between the grammatical system that, in the minds of all speakers of a particular language, allows the generation of grammatical utterances and the recognition of non-grammatical ones (*langue*), and those specific grammatical utterances that are so generated (*parole*). Applying this to literary works has proved to be at best problematic and at worst misleading and ill-judged. (There is, to state one objection, no literary ability equivalent to linguistic native-speaker competence that allows the instant recognition of a 'non-grammatical' novel or short story.)

If structuralist narratology can be said to have been enormously productive, then, its limits and shortcomings have also inspired some narratologists to find an alternative model for narrative than structuralist linguistics. And this search for an alternative narratological model is one of the forces that has powered the shift from the linguistic paradigm to the rhetorical paradigm. Instead of the model being that of the grammar of a language as it exists in the heads of native speakers at a given time, the model is that of the persuasive (or at least considered) delivery by one person of an utterance to another person or persons – known from antiquity as the art of rhetoric.

Rhetorical narratology

A more and more commonly perceived problem with structuralist narratology has involved the terminology that it imported from structuralist linguistics, an issue that I have mentioned earlier in this book (see p. 112). The rhetorical narratologist James Phelan makes the following comment in relation to a term that he himself has proposed.

> ... I want to explain why I use the term 'character narration' rather than the more common 'first-person narration' or narratology's more specialized 'homodiegetic narration.' 'First-person narration' is, as Genette points out, insufficiently precise because any narrator, regardless of the grammatical person used to refer to the protagonist, can say 'I.' But Genette's more precise terms have not caught on beyond the field of narratology; they have simply proven to be infelicitous coinages for most other contemporary critics in the United States. (Phelan, 2005, xi)

Other structuralist-narratological terms, such as 'tense' and 'mode', have never enjoyed general acceptance in English because they are already used to express different meanings. The critic Robert Burden, writing about Joseph Conrad's *Heart of Darkness*, has, while making a set of absolutely correct and important distinctions, displayed something of the off-putting nature of the terminology of structuralist narratology.

> [T]he first [frame] narrator is *extra-diegetic* but also *homo-diegetic* (located outside the main story as narrator, while participating in it as narratee). Marlow ... is ... *intra-diegetic* and also *auto-diegetic* (located in the main story as narrator while participating in it as its central character or protagonist). (Burden, 1991, 54)

The presence of the explanatory notes in parentheses doubtless acknowledges the writer's awareness that his readers are in need of help at this point, but if use of the terms requires such glosses then one must ask whether one might not dispense with the terms altogether and use just the glosses.

However, the rise of a rhetorical narratology that, while recognizing and incorporating many of the insights and conceptual tools of structuralist narratology, has moved to supplant some of these and to build on others is not just a matter of terminology. Richard Walsh has suggested in a recent book that, in many respects, 'the structuralist enterprise is now as much a part of the history of literary theory as Russian Formalism: narratology's figuration of narrative as a language (in accordance with structuralism's linguistic paradigm) has proved unsustainable …' (Walsh, 2007, 54). The title of the book from which this comment is taken – *The Rhetoric of Fictionality: Narrative Theory and the Idea of Fiction* (2007) – makes Walsh's affiliations with a rhetorical approach clear. Walsh's funeral oration over structuralist narratology may be premature, but there is no doubt that the rise of rhetorical narratology has exposed some of the problems associated with structuralist narratology.

So what is rhetorical narratology? At bottom, one can say that whereas structuralist narratology can be understood as a *textual* approach to narrative, rhetorical narratology is a *communicative* approach to the same topic. Whereas the structuralist narratologist homes in on the text, and analyses it with little or no direct reference to the writer, the reader or the different social and cultural contexts in which these individuals have lived, written and read, the rhetorical narratologist sees the text in terms of its *mediating function* – that is to say, in terms of the ways in which it forms a link in contact between human beings living in different times and places.

In his book *Narrative as Rhetoric: Technique, Audiences, Ethics, Ideology* (1996), James Phelan asks the (rhetorical!) question: 'What does it mean to treat narrative as rhetoric?' (1). He answers this question by taking a short fiction (Katherine Anne Porter's 'Magic' [1928]) that is itself 'a narrative of rhetoric, that is, a narrative whose central event is the telling of a story' (1). He then draws attention to parallel acts: a character in the story, a maid, tells a story. As he comments, she is telling '*a particular story to a particular audience in a particular situation for, presumably, a particular purpose*' (4). But so too, he reminds us, is Katherine Anne Porter. After an extended discussion of the story and of its different levels of rhetoric, Phelan provides a summarizing comment. '[T]he phrase "narrative as rhetoric" means something more than that narrative uses rhetoric or has a rhetorical dimension. It means instead that narrative is not just story but also action, *the telling of a story by someone on some occasion to someone for some purpose*' (7–8). Narratives are designed to have some effect on readers, and readers are indeed affected by the narratives they read. Moreover, writers' purposes and readers' responses are not independent of 'occasions' – when a work is written and read, and in what situation, broadly understood.

The Canadian poet and novelist Margaret Atwood has an amusing prose poem entitled 'Murder in the Dark' in which she reminds us of the fact that authors have designs on their readers. Her title refers to the game in which a group of people are dealt out pieces of paper. All but two of these are blank, but one has a black spot on it indicating 'murderer', while another has an 'X' written on it indicating 'detective'. The lights are turned out, the murderer puts his or her hands round a victim's neck, the victim screams. At this point everyone must stand still except the murderer, who can reposition him- or herself. The lights are then switched on and the detective must, by questioning people, find out who the murderer is. Everyone must tell the truth except the murderer.

Atwood suggests a number of ways to relate this game to books, writers and readers. In one version the murderer is the writer, the detective is the reader and the victim is the book. In another, perhaps more worrying version, the murderer is the writer, the detective is the critic and the victim is the reader. It is this latter pattern that clearly appeals to Atwood, who proceeds to portray herself (the author) as hiding in the dark, with designs on the reader and with her hands reaching for the reader's neck. And she reminds her own, present, reader, that when questioned, the murderer must always lie.

'Murder in the Dark' is amusing and thought-provoking, and its perspective has a lot in common with the perspective of the rhetorical narratologist, who is always reminding us that authors and their narrators are not friendly, transparent, innocent collaborators with the reader, but are often pretending to be what they are not, misleading the reader about their motives, and never switching the lights on but forcing the reader to stumble about in the dark. Rhetorical narratologists have reminded us that just as a structuralist linguist is uninterested in meaning but is concerned with the system that makes meaning possible, so too a structuralist narratology may tell us something about the formal tools available to the writer of fiction but little or nothing about how and why these are used in a particular case, and with what effects on the reader.

How different are the results – the readings – that a rhetorical narratological approach generates from those enabled by other approaches? Let me take one example, again from James Phelan's book *Narrative as Rhetoric: Technique, Audiences, Ethics, Ideology*. In a chapter of this book on Joseph Conrad's novella *The Secret Sharer* (1910), Phelan discusses what he calls 'the homosexual secret' of (or in) this story. Conrad's tale ostensibly gives a first-person narrator's account of how, in his first voyage as a sea captain, he rescued and hid a fugitive murderer, and finally helped him to escape. In recent years a number of critics, including Phelan, have considered the possibility that the tale hints at a homoerotic or even homosexual relationship between captain-narrator and fugitive. Phelan admits that Conrad's relation to this homosexual secret is 'hard to pin down', and he comments as follows.

> If we opt for the understanding of the captain as in control of his
> narrative, we will also see Conrad as carefully in control behind the
> captain. If, however, we see the captain's revelation as unwitting, we
> may decide that Conrad has planned it that way or that Conrad himself
> is not fully aware of the homosexual subtext. In fact, articulating the
> secret and specifying the evidence for it helps to illuminate one of
> the fault lines in rhetorical reader response: the one running between

> the authorial and the flesh-and-blood audiences. On the one hand,
> the evidence points to a design on Conrad's part that the authorial
> audience needs to discern; indeed, without such a pattern of evidence,
> I would not suggest that this secret is a plausible one. On the other
> hand, I can't help wondering how much my perception of this secret is
> a consequence of my historical moment, in particular, the way in which
> the gay studies movement has made me and numerous other academic
> readers especially attuned to representations of same-sex desire. (127–8)

Note here that Phelan's approach does not abandon close attention to Conrad's
text; his skills as a close reader would satisfy the most rigorous of old-fashioned
'words-on-the-page' critics. But he extends his concern from Conrad's captain-
narrator to Conrad as author, wondering also about Conrad's conscious control
over what lies under the surface of his text (its 'subtext'). Moreover, these three
instances – author, narrator and text – are interrelated: change your view of the
level of control exerted by the author, and you may need to change your understanding of the narrator's control over *his* (or *her*) story.

Then there is the reader and his or her 'moment'. Phelan asks himself
whether what he detects in Conrad's tale is partly or wholly the product of his
own historical circumstances, including the ways in which his awareness of the
possibility of 'representations of same-sex desire' has led him to detect just such
a representation here. In this case we have come to what, in his earlier formulation, he uses the term 'occasion' to denote: here the occasion of his own reading
of Conrad's tale.

But there is yet another step to be taken, and perhaps here the most challenging aspects of a rhetorical narratology become apparent. The above-quoted
passage continues as follows.

> Is the secret constructed by the implied Conrad or the flesh-and-blood
> critic? I don't fully know. Furthermore, there is a sense in which, within
> the rhetorical approach, it is not all that important to know. When the
> situated subjectivity of the reader encounters the otherness of the text,
> the analyst cannot always definitively locate the boundaries that mark
> off flesh-and-blood and authorial audiences – or more generally, reader,
> text, and author – from each other. The synergy among these different
> elements of the rhetorical transaction is precisely what the rhetorical
> approach wants to acknowledge. (128)

It is at this point that those I have termed 'old-fashioned "words-on-the-page"
critics' would undoubtedly throw up their hands in horror. For here the 'old-
fashioned' view that a single text may be complex and resistant but can nonetheless be analysed correctly or incorrectly gives way to the text as a component
in a complex chain of mediated and creative relationships. 'Creative', because a
reading now does not just respond to what is already 'in' the text, but may insert

things in it depending upon who the reader is and what the occasion is. Whether an element is already 'in' the text – put there by the author – and whether it is inserted in the text by the critic (or, we may add, the reader), cannot be known for sure. Not only that, but as Phelan challengingly declares: 'it is not all that important to know'.

The student reader may be forgiven for responding that it may be very important 'to know' (or to pretend to know) such things in certain specific contexts: writing an examination answer, for example. The rhetorical narratologist may respond that novels and short stories are not composed in order that they should be written about in examinations, but for the pleasure and enlightenment of readers. And if the usage for which they are intended causes problems for those sitting, or grading, examinations, then this should serve to remind us that writers and readers are more important than examiners and examinees.

The literary-critical tradition

Narratology is a recent development in terms of the history of the novel and prose fiction, although those who have interested themselves in what Henry James termed 'the art of fiction' have always taken an interest in many of prose fiction's technical and formal characteristics. A concern with narrators, point of view, plot, chronology, characterization and so on did not first emerge with the development of modern narratology.

There is a sense, however, in which the differences between structuralist and rhetorical narratology can be compared to a major division in more traditional approaches to prose fiction – that between textual and contextual approaches. This is a crude distinction, but it serves as a useful starting point for considering differences in the ways that prose fiction and, to some extent, other literary genres have been studied by literary critics.

Textual approaches

Textual critics concentrate on the actual words of the novel or short story that they are studying rather than bringing what is called extrinsic information into their criticism. They thus pay little or no attention to biographical information about the author (including other writings by him or her), information about the author's society and historical period, the history of readers' responses to the novel and so on. Critics known as *formalists* take a particularly exclusivist attitude to the text. A formalist critic is one who pays great attention to the *form* of a literary work, but the term has been applied mostly to three groups of critics: the Russian and Czech formalists whose most influential work was written in the second two decades of the twentieth century, and the Anglo-American

New Critics who flourished in the 1940s and 1950s. Because the Czech formalists (often referred to as the 'Prague School') were influenced by the work of Ferdinand de Saussure there are important connections between formalism and structuralist narratology.

Russian and Czech formalism

Russian formalism developed during the First World War and lasted into the 1920s, but by 1930 antagonism from Soviet authorities had forced its most prominent members into exile. One Russian formalist, Roman Jakobson, moved first to Czechoslovakia and then to the United States, and René Wellek's migration from Prague to the United States established important lines of indirect influence from Russian and Czech formalism through to Anglo-American New Criticism.

The importance of Russian formalism for critics of the novel is that members of this critical and theoretical grouping paid serious attention to the novel, and developed an analytical terminology which has remained important. It is the Russian formalists we have to thank for the distinction between *fabula* and *sjužet* (story and plot in my terminology, see p. 140).

The Czech formalists of the 'Prague School' flourished from the late 1920s through to the German invasion of Czechoslovakia, and had less to say about prose fiction than their Russian predecessors. However, they developed certain concepts of the Russian formalists such as that of *defamiliarization*, producing their own concept of *foregrounding*, which has played a useful role in criticism of prose fiction.

New Criticism

The New Critics – to oversimplify somewhat – at least in theory rejected what they termed 'external' or 'extrinsic' information more or less *in toto*, preferring to concentrate upon 'the work itself' in relative isolation. In certain ways New Critical approaches resemble structuralist-narratological approaches: they pay little or no attention to extrinsic factors, and consider either 'literature' or a genre such as the novel as a self-enclosed system that can be studied in terms of itself. Thus, just as the New Critics argued against 'The Intentional Fallacy' of granting extratextual statements of intent any prioritized weight in interpreting that text, so too structuralist critics have followed Roland Barthes in agreeing to announce 'The Death of the Author' (see Glossary) so far as the interpretation of his or her text is concerned. In terms of method the New Critics typically use what has been called *close reading* – taking a small section of a novel or a recurrent verbal feature and analysing this in exhaustive detail, drawing attention to the sort of issues that I outlined in the checklist in Chapter 7. Because the New Critics (unlike the Russian formalists) developed their critical ideas and practices mainly in connection with the interpretation and analysis of poetry, they tended to bring to the criticism of the novel a new concern with such matters as linguistic detail, paradox, tension, irony, symbolism and so on. The title of an essay written by the New Critic Robert Heilman and first published in 1948, '"The Turn of the Screw" as Poem', can be seen to announce a representative critical trajectory.

Such critics have, by common consent, contributed enormously to our understanding of the complexity and subtlety of great works of fiction, moving us away from merely discursive discussion of plots and characters and demonstrating that the novel is as receptive to detailed analysis as is poetry. Chapter 6 in the present book, 'Analysing Fiction', could not have been written without the work of such critics. The analytical methods of structuralist narratologists also owe a considerable debt to the New Critics. Jonathan Culler summed up this debt in 1981 when he admitted that '[w]hatever critical affiliations we may proclaim, we are all New Critics, in that it requires a strenuous effort to escape notions of the autonomy of the literary work, the importance of demonstrating its unity, and the requirement of "close reading"' (1981, 3).

Post structuralism and deconstruction

For the purpose of a brief survey such as this, 'post-structuralism' and 'deconstruction' will be treated as synonymous. However, certain usages distinguish between the two terms in important ways and make post-structuralism a more general position of which deconstruction represents one possible variant.

Again, to simplify, we can say that post-structuralism extends and even universalizes the structuralist assumption that no element in a system of meaning has significance in and for itself but only as part of the system. If this is so, then there are (or should be) no elements in any text whose fixity of meaning can be used as a foundation stone or interpretative bedrock. Jacques Derrida, the French high priest of deconstruction, called such a desired point of stability in the swirl of meanings generated by the play between the different components of the system a *transcendental signified*, in other words an element that has meaning in and for itself rather than a meaning that is defined by relations to other elements. For Derrida, meaning is always relational, and thus when he, famously (or infamously), declared that there was nothing outside of the text, he was arguing that there was no such fixed, extratextual point by reference to which the meaning of a text could be plotted and fixed.

Deconstructionists are accordingly committed to the unweaving of apparently firm and solid interpretations through a display of the way in which such interpretations rely upon such a transcendental signified. Examples of such transcendental signifieds in the criticism of the novel would be such things as 'the intended meaning of the author', 'how contemporary readers read the work', 'what the work means to a competent reader' and so on. In practice, deconstructionist readings very often involve dispensing with such traditional critical points of reference as these, and responding to the work in a way that is unconstrained by them.

At an early stage in undergraduate study such post-structuralist readings are either terrifying or exhilarating or both. The terror can be reduced by noting that post-structuralist readings often rely upon relatively simple processes of de- or recontextualization of a work or an element in a work, playing with the interpretations that can be generated once the work or the passage is unhooked from a fixed textual or other context that restricts its possible meanings. The exhilaration can be eye-opening, revealing how our readings and responses are often channelled into familiar paths by reliance upon familiar but unregarded anchor points.

Contextual approaches

If the most valuable aspect of the work of textual critics has been their development of sophisticated methods of detailed critical analysis, the aspect of their work which has gone least unchallenged by others has been their rejection or playing down of 'extrinsic' information as an adjunct to the reading and criticism of literature.

Socio-historical approaches

Sociological and historical critics have placed great stress upon the need to understand the context of the author's own society and his or her position within it, both as an individual (a member of a particular social group or class) and as an author (a member of a literary group, relying on certain publishers, libraries, readers and so on).

Let us return to Joseph Conrad's *Heart of Darkness*. Recent critics have suggested that the novella can only be fully appreciated in the context of what European powers were doing in Africa in the last part of the nineteenth century, and in particular in the context of statements made by prominent Belgians – including King Leopold II – concerning the Belgian exploitation of the Congo (in which Conrad himself had worked). Thus some of Leopold's statements concerning the (extremely brutal) Belgian exploitation of the Congo include comments about opening to civilization the only part of our globe where Christianity has not penetrated, and piercing 'the darkness which envelops the entire population'. Conrad's ironic use of words such as 'civilization' and 'darkness' in the novella, it has been argued, can only fully be appreciated in the light of his aim to mock and expose statements such as Leopold's.

Some contextual critics argue that more than this is needed. The narrative indirection in the novella – Marlow's inability to tell the truth to Kurtz's

'Intended' and his feeling that he cannot make himself understood to his auditors – mirrors a situation in which comfortable Europeans who had never witnessed colonial brutality at first hand in Africa were unable to hear the truth spoken by such as Marlow. This argument raises some problems in its turn. Conrad deliberately left out localizing information such as the name of the European country or the part of Africa in which the novella was set, and with regard to his short story 'Youth', he made it clear that he very much objected to having such information reinserted (Curle, 1928, 297). Novelists themselves tend, like Conrad, to be suspicious of critics who fill in background information claimed to be relevant to their works. Asked whether it is important to know the history of Czechoslovakia to understand his novels, Milan Kundera replied: 'No. Whatever needs to be known of it the novel itself tells' (Kundera, 1988, 39). Key issues to be confronted are: does the information point to material that had a *determining* effect on the writing of the work? What information is *relevant*?

Sociological critics have also drawn attention to the important influence that factors referred to collectively as the 'sociology of literature' can have on the creation of works of literature: publishers, patronage (see Glossary), literacy rates, readership profiles, libraries, booksellers and so on. It is clear that if only a part of society is literate and thus able to read novels, then this will affect the sort of novels that are written – as was the case in eighteenth-century England. If the habit of listening to novels read aloud by a friend or family member becomes customary in a society, this will alter the importance of the fact that many members of that society are illiterate. If success as a novelist depends upon having your work accepted by the circulating libraries, and these do not accept anything that does not conform to a set of rigidly moralistic views, then the reader should know this before expressing dissatisfaction with the portrayal of sexual relationships in a novel – and should also be on the lookout for concealed hints and suggestions!

Cultural materialism and New Historicism

Cultural materialist and New Historicist critics allow some of the insights (or claims) of post-structuralism concerning the difficulty or impossibility of confronting or interrogating reality other than through texts of some sort, while retaining a degree of what we can call a realist commitment – a belief that reality is not just texts or closed systems of meaning. New Historicists typically juxtapose literary and non-literary texts in ways that produce unexpected and frequently highly illuminating flashes of insight. Cultural materialists are especially interested in following the life of literary works through successive ages and varied cultures, and often responses to and interpretations of a literary work are as much of interest to them as is 'the work itself'. It has to be said, however, that up to now these critics have paid proportionately less attention to the novel than to other literary genres.

Postcolonial theory

The field of postcolonial theory is fashionable, fast-growing and riven with debates. At its best it has confronted readers and critics with the hidden or unstated implications of colonial and imperialist relations between lands and people for the reading and interpretation of literary works. Thus my earlier discussion of the way in which Jean Rhys's *Wide Sargasso Sea* interrogates Charlotte Brontë's *Jane Eyre* owes much to the new perspectives brought to literary and cultural criticism by postcolonialism. A key text is Edward Said's *Orientalism* (1978), which attempted to describe how Western domination of subject lands required not just physical force but also a discourse, a system of ideas by which European culture was able to manage and even to produce 'the Orient' for itself.

Following Said's example, many writers attempted to use the vantage point of a period after colonialism ('post' colonialism) to interrogate literature written both during and after the classic forms of colonialism, and also to draw attention to the silenced voices of those who wrote from the standpoint of the oppressed.

This much is unproblematic – but much else is not. Earlier in this book (p. 43) I made reference to Ngũgĩ Wa Thiong'o's dedication of his novel *Devil on the Cross* 'To all Kenyans struggling against the neo-colonial stage of imperialism'. If there are such things as neo-colonialism and imperialism, is not the 'post' in postcolonialism a little optimistic? Does it refer to a historical or merely a mental and ideological supersession of colonialism? If Australia and the United States are just as much postcolonial countries as are Kenya and India, then is not the term in danger of becoming so all-embracing that it loses any effective specificity? Many have pointed out that the term has become very popular precisely because few objections to it are raised in the academy: it avoids sensitive words such as 'imperialism' and it raises the topic of colonialism only to suggest that all that is safely in the past.

Generic approaches

A genre is a type or kind of literature, and we often refer to prose fiction itself as one of the three main literary genres, along with poetry and drama. There are many different ways to classify literature generically, and the novel has been divided into a number of sub-genres by various critics – the gothic novel, the epistolary novel, the postmodern novel and so on. Note that these generic divisions involve different sorts of category: there is no single set of principles that are available for dividing novels into sub-genres, and as a result a single novel can usually be classified in more than one way.

A generic approach to prose fiction insists that we cannot begin to read or understand a novel until we are clear as to what sort of novel it is. This typically means getting clear about the author's intentions with regard to his or her work, although it can also involve seeing how successive generations of readers have classified a work. Thus – the argument goes – unless we understand the picaresque tradition (see the Glossary) within which Defoe's *Moll Flanders* is written, we will run the danger of misreading and misunderstanding this novel.

I list this under 'Contextual approaches' because a genre is a sort of context: it helps us to understand the aims of a writer and the expectations of readers, to recognize conventional elements as well as divergences from what is conventional. Obtaining a better understanding of a work's generic associations can often be one of the most useful benefits of reading critics.

Biographical approaches

A writer's life is also a sort of context. The more books by the same novelist that we read, the more we become conscious of common or similar elements in them (as well as of contrasts, new directions, surprise variations), and the more we begin to build up a picture of the man or woman behind the printed text, constructing an idea of his or her values, interests and attitudes. We can, in short, start to use the life as a sort of explanatory context for the work.

Such an interest in an author can lead us to want to know more about the person in question in his or her own right, and then we may start to read the novels in the light of what we have learned about the author – even in terms of what he or she has said about them explicitly. Such a biographical approach to the study of the novel – reading fictional works with explicit reference to the life, personality and opinions of the author – seems straightforward enough, yet it is fraught with problems and has involved many sharp debates. In a piece entitled 'The Spirit of Place', D.H. Lawrence advised: 'Never trust the artist. Trust the tale' (Beale, 1961, 297), and generations of critics have pointed out that novelists can be very bad guides to their own work.

Why should this be so? We can isolate a number of possible explanations. First, there is the issue of *inspiration*. The writer seems often not to use the conscious and rational part of his or her mind for literary composition – something that has been appreciated since the days of antiquity when a term equivalent to 'inspiration' was first used. As a result, secrets of the created work may not be accessible to the rational, enquiring mind in the same way that details of other actions and utterances are. Second, the author may want actually to *conceal* something: a real-life model, a confessional element in the work or whatever. Third, the author may comment on his or her work a very long time after writing it.

When it is a matter of relating a novelist's work to his or her life, similar problems may emerge. How do we know which experiences in a writer's life were reflected (or transformed) in his or her work? Experiences which seem minor to us may have been crucial to the person who had them – but, even so, they may not have influenced the writing of a given work.

If all this sounds like a counsel of despair I should add that it is not meant to be. Biographical information can be of very great help in enabling us to respond more fully to a novel or a short story. However, we should be fully aware of the problems involved in such critical procedures, and we need always to be sensitive to what the work itself can tell us.

Take D.H. Lawrence's novel *Women in Love*. It seems very likely that Lawrence's experiences in the period of the First World War had a crucial effect on the writing of this novel even though the war is not mentioned at all in it (in spite of the fact that it was written in the middle of these experiences). Lawrence was medically unfit for service in the war, and came under suspicion from the authorities for his anti-war views and because his wife Frieda (*née* von Richthofen) was the cousin of 'the Red Baron' – a man notorious for shooting down scores of British aeroplanes. Lawrence and Frieda were even forced to leave their cottage on the Cornish coast, allegedly because they were suspected of signalling to German U-boats. Now although none of this is directly referred to in *Women in Love*, it is arguable that much of the tone of that novel – in particular its dismissive remarks about England – can only be fully understood in the light of these experiences of Lawrence's. Moreover, the comments in the novel by Birkin about the destructiveness of the 'mechanical principle' have, too, to be seen in the context of Lawrence's complex responses to the slaughter of the war – a slaughter that is not mentioned directly in the novel at all.

Psychological and psychoanalytic approaches

In broad terms the distinction between psychology and psychoanalysis is that between theories of how the mind functions and theories of how the secrets of the mind can be unlocked through analysis. The question is then: which mind – the author's, the reader's or a character's? Let us again consider Henry James's novella *The Turn of the Screw*. A succession of critics have attempted to psycho-analyse the governess in this tale, finding evidence of mental instability of a sort that leads her to hallucinate and to imagine the ghosts that she reports on to the reader. But given James's clearly reported intention to make the reader 'think the evil' in this tale, it is possible to concentrate on the way in which readers and crit-ics have responded to and interpreted the work, and to thus use the *work* as a way of analysing *readers*. (Compare the way in which the Rorschach 'ink-blot test' is used; the interpretive responses of different individuals to the same 'blot' are used to tell us something about these individuals rather than anything about the blot itself, which is normally possessed of an appropriately Jamesian ambiguity.) Finally, it is possible to use James's novella as a way of psychoanalysing James himself, and there is no shortage of critics who have attempted to do just this.

Certain short stories and novellas have been much used by psychological and psychoanalytic critics: Sigmund Freud wrote an influential essay on E.T.A. Hoffmann's 'uncanny' tale 'The Sandman', while Marie Bonaparte's study of the tales of Edgar Allan Poe remains much-quoted. More recently Jacques Lacan's analysis of Poe's 'The Purloined Letter' has confirmed the American writer's work as a richly seamed mine waiting for psychoanalytical excavation.

Children's literature, fairy tales and folktales have also provided material for analysis by writers such as Bruno Bettelheim. Generally speaking, though, psychological and psychoanalytical criticism has had most impact on criticism of the longer novel through incorporation in other approaches, such as those of feminism and deconstruction.

Ideological approaches

I choose the word 'ideological' for want of a better one, but I recognize that the problem with it is that it has a pejorative ring, suggesting narrow-mindedness and a lack of impartiality. These suggestions are not intended: all that I want to imply by my choice of this word is that certain critical schools and approaches carry with them an overt and conscious commitment to ideas, values, systems of belief that generally have a wider scope than the purely literary. Putting the matter crudely, knowing that a critic is a narratologist or a psychoanalytic critic does not help us to work out how they would vote or whether they are in favour of equal rights for men and women, whereas knowing that a critic calls him- or herself a feminist does give us information that may be relevant to an enquiry into such questions.

'Ideological' schools and approaches are often accused of imposing beliefs and positions onto innocent and resisting literary works, and there is no doubt that such accusations are sometimes justified. On the other hand, an ideologically committed critical approach may just as well illuminate something in a novel or a short story that has gone unnoticed by more seemingly impartial critics. In my personal opinion, for example, much criticism that can loosely be associated with Queer Theory (see p. 216) has indubitably revealed aspects of the work of canonical writers that have lain undiscovered for many years, and much the same can certainly be argued about feminist criticism.

Marxist approaches

Like sociological critics, Marxist critics are interested in relating literary works to the societies in which they were written. Marxism is a materialist philosophy, one which insists upon the primacy of material living conditions rather than ideas or beliefs in the life of human beings. It sees history as, in Marx's words, 'the history of class struggle' – the history of struggle for control of the material conditions upon which life rests. It is on the basis of these material conditions, and in response to the struggle for them, that ideas, philosophies, mental pictures of the world develop – as secondary phenomena. These secondary phenomena may provide human beings with an accurate picture of reality, including themselves and their situation, but they may not. Ideologies are all related to class positions and thus, in turn, to material conditions and the struggle for their control, but this is not to say that they provide a reliable picture of these. Traditional Marxists have laid great stress upon the distinction between base (or basis) and superstructure, seeing the social base as essentially economic in nature, and the superstructure as constituting the world of mental activities – ideas, beliefs, philosophies, and (in the opinion of some but not all Marxists) art and literature.

Marxists have been particularly interested in the novel because the novel can be argued to have emerged in response to a changed social situation and to the needs of an emergent class – the bourgeoisie created by the capitalist system that replaced feudalism. The Hungarian Marxist Georg Lukács, who remains an important critic of the novel, clearly also values the novel because of its association with realism, an association that holds out the promise of finding accurate rather than distorted analyses of social structures within realist (or 'classical') novels. More generally it seems clear that the novel typically (although not inevitably) raises issues concerning the relationship between the individual and society in a more historically detailed and specific way than do poetry or drama.

Feminist approaches

Over seventy years ago Virginia Woolf's extended essay *A Room of One's Own* (1929) startled many readers by claiming that they lived in a patriarchy and that this fact conditioned the ways in which novels were written (or not written) and read. In more recent years a growing number of feminist critics have offered challenging accounts of the novel in general and of particular novels. Feminist critics have argued that not only have women had to overcome severe difficulties to become writers, but also that once they have produced novels, these have consistently been read in dismissive ways by male readers. Thus once a woman had managed to become literate (no easy matter in the past), she had to overcome all sorts of male prejudices in the reception accorded to her work. As Virginia Woolf expresses it in *A Room of One's Own*, 'This is an important book, the critic assumes, because it deals with war. This is an insignificant book because it deals with the feelings of women in a drawing-room.' Moreover, as Woolf points out, it may be difficult for a woman to write about such things as war because of the domestic role to which she has been confined, and she declares that a woman could not have written *War and Peace*.

Feminist critics have also done much to show the ways in which male views of reality have dominated much fiction – especially, of course, that by men, and especially their views of women. Women are typically portrayed *in relation to men*, and are often seen in certain stereotyped ways – as passive, hysterical, emotional, 'bitch' or 'goddess'. Thus it seems fair to say that it is only as a result of the efforts of feminist critics in recent years that the portrayal of women in D.H. Lawrence's major novels has been interrogated and criticized, and that the work of many other authors have been looked at with eyes more open to gender differences.

One of the works which introduced the new wave of feminist literary criticism was Kate Millett's *Sexual Politics*, first published in 1970. Millett's book is divided into three connected sections: 'Sexual Politics', giving a theoretical basis for what follows; a section on the historical background detailing the movements towards female emancipation and those seeking to reverse their effects; and finally a section entitled 'The Literary Reflection'. In this final section Millett looks at the work of D.H. Lawrence, Henry Miller, Norman Mailer and Jean Genet. In the writing of all of these she detects what we now familiarly refer to as patriarchal ideas – frequently linked to portrayals that debase, ridicule and humiliate women. The following comments on Lawrence's *Lady Chatterley's Lover* are representative:

> In *Lady Chatterley*, as throughout his final period, Lawrence uses the
> word 'sexual' and 'phallic' interchangeably, so that the celebration of
> sexual passion for which the book is so renowned is largely a celebration
> of the penis of Oliver Mellors, gamekeeper and social prophet. While
> insisting his mission is the noble and necessary task of freeing sexual
> behavior of perverse inhibition, purging the fiction which describes it
> of prurient or prudish euphemism, Lawrence is really the evangelist
> of quite another cause – 'phallic consciousness'. This is far less
> a matter of 'the resurrection of the body', 'natural love', or other
> slogans under which it has been advertised, than the transformation of
> masculine ascendancy into a mystical religion, international, possibly
> institutionalized. (1971, 238)

Millett's book is a fine piece of polemic, and one which jolted both men and women into reconsidering various canonical authors from previously unconsidered perspectives.

A variety of feminist criticism which believes 'gendering' to take place at a fundamental level concerns itself with what, using a French term, is termed *écriture féminine* – 'feminine writing'. Theorists of *écriture féminine* believe that men and women use language in fundamentally different ways, and that the task of the feminist critic is to give women writers the self-confidence to write as their femaleness requires, and not to ape the writing habits and style of men. As the term suggests, the concept in its modern form has originated in France, especially in the writing of Hélène Cixous. It has, however, antecedents and parallels outside France, and it is interesting in this context to see how many of the recent formulations about 'writing and the body' have parallels in Virginia Woolf's essay 'Professions for Women' (first published in 1942).

A further task undertaken by feminist critics has been that of the 'rediscovery' or reinstatement of a number of (mainly women) writers whose works have been undervalued or forgotten.

Ecocriticism

A relatively new development, ecocriticism is less than half a century old. As the name suggests, its concern is with the relationship between literature and our changing physical environment. This concern includes, most obviously, depictions of the physical environment in literature. But it also includes the ways in which ideas of nature are preserved and disseminated in and by literary works. The tradition of portraying a nature that has been ravaged by human beings is not just a recent one; Richard Jefferies's *After London, or Wild England* (1886) is a strikingly modern-seeming account of a London that has been abandoned by human beings following some unspecified catastrophe and that is being recolonized by non-human nature. Behind Jefferies's portrayal, of course, is a polemic against what human beings have done to nature and, indirectly, to themselves.

Much literature, of course, has used comparisons and contracts involving humanity and nature to make points about humanity; the new force of ecocriticism is that while it clearly includes the condition and fate of humanity in its agenda, it is also interested in the fate and condition of nature for its own sake.

Queer Theory

If Marxist criticism has sought to expose hidden links with class or economic interests in novels and short stories, Queer Theory attempts to expose different sorts of concealed or disguised elements in literary works. Although 'queer' was originally used as a term of abuse to stereotype homosexuals, it has now been reclaimed by gay men and women and used to express pride in their sexual identity.

Since the legalization of homosexuality in Britain, the United States and many other societies, it has been possible to write far more openly about issues of sexual orientation. This, combined with the fact that many writers in the past have not enjoyed this freedom, has meant that criticism aimed at exposing gay subtexts in the works of canonical writers has flourished in the course of recent decades. When I was an undergraduate studying English in the 1960s, no one mentioned the fact that E.M. Forster was homosexual, and no one considered the extent to which this might have a bearing on the novels that he wrote. Today this is a factor that is hard not to take into account in reading and responding to Forster's novels, and this shift of reading perspective has illuminated aspects of these novels that had previously gone unregarded.

On a rather more sophisticated level, Queer Theorists have done much to destabilize our sense of the fixity of gender divisions – partly by drawing attention to the sort of gender destabilization that can be traced in important novels and short stories. Much very important recent work on the fiction of Henry James is of this sort, and goes far beyond the treatment of James's tales and novels as a sort of homoerotic *roman à clef* (see the Glossary). Instead, the binary gender divisions fixed by social convention are seen to match up very imperfectly with the personal gender preferences and identities of James's characters, while the interplay of gender, class and culture can be traced in the convolutions of Jamesian narrative. Here for example is a passage from James's short story 'The Death of the Lion' (1894). In this story, the narrator discovers that a newspaper journalist named Guy Walsingham is actually a woman, while one named Dora Forbes is referred to as 'he'.

> I was bewildered; it sounded somehow as if there were three sexes.
> My interlocutor's pencil was poised, my private responsibility great.
> I simply sat staring, none the less, and only found presence of mind
> to say: 'Is this Miss Forbes a gentleman?'
>   Mr Morrow had a subtle smile. 'It wouldn't be "Miss" – there's a wife!'
>   'I mean is she a man?'
>   'The wife?' – Mr Morrow was for a moment as confused as myself.
> But when I explained that I alluded to Dora Forbes in person he
> informed me, with visible amusement at my being so out of it, that
> this was the 'pen-name' of an indubitable male – he had a big red
> moustache.

While not rejecting a more traditional reading that sees this and comparable passages as examples of James's whimsical humour, Queer Theorists have shown how effectively (and, I think, deliberately) they chip away at a conventional sense that the sexual diversity of the human race can be neatly divided into two standard genders.

Topics for discussion

- ↤ Are the most useful critics the ones who share your own beliefs and opinions?
- ↤ 'If I want to quote a critic, should I say something about his or her theoretical position? How do I find out what it is?'
- ↤ When two critics disagree about a novel, how are we expected to decide who is right?
- ↤ Is 'close reading' an unnatural way to deal with a novel or short story?
- ↤ 'I always want to find out more about the author, but my lecturer disapproves of this approach.'

Timeline of the novel

The following list includes the dates of birth and death of major figures connected to the novel. It also lists key works of fiction, key critical studies and significant public events. Titles of novels are those by which they are commonly known – thus *Gulliver's Travels* rather than *Travels into Several Remote Nations of the World, in Four Parts, by Lemuel Gulliver, first a Surgeon, and then a Captain of several Ships*. Unless otherwise stated, publication dates are for first book publication in the original language. The list is inevitably selective, and to a certain extent anglocentric. It is included to provide readers with a general sense of 'what was happening' and 'who was active' from year to year. Those looking for more detailed biographical or encyclopaedic information should consult specialist sources.

c. 1494 — François Rabelais born
1508 — *Amadis de Gaula* (first known printed edition published in Zaragoza)
1532 — François Rabelais, *Pantagruel* (followed in 1534 by *Gargantua*)
1547 — Miguel de Cervantes (Miguel de Cervantes Saavedra) born
1553 — François Rabelais dies
1594 — Thomas Nashe, *The Unfortunate Traveller*
1597 — Thomas Deloney, *Jack of Newberry*
1605 — Miguel de Cervantes, *Don Quixote* (Part 1; Part 2 followed in 1615)
1616 — Miguel de Cervantes dies
1628 — John Bunyan born
1640 — ? Aphra Behn born
1662 — Cyrano de Bergerac, *Voyages to the Moon and the Sun*

1678 — John Bunyan, *The Pilgrim's Progress* (Part 1; Part 2 followed in 1684)

1688 — John Bunyan dies; Aphra Behn, *Oroonoko, or The Royal Slave*

1689 — Samuel Richardson born; Ahra Behn dies

1703 — Daniel Defoe sentenced to stand in the pillory, largely because of his ironic pamphlet 'The Shortest Way with the Dissenters'

1707 — Henry Fielding born

1713 — Laurence Sterne born

1715 — Alain-René Lesage, *Gil Blas*

1719 — Daniel Defoe, *Robinson Crusoe*

1721 — Tobias Smollett born

1722 — Defoe, *Moll Flanders*

1726 — Jonathan Swift, *Gulliver's Travels*

1731 — L'Abbé Prévost, *Manon Lescaut*

1740 — Samuel Richardson, *Pamela*

1742 — Henry Fielding, *Joseph Andrews*

1748 — Samuel Richardson, *Clarissa Harlowe*; Tobias Smollett, *Roderick Random*

1749 — Johann Wolfgang von Goethe born; Henry Fielding, *Tom Jones*

1750 — Johnson's *Rambler* essay number 4 on the 'works of fiction, with which the present generation seems more particularly delighted'

1752 — Frances Burney born

1754 — Henry Fielding dies

1760–7 — Laurence Sterne, *Tristram Shandy*

1761 — Samuel Richardson dies

1768 — Laurence Sterne dies

1771 — (Sir) Walter Scott born; Tobias Smollett dies

1774 — Johann von Goethe, *The Sorrows of Young Werther*

1775 — Jane Austen born

1782 — Frances Burney, *Cecilia*

1794 — Ann Radcliffe, *The Mysteries of Udolpho*

1804 — Nathaniel Hawthorne (Hathorne) born

1812 — Charles Dickens born

1813 — Jane Austen, *Pride and Prejudice* (the title of which Austen took from a passage towards the end of Frances Burney's *Cecilia*)

1816 — Charlotte Brontë born

1817 — Jane Austen dies

1818 — Emily Brontë born; Mary Shelley, *Frankenstein*

1819 — George Eliot (Mary Ann, or Marian, Evans) born

1820 — Sir Walter Scott, *Ivanhoe*

1821 — Fyodor Mikhaylovich Dostoyevsky born

1830 — Stendhal (Henri-Marie Beyle), *The Red and the Black*

1832 — Sir Walter Scott dies

1835 — Mark Twain (Samuel Langhorne Clemens) born

1837 — Charles Dickens, *The Pickwick Papers*

1839 — Edgar Allen Poe, 'The Fall of the House of Usher'

1840 — Frances Burney dies; Thomas Hardy born

1842 — Johann Wolfgang von Goethe dies; Nicolai Gogol, *Dead Souls*; Alessandro Manzoni *The Betrothed*. A London bookshop opened by Charles Edward Mudie in 1840 starts to lend rather than sell books, and 'Mudie's Lending Library' is born

1843 — Henry James born

1846 — Herman Melville, *Typee*

1847 — Emily Brontë, *Wuthering Heights*, Anne Brontë, *Agnes Grey* and Charlotte Brontë, *Jane Eyre* are all published pseudonymously (Ellis Bell, Acton Bell and Currer Bell)

1847–8 — William Makepeace Thackeray, *Vanity Fair*

1849 — Emily Brontë dies

1850 — Robert Louis Stevenson born; Nathaniel Hawthorne, *The Scarlet Letter*; Charles Dickens, *David Copperfield*

1851 — Herman Melville, *Moby Dick*

1855 — Charlotte Brontë dies

1857 — Joseph Conrad (Józef Teodor Konrad Korzeniowski) born; Gustave Flaubert, *Madame Bovary*. Unsuccessfully prosecuted in France, for obscenity

1859 — Charles Darwin, *On the Origin of Species*

1860 — George Eliot, *The Mill on the Floss*

1860–1 — Charles Dickens, *Great Expectations*

1861–5 — American Civil War

1864 — Nathaniel Hawthorne dies

1865 — Lewis Carroll, *Alice's Adventures in Wonderland*

1865–72 — Leo Tolstoy, *War and Peace*

1866 — Fyodor Dostoyevsky, *Crime and Punishment*

1870 — Charles Dickens dies; Jules Verne, *Twenty Thousand Leagues under the Sea*

1872 — George Eliot, *Middlemarch*; Thomas Hardy, *Under the Greenwood Tree*

1873 — Ford Madox Ford (Ford Hermann Hueffer) born

1874 — Thomas Hardy, *Far from the Madding Crowd*

1875–6 — Leo Tolstoy, *Anna Karenina*

1876 — Mark Twain, *The Adventures of Tom Sawyer*

1879 — E.M. Forster born

1880 — Fyodor Dostoyevsky, *The Brothers Karamazov*

1881 — Fyodor Dostoyevsky dies; Henry James, *The Portrait of a Lady*

1882 — James Joyce born; Virginia Woolf born

1883 — Franz Kafka born; Robert Louis Stevenson, *Treasure Island*

1884 — Henry James, 'The Art of Fiction'; Mark Twain, *Huckleberry Finn*

1885 — D.H. Lawrence born; Guy de Maupassant, *Bel-Ami*

1888 — Katherine Mansfield (Kathleen Mansfield Beauchamp) born

1890 — Jean Rhys (Ella Gwendolyn Rees Williams) born; George Eliot dies; Knut Hamsun, *Hunger*

1891 — Thomas Hardy, *Tess of the D'Urbervilles*

1892 — Arthur Conan Doyle, *The Adventures of Sherlock Holmes*

1894 — Robert Louis Stevenson dies; Stephen Crane, *The Red Badge of Courage*

1895 — Mikhail Mikhailovich Bakhtin born; H.G. Wells, *The Time Machine*

1896 — F. Scott Fitzgerald born

1897 — William Faulkner born

1898 — Henry James, *The Turn of the Screw*

1899 — Ernest Miller Hemingway born

1900 — Joseph Conrad, *Lord Jim*

1901 — Lewis Grassic Gibbon (James Leslie Mitchell) born

1902 — Joseph Conrad, *Heart of Darkness*

1905 — Edith Wharton, *The House of Mirth*

1910 — Mark Twain dies

1913 — D.H. Lawrence, *Sons and Lovers*

1913–27 — Marcel Proust, *A la recherche du temps perdu*

1914 — James Joyce, *Dubliners*; Robert Tressell (Robert Noonan), *The Ragged Trousered Philanthropists* published in expurgated form, first complete edition 1955

1914–18 — First World War

1915 — Franz Kafka, 'The Metamorphosis'; D.H. Lawrence, *The Rainbow*, published then seized by the police and banned by court order, unavailable in Britain for the following 11 years

1916 — Henry James dies

1917 — Russian revolution

1919 — Virginia Woolf, 'Modern Novels' published in the *Times Literary Supplement*. Published in revised form as 'Modern Fiction' in 1925

1920 — The New York Society for the Suppression of Vice initiates a prosecution of a literary magazine for publishing the 'Nausicaa' section of James Joyce's *Ulysses* (the book is banned in USA until 1933); Georg Lukács, *Theory of the Novel* published in German, English translation 1971

1921 — Percy Lubbock, *The Craft of Fiction*

1922 — James Joyce, *Ulysses*

1923 — Katherine Mansfield dies

1924 — Franz Kafka dies; Joseph Conrad dies; Virginia Woolf, 'Mr Bennett and Mrs Brown' read as a paper at Cambridge; E.M. Forster, *A Passage to India*

1925 — Franz Kafka, *The Trial*; Virginia Woolf, *Mrs. Dalloway*

1927 — E.M. Forster's *Aspects of the Novel*; Jean Rhys, *The Left Bank and Other Stories*

1928 — Thomas Hardy dies

1929 — William Faulkner, *The Sound and the Fury*

1930 — D.H. Lawrence dies

1933 — US Customs seize copies of James Joyce's *Ulysses* that the publisher Random House is attempting to import. In a subsequent trial the novel is found not to contravene the obscenity laws and can be published in USA

1935 — Lewis Grassic Gibbon dies; Christopher Isherwood, *Mr Norris Changes Trains*

1936 — Walter Benjamin, 'The Storyteller: Reflections on the Works of Nikolei Leskov'

1937 — Georg Lukács, *The Historical Novel*, published in Russian 1937. English translation 1962

1938 — Ngũgĩ wa Thiong'o (James Ngugi) born

1939 — Ford Madox Ford dies; James Joyce, *Finnegans Wake*

1939–45 — Second World War

1940 — F. Scott Fitzgerald dies; Angela Carter born; Richard Wright, *Native Son*; Ernest Hemingway, *For Whom the Bell Tolls*

1941 — James Joyce dies; Virginia Woolf dies

1942 — Albert Camus, *The Outsider* (also translated as *The Stranger*)

1945 — George Orwell, *Animal Farm*

1947 — Ahmed Salman Rushdie born

1948 — Ian McEwan born; F.R. Leavis, *The Great Tradition*. Included in Leavis's great tradition are Jane Austen, George Eliot, Henry James and Joseph Conrad; excluded are Sterne, Hardy and Dickens, although Dickens is granted belated recognition in *Dickens the Novelist* (1970), co-written with his wife Q.D. Leavis

1949 — George Orwell, *1984*

1951 — Hanif Kureishi born

1955 — Alain Robbe-Grillet, *The Voyeur*

1957 — Ian Watt, *The Rise of the Novel*

1958 — Chinua Achebe, *Things Fall Apart*

1959 — Jeanette Winterson born

1960 — Trial of Penguin Books for having published D.H. Lawrence's *Lady Chatterley's Lover*. The 'not guilty' verdict allows the book to be published legally in Britain for the first time since its Italian publication in 1928, and heralds a relaxation of the laws governing obscenity

1961 — Ernest Hemingway dies; Wayne C. Booth, *The Rhetoric of Fiction*

1962 — William Faulkner dies

1966 — Jean Rhys, *Wide Sargasso Sea*

1969 — Maya Angelou, *I Know Why the Caged Bird Sings*; Philip Roth, *Portnoy's Complaint*

1970 — E.M. Forster dies

1975 — Mikhail Bakhtin dies

1979 — Jean Rhys dies; Sandra M. Gilbert and Susan Gubar, *The Madwoman in the Attic*

1980 — Gérard Genette, *Narrative Discourse: An Essay in Method* published in English (first published in French as a part of *Figures III* in 1972)

1981 — Mikhail Bakhtin's *The Dialogic Imagination*, containing four essays, introduces Bakhtin's ideas on the novel to the English-speaking world; Salman Rushdie, *Midnight's Children*

1982 — Ann Banfield, *Unspeakable Sentences: Narration and Representation in the Language of Fiction*

1983 — Alice Walker, *The Color Purple*

1987 — Toni Morrison, *Beloved*

1988 — Salman Rushdie, *The Satanic Verses*

1989 (14 February) — 'Fatwah' demanding Salman Rushdie's death proclaimed on Radio Tehran by Ayatollah Ruhollah Khomeini, the spiritual leader of Iran, in response to the 'blasphemous' *The Satanic Verses*

1992 — Angela Carter dies

1999 — J.M. Coetzee, *Disgrace*

Glossary of terms

Where terms have been defined and discussed in earlier chapters, I limit entries to a brief comment and a cross-reference to the relevant page(s). Cross-references within the Glossary are indicated by the use of small capitals. To avoid repetition, terms such as 'novel', 'short story' and 'fiction' are not cross-referenced.

Achronicity/achrony ↦ Achronicity is a state in which temporal relationships cannot be established; applied to a NARRATIVE it implies the impossibility of establishing an accurate chronology of EVENTs. An achrony is an event in a narrative which cannot be located on a precise time scale, and cannot be temporally related to other events in the narrative.

Anachrony ↦ Also, following Bal (1985), *chronological deviation*. Any lack of fit between the order in which EVENTs are presented in the PLOT or *sjužet*, and that in which they are reported in the story or *fabula*, is termed an anachrony. Both analepsis and prolepsis are examples of anachrony. See also STORY AND PLOT.

Bal isolates two sorts of anachrony: *punctual anachrony*, when only one instant from the past or future is evoked, and *durative anachrony*, when a longer span of time or a more general situation is evoked.

Analepsis and prolepsis ↦ Both terms denote a divergence from strict chronological sequence in a NARRATIVE. An analepsis (otherwise flashback) moves out of the present of STORY-time to describe or evoke something from the 'past' of the story being told. A prolepsis (or anticipation, or flashforward) moves out of the present of story-time to describe or evoke something from the 'future' of the story being told.

225

Anisochrony ↔ See ISOCHRONY.

Anti-novel ↔ A now outdated term used in the mid-twentieth century to describe experimental fiction that frustrated reader expectations by refusing to conform to accepted conventions – often by containing self-contradictions which could not be resolved by the reader. Compare *NOUVEAU ROMAN*.

Bildungsroman ↔ The German term *Bildungsroman* is now generally used in English to denote that sort of novel which concentrates upon one CHARACTER's development from early youth to some sort of maturity. Goethe's *Wilhelm Meister's Apprenticeship* (1795–6), Dickens's *David Copperfield* (1849–50) and James Joyce's *Portrait of the Artist as a Young Man* (1916) can all be described as examples of the *Bildungsroman*.

This type of novel clearly attracts the writer interested in depicting the close relationship between early influences and later character development, and its emergence can be related to the growing interest in the THEME that 'the child is father to the man' that accompanies the late eighteenth- and nineteenth-century interest in the young.

Campus novel ↔ A novel which takes place within a university or college, or which involves CHARACTERS drawn from such an academic milieu.

Character ↔ An actor in a literary NARRATIVE. If this seems like stating the obvious, it should be pointed out that genres such as science fiction provide borderline cases of entities which from a narrative point of view function as characters (they initiate actions, engage in communication or even speech and form relationships), but are non-human in other ways.

E.M. Forster's *Aspects of the Novel* provides the now-familiar distinction between the round and the flat character; the former having depth, complexity and unpredictability, and the latter being reduced almost to a single quality. Flat characters are often compared to *types*. See the extended discussion on p. 130.

A *chorus character* is a character used by a writer to comment authoritatively on EVENTS; for *cancelled* or *erased character* see p. 131. For *synonymous character* see p. 134. For *projection character* see p. 135. For *character narrator* see p. 112.

Character zone ↔ A term coined by Mikhail Bakhtin to describe the way in which a fictional CHARACTER is surrounded by various verbal and stylistic elements which create a 'zone' that is 'the range of action of the character's voice, intermingling in one way or another with the author's voice' (quoted in Todorov, 1984, 73).

Chronotope ↔ Coined by Mikhail Bakhtin to designate 'the distinctive features of time and space within each literary genre' (Todorov, 1984, 83).

Closure ↔ That sense of satisfying or reassuring finality that accompanies the end of a traditional REALIST novel, when no problems remain to be solved. It is typical of MODERNIST and POSTMODERNIST novels that they postpone or frustrate closure by giving their works *open endings*.

Colouring ↔ The modification of the language of (say) a NARRATOR by the linguistic characteristics of (say) a CHARACTER. Also referred to as the 'Uncle

Charles Principle', after a sentence in James Joyce's *A Portrait of the Artist as a Young Man*: 'Uncle Charles repaired to the outhouse', in which the word 'repaired', which is typical of Uncle Charles's usage, 'colours' the narrator's description. See also the discussion on p. 129.

Conte ↔ The *conte* was originally distinguished from the novel by its (often quirky) wit and its more fantastic, less REALISTIC nature, and by a strongly didactic element normally focussed in a moral point or use of allegory. Typical examples are two works both first published in 1759: Samuel Johnson's *Rasselas* (first published as *The Prince of Abissinia. A Tale*) and Voltaire's *Candide*. For the past century or so, however, the term in English has become roughly synonymous with 'short story', although Frank O'Connor (whose views on the short story I discuss in Chapter 3) categorizes Robert Browning's poem 'My Last Duchess' (1842) and Ernest Hemingway's 'Hills Like White Elephants' (1927) as *contes* (O'Connor, 1963, 26).

Covert plot ↔ See SUBPLOT.

Cyberpunk/cyberfiction In both terms the 'cyber' is taken from the word 'cybernetics', itself a coinage by Norbert Wiener, whose book *Cybernetics: Or Control and Communication in the Animal and the Machine* was first published in 1949. 'Cyber' comes from the Greek word for 'steersman', and Wiener's book was particularly concerned with what are known as feedback systems. The yoking together of animals and machines in Wiener's title may be one reason why 'cyber' has been hooked on to 'punk' and 'fiction' to refer to recent developments of SCIENCE FICTION that involve various graftings of the inorganic on to the human or organic. According to Austin Booth and Mary Flanagan, cyberfiction is 'writing that explores the relationship between people and virtual technologies' (Booth and Flanagan 2002, 1), but some works defined as cyberfiction, especially earlier ones, are concerned with technology rather than virtual technology.

So far as cyberpunk is concerned, the second part of the term focuses attention on to the 'young male outlaws who hack and crack computer networks to steal, manipulate, or erase the information they find' (Booth and Flanagan 2002, 7). Such works are generally set in the desolate urban spaces of technologically advanced but culturally and morally decayed societies of the future, and they implicitly draw critical attention to what are seen as negative trends in today's world, in which large impersonal corporations control more and more of human life. The American Marxist critic Fredric Jameson has suggested that cyberpunk 'is fully as much an expression of transnational corporate realities as it is of global paranoia' (Jameson, 1991, 38).

The term 'cyberpunk' seems first to have been used by the writer Bruce Bethke, who published a story of this name in the magazine *Amazing* in 1983 (Butler, 2000, 9). The most influential early cyberpunk author, however, is generally agreed to be William Gibson. Cyberpunk has moved from being the preserve of a small band of enthusiasts to a generic term more widely known as a result of the very successful filming of certain key cyberpunk texts. Philip

K. Dick's 1968 novel *Do Androids Dream of Electric Sheep?* was made into the blockbuster film *Blade Runner* (1982, directed by Ridley Scott).

Apart from its debt to science fiction, the style and ambience of cyberpunk owe much to the so-called 'hard-boiled' detective fiction and its cinematic offshoot *film noir*. But going further back, the PICARESQUE NOVEL also shares common elements with cyberpunk: in particular, that of the central figure of a mobile, outcast, young male. There are also intriguing parallels to be argued concerning the way in which both of these sub-genres seem to have been inspired by rapid and disruptive social changes.

Cyberpunk has attracted the attention of women writers, who see in its concern with bodily modification and gender adaptation possibilities for feminist development. Again in the words of Booth and Flanagan, '[w]omen writers are appropriating the cyberpunk aesthetic – metaphors of jacking in, figures of outlaws and outsiders, and film noir rhetoric – for their own ends' (2002, 2). The work of writer Donna Haraway is often seen as forging a bridge between cyberfiction ('cyberfeminism') and postmodernism. Haraway has fixed on the concept of the cyborg – part-human, part-machine – as a figure that uses technology to break down divisive binaries, especially those connected with gender. It is interesting to note that the work that can claim to have had a founding function so far as the concept of the cyborg is concerned – Mary Shelley's *Frankenstein* (1818) – was written by a woman.

Haraway's optimism has not been shared by all: others have suggested that bodily modification is today more testimony to the control of women's bodies by patriarchal forces than evidence of a potential liberation.

Death of the author ↦ A term taken from an essay by Roland Barthes, 'The Death of the Author' (1977, in French 1968). One commentator (Carlier, 2000) has suggested that Barthes's essay had a satirical intention, but it continues to be taken as a serious argument advocating that the author be relieved of any authority over his or her work once it has been published, and that it is language, rather than the author, that speaks in a work. Barthes's arguments are often associated with those of his fellow countryman Michel Foucault, whose essay 'What is an Author?' was also published in English in 1977.

Defamiliarization ↦ From the Russian meaning 'to make strange', the term originates with the Russian Formalists and, in particular, the theories of Viktor Shklovsky. In his essay 'Art as Technique', Shklovsky argues that perception becomes automatic once it has become habitual, and that the function of art is to challenge automization and habitualization, and return a direct grasp on things to the individual perception. Of interest to students of the novel is that the Russian Formalists exemplified defamiliarization by reference to the work of novelists such as Tolstoy, and Boris Tomashevsky, one of Shklovsky's fellow Russian Formalists, refers to Swift's defamiliarizing techniques in *Gulliver's Travels* in his essay 'Thematics' (the scene in which the Lilliputians discover Gulliver's watch and describe it without understanding what it is – thus encouraging the reader to see something familiar as if it were strange).

Deixis ↔ Those features of language which fasten utterances temporally or spatially: 'here' and 'now', for example. Deictics, or deictic elements (deictic can perform as either noun or adjective) play an important role in NARRATIVE; they constitute an important token of Free Indirect Discourse, for example.

Delayed decoding ↔ A term coined by Ian Watt in his *Conrad in the Nineteenth Century* (1980) to describe a particular impressionist technique used by Joseph Conrad by means of which the experiences of a CHARACTER who understands what is happening to him or her only while these experiences are taking place (or afterwards) are recreated in the reader. Thus in Conrad's *Heart of Darkness* we share Marlow's belief that lots of little sticks are dropping on the ship, up to the point when Marlow realizes that the 'sticks' are in fact arrows, and that the ship is being attacked.

Dialogue ↔ The standard meaning of this term with regard to prose fiction concerns the representation of the speech of CHARACTERS, either interactively between two or more characters, or monologically addressed by one character to him- or herself. See the extended discussion on p. 154, and compare also INTERNAL/INTERIOR DIALOGUE.

The writings of Mikhail Bakhtin have helped to make the term fashionable by suggesting that language itself is naturally dialogic, and that all use of language involves interaction with those others who have left traces on the words and phrases they have used.

Diegesis and mimesis ↔ These are terms that present a number of problems of usage, as the meanings attached to them have changed since their appearance in the third book of Plato's Republic, in which Socrates uses them to distinguish between two ways of presenting speech. For Socrates, diegesis stands for those cases where the poet himself is the speaker and does not wish to suggest otherwise, and mimesis stands for those cases in which the poet attempts to create the illusion that it is not he who is speaking. Recent usage among critics and theorists of prose fiction is rather different: diegesis is commonly used to denote 'the world of the story'. Thus in *Wuthering Heights* we can describe Lockwood and Nelly Dean as intradiegetic NARRATORS, because they are also CHARACTERS occupying the same reality as Heathcliff and Cathy. The narrator of Fielding's *Tom Jones*, in contrast, clearly belongs to a reality that represents the STORY he tells as fictional, and thus he is described as an extradiegetic narrator.

In like manner, mimesis has come to be used to describe the more general capacity of literature to imitate reality, and has on occasions accumulated a somewhat polemical edge as a result of its use by those wishing to establish imitation as central or essential to art – by Marxist critics intent on stressing that literature and art 'reflect' extra-literary reality, for example.

For a range of compound terms that use 'diegesis' as their root, such as *extradiegetic*, *autodiegetic* and *homodiegetic*, see p. 111.

Distance ↔ A term used in a number of different ways to suggest varying levels of involvement (emotional, intellectual, ideological) with what goes on in a STORY on the part *either* of a NARRATOR *or* a reader. See also p. 122.

Duration ↔ In NARRATIVE theory, the relation between the time covered by the STORY or part of it (such as an EVENT), and the 'time' allotted to it by the text (story-time and text-time). Thus three years of story-time may be covered by three pages of text, while further on in the same text one hour of story-time may occupy fifty pages. Unfortunately 'pages' do not give a particularly reliable measure: some readers read more quickly than others and the same reader will read more or less quickly depending upon textual complexity, reader involvement and tension, and so on. As a result many writers on narrative find *speed* or *tempo* more fruitful concepts.

See also p. 141, and compare ISOCHRONY.

Ecocriticism ↔ See p. 216.

Ellipsis ↔ A gap in the information provided for the reader, which may be permanent (we never learn what Heathcliff did after he left Wuthering Heights and before he returned) or temporary (as with most detective stories, when the missing details about the crime are provided in the book's concluding pages). Ellipses can be marked or unmarked – that is to say the reader may or may not be made aware of the gap. See also p. 140.

Epic ↔ Traditionally a long NARRATIVE poem presenting a heroic subject in an elevated style. Among the earliest epics are the *Odyssey* and the *Iliad*, although earlier examples exist. Some commentators distinguish between primary and secondary epics, where secondary epics have a single author rather than a collective origin, and are written within a literate culture rather than sung or recited in an oral culture. The novel has been approached as a modern epic, and some authors have attempted to give their works something of an epic status, although Mikhail Bakhtin (see p. 5) has argued for a sharp dividing line between epic and novel.

Epitext ↔ See Chapter 4, p. 78.

Epistolary novel ↔ An epistolary novel is told through letters ('epistles') exchanged between different CHARACTERS. The form flourished in the English novel in the eighteenth century. Samuel Richardson's *Pamela* (1740) and *Clarissa* (1747–8), Tobias Smollett's *Humphry Clinker* (1771) and Frances Burney's *Evelina* (1778) are classic epistolary novels. Writers in subsequent periods have made sporadic attempts to adapt the technique to their own needs, and one of the most successful examples of a recent epistolary novel is Alice Walker's *The Color Purple* (1982).

Given how important letters were in English society in the eighteenth century, it is not surprising that the novel should have been heavily influenced by this form of communication in its early development. In his novel *Clarissa* Samuel Richardson gives a comment to his character Mr Belford, writing to Lovelace about Clarissa, which helps to explain why Richardson (and his readers) favoured the technique:

> Such a sweetness of temper, so much patience and resignation, as she seems to be mistress of; yet writing of and in the midst of *present* distresses! How *much more* lively and affecting, for that reason, must her style be, her mind tortured by the pangs of uncertainty (the events then hidden in the womb of fate), *than* the dry narrative, unanimated style of a person relating difficulties and dangers surmounted; the relater perfectly at ease; and if himself unmoved by his own story, not likely greatly to affect the reader. [Italics in original]

Clearly the personal insight, self-display and dramatic effectiveness of the epistolary technique are what appeal to Richardson. On the negative side, a novel told exclusively through letters (Richardson allows himself the occasional authorial footnote and square-bracketed interpolation) can be unwieldy and inflexible. The characters have to be kept apart (otherwise they have no reason to write to one another), and sometimes this involves artificiality: Richardson's heroines are banished to locked rooms with disturbing regularity. When they actually meet their loved ones Richardson has somehow to arrange for someone else to write a letter about the encounter. Moreover, whatever else the characters do they must always have access to pen and paper. As Clarissa on one occasion writes to Miss Howe: 'And indeed, my dear, I know not how to *forbear* writing. I have now no other employment or diversion. And I must write on, although I were not to send it to anybody.' It was this element in Richardson's *Pamela* that was so cruelly but effectively satirized by Henry Fielding in his parody *An Apology for the Life of Miss Shamela Andrews* (1741), in which the heroine continues to write a letter while the man who is assaulting her virtue climbs into bed with her.

If the 'pure' epistolary novel is rare after the eighteenth century, the technique taught novelists how very useful letters could be as an element within the NARRATIVE variety of a novel. Two good examples are Isabella's letter about her marriage to Heathcliff in Emily Brontë's *Wuthering Heights*, and Decoud's letter to his sister in Joseph Conrad's *Nostromo*.

Event and existent ↦ The two are distinguished by NARRATOLOGISTS. 'Events' are those things that are 'done' or that 'occur' in a narrative, while 'existents' are those things in a narrative that 'are'.

Fabliau ↦ A short medieval tale in verse, usually humorous and satirical and often bawdy. Geoffrey Chaucer's 'The Miller's Tale' from the late fourteenth century is frequently cited as a typical example of the form.

Fabula **and** *sjužet* ↦ See STORY AND PLOT.

Fabulation and surfiction ↦ These two terms are used relatively interchangeably. Both imply an aggressive and playful luxuriation in the non-representational, in which the writer takes delight in the artifice of writing rather than attempting to describe or make contact with a perceived extra-fictional reality. Both terms are normally used in connection with relatively recent fiction.

Faction ↔ The term comes from the American author Truman Capote and is a portmanteau word (= fact + fiction) which describes novels such as his own *In Cold Blood* (1966). In this work primarily novelistic techniques are used to bring actual historical EVENTS to life for the reader. The term has thus come to denote a work that is on the borderline between fact and fiction, concerned primarily with a real event or persons, but using imagined detail to increase readability and verisimilitude.

Fantastic ↔ Characteristic of the fantastic is that it *hints* at a supernatural explanation without actually confirming that the supernatural has been involved in the EVENTS and experiences described. It thus constitutes one of the more recent movements away from a view associating the novel with classic realism. According to some theorists – especially those influenced by Tzvetan Todorov – to be classified as a genuine example of the fantastic, a novel or short story must retain a sense of ambiguity to the end, never allowing the reader finally to establish that the depicted events can only be accounted for by natural or, alternatively, by supernatural explanations. From this perspective there are few pure examples of the fantastic; according to some (but not all) accounts one would be Henry James's *The Turn of the Screw*. Recent interest in the fantastic has been encouraged by feminist writers and critics interested in exploring alternative 'realities' in which the gender conventions of past and existing societies are challenged or held up to scrutiny. I discuss the ways in which the new electronic media have developed more traditional forms of the fantastic in Chapter 5. See also MARVELLOUS.

Ficelle ↔ From the French meaning 'string', the term is used by Henry James to denote a minor CHARACTER in a novel whose FUNCTION is that of helping the reader with information, as an anchor point, and so on.

Fiction ↔ See Chapter 1.

Flat character ↔ See CHARACTER.

Focalization ↔ A term used by structuralist NARRATOLOGISTS to specify what used to be known as 'point of view'. See PERSPECTIVE AND VOICE.

Frame ↔ Used within NARRATIVE theory to describe the way in which certain works present the reader with 'narratives within narratives', or *framed* or *nested* narratives. Thus Marlow's telling in Conrad's *Heart of Darkness* is framed by introductory, interjected and concluding comments from an unnamed 'frame NARRATOR'.

Free Indirect Discourse ↔ The term denotes a NARRATIVE technique for providing the reader with a CHARACTER's speech, thoughts or even unconsidered attitudes without the use of direct attribution by tag-phrase ('she thought', 'he said') or even quotation marks. Discussed in more detail on p. 126. Often abbreviated to FID.

Frequency ↔ The numerical relationship between 'EVENTS in a PLOT' and 'events in a STORY'. See p. 141.

Function ↔ According to Vladimir Propp, 'an act of a character, defined from the point of view of its significance for the course of the action'. See p. 134.

Gothic novel ↔ See *ROMAN NOIR*.

Historical novel ↔ As its name suggests, the historical novel sets its EVENTS and CHARACTERS in a well-defined historical context, and it may include both fictional and real characters. It is often distinguished (in its more respectable forms) by convincing detailed description of the manners, buildings, institutions and scenery of its chosen SETTING, and generally attempts to convey a sense of historical verisimilitude. Its most respected practitioner in Britain has been Sir Walter Scott.

In its more recent popular, 'pulp' and electronic forms it tends to abandon verisimilitude for fantasy, and in some ways can be seen as the present-day version of the romance.

Image and imagery ↔ Terms with a range of meanings in literary critical discussion, but generally implying the use of language to evoke sensuous (often visual) experiences in the reader. More loosely, any examples of figurative language, especially those with a repetitive or cumulative effect in a work. See the discussion on p. 153.

Implied author/reader ↔ These terms were coined by the American critic Wayne C. Booth. The term 'implied author' is used to refer to that picture of the creating author behind a literary work that a reader builds up solely on the basis of a reading of that work. The term 'implied reader' is used to refer to that sense of the reader that the author (or the work) appears to want or require – again based solely on 'internal information', that is on the reader who seems to be implied by a sympathetic reading of a work.

In medias res ↔ From the Latin meaning 'in the middle of things', the term is generally applied to beginnings (or works, chapters, or sections) that plunge the reader into a scene without any explanatory or introductory material.

Instalment, ↔ Publication by: see PERIODICAL PUBLICATION.

Internal/interior dialogue ↔ Generally used to refer to a DIALOGUE between two well-defined voices within the single consciousness of a literary CHARACTER (or, in a wider usage, of a real human being), and the NARRATIVE representation of this process. Interior dialogue involves more than the representation of a character's verbalized thought processes in which questions are asked and answered. To count as genuine interior dialogue the questions and answers must stem from two voices which represent different and as it were *personified* attitudes, beliefs or characteristics. A good example occurs towards the beginning of the tenth chapter of Charlotte Brontë's *Jane Eyre*, in which we have represented a long dialogue between different and personified aspects of Jane Eyre's personality or identity.

Internal/interior monologue ↔ A NARRATIVE technique for representing the unexpressed thoughts of a CHARACTER. Strictly speaking interior monologue, unlike the broader term STREAM OF CONSCIOUSNESS, applies when the words used to express the thoughts are those that the character is assumed to be using for thinking. The term is often used more loosely, however, as a synonym for stream of consciousness. See also p. 124.

Intertextuality ↔ A relation between two or more texts which has an effect upon the way in which the *intertext* (that is, the text within which other texts reside or echo their presence) is read. In some usages the term *transtextuality* is reserved for more overt relations between specific texts, or between two particular texts, while intertextuality is reserved to indicate a more diffuse penetration of the individual text by memories, echoes, transformations, of other texts. Gérard Genette uses his coinages *hypertext* and *hypotext* such that the relationship between James Joyce's *Ulysses* and Homer's *Odyssey* is that of hypertext to hypotext.

Intrusive narrator ↔ Used to refer to a NARRATOR who is generally situated outside the world of the action, and who intrudes his or her own thoughts, opinions, comments about a CHARACTER or a situation. Thus Lockwood, in *Wuthering Heights*, is not generally thought of as an intrusive narrator in spite of his frequent sententious comments, because he is an intradiegetic (see DIEGESIS AND MIMESIS) narrator, and not situated outside the world of the action. Compare METALEPSIS.

Isochrony ↔ Borrowed by recent NARRATIVE theorists from a term used to describe poetic rhythm, isochrony denotes an *unvarying* or an *equal* relationship between narrating-time and STORY-time. The two are not the same: if a story covers three hours and each hour is narrated by means of five thousand words, then the relationship between narrating-time and story-time is unvarying. If a story covers three hours and each hour of the story takes approximately an hour to read, then the relationship between narrating-time and story-time can be said to be equal. The opposite of isochrony is *anisochrony*: either a varying or an unequal relationship between narrating-time and story-time – normally the former. Compare DURATION.

Iterative ↔ See FREQUENCY.

Künstlerroman ↔ From the German meaning 'a novel about an artist'. A *BILDUNGSROMAN* which has an artist as its hero or heroine, and which often contains a concealed or partly concealed autobiographical element, can be described as a *Künstlerroman*. A good modern example of the *Künstlerroman* would be Philip Roth's *The Ghost Writer* (1979).

Local colour ↔ Realistic detail, often concerned with such matters as dress, scenery, customs, which has no THEMATIC significance but which is there to give the reader a greater sense of verisimilitude.

Magic realism ↔ A blending of the FANTASTIC or fantasy with realism, which today is particularly associated with certain Central and South American novelists such as Gabriel García Márquez and Isabel Allende but which has also been applied to some of the later work of the Kenyan novelist Ngũgĩ Wa Thiong'o and to various European novelists including the German Günther Grass and the British Angela Carter – and even retrospectively to a novel such as Virginia Woolf's *Orlando* (1928) and to the female GOTHIC NOVEL. In Europe the term is particularly associated with certain recent female and feminist novelists. 'Blending' is perhaps misleading; magic realism seems typically to involve the sudden incursion of fantastic elements into an otherwise realistic PLOT and SETTING.

Marvellous ↔ A MODE in which the non-realistic and other-worldly is presented in such a way as to exclude any possible realistic or rational explanation. See also FANTASTIC.

Metafiction ↔ Literally, fiction about fiction – normally denoting the sort of novel or short story which deliberately breaks fictive illusions and comments directly upon its own fictive nature or process of composition. The English father figure of metafiction is Laurence Sterne, in whose *Tristram Shandy* (1759–67) the NARRATOR jokes with and teases the reader in various ways – advising him or her to turn back several pages to read a passage afresh, for example (see p. 94). Metafictional techniques are common to much MODERN-IST and, especially, POSTMODERNIST writing.

Metalepsis ↔ According to Gérard Genette, any transgressing of NARRATIVE levels, such as when Laurence Sterne (or his NARRATOR) implores the reader of *Tristram Shandy* to help the CHARACTER Mr Shandy get back to his bed. Compare INTRUSIVE NARRATOR.

Mode ↔ A term that is used in a confusing variety of ways. It is commonly used in a loose sense to denote a manner of writing characterized by a particular tone or attitude, as in 'the ironic mode'. It can also refer to a specific type of 'fictional world', such as the ROMANCE or the FANTASTIC. Structuralist narratologists, however, use it as a rough way of categorizing different sorts of DISTANCE, and Gerald Prince names TELLING AND SHOWING as two different modes (1988, 54). See also p. 201.

Modernism ↔ See Chapter 4, p. 69.

Mood ↔ Apart from being used as a rough synonym for 'atmosphere', mood is a term adapted by STRUCTURALIST NARRATOLOGISTS from its grammatical sense, which distinguishes between grammatical moods such as the subjective or the indicative. In NARRATIVE theory, mood is roughly equivalent to the old-fashioned 'point of view' (see PERSPECTIVE AND VOICE).

Motif ↔ In discussion of prose fiction 'motif' is often used as a synonym for the German *leitmotif*, to refer to recurrent elements that are not quite SYMBOLS or THEMES, but that have a cumulative effect on the reader. Thus in the Penguin edition of Joseph Conrad's *Lord Jim*, Cedric Watts provides the reader with a useful list of *leitmotifs*: 'butterflies and beetles'; 'dream, dreams'; 'glimpse (of Jim's character) through mist or fog'; 'in the ranks'; 'jump, leap'; 'nothing can touch me'; 'one of us'; 'romance, romantic'; 'under a cloud'; 'veiled opportunity'.

Narratee ↔ The 'target' at whom a NARRATIVE is directed. A narratee is not just the actual individual by whom a narrative is received; there has to be some textual evidence that the narrative is actually intended for a particular person or target for this to count as the (or a) narratee.

Narrative ↔ See Chapter 1, p. 6.

Narrative situation ↔ Defined according to the NARRATOR's relationship to the narrative and the STORY. Is the narrator diegetic or extradiegetic (see DIEGESIS AND MIMESIS)? Is the NARRATIVE ostensibly spoken or written?

Narratology ↔ Used to refer (i) to the structuralist inspired theory (or theories) of NARRATIVEs that have flourished in the past three decades, and (ii) to the rhetorical narratology that is a more recent development. The term is also used more loosely to describe any body of theory concerned with the analysis of narratives, literary or other. See the extended discussions in Chapter 6, pp. 108–113, and Chapter 9, p. 198.

Narrator ↔ The person, voice or language source that tells the STORY. This awkward formulation stems from the fact that some novels and short stories have no clearly personified or human teller, but it is still conventional to refer to their having a narrator. Some recent theorists have, however, argued that the term should be reserved for human or personified tellers. See also INTRUSIVE NARRATOR. See p. 109.

Naturalism ↔ Naturalism is a variety of realism, and the term is used in much the same way but with a narrower focus. Strictly speaking, naturalism should be restricted to a description of those literary works which were written according to a method founded upon the belief that there is a natural (rather than supernatural or spiritual) explanation for everything that exists or occurs. Naturalist novelists include the Goncourt brothers, Émile Zola, George Moore, the German Gerhard Hauptmann, and Americans such as Theodore Dreiser and Stephen Crane.

Nouveau roman ↔ (French for 'new novel') In the *nouveau roman* the accepted conventions of fictional composition are deliberately distorted or flouted in order to disorient the reader and to foreground certain processes of artistic illusion or NARRATIVE convention. As such it can be seen as a post-Second World War development of MODERNISM. It is associated particularly with France.

The best-known exponents of the *nouveau roman* are Alain Robbe-Grillet (whose book *Pour un Nouveau Roman* [1963] originated the term), Michel Butor and Nathalie Sarraute. Compare ANTI-NOVEL.

Nouvelle ↔ A *nouvelle* is characterized by a concern with a single episode or state of affairs, although its treatment of this (which conventionally moves to a surprise ending of one sort or another) may cover many pages. The genre is generally agreed to achieve a recognized form in the middle of the sixteenth century, with the publication of *Nouvelles Récréations et Joyeux Devis*, a collection ascribed to Des Périers. The term can be a little treacherous as in some usages it has come to be seen as synonymous with CONTE, while in others it is used interchangeably with NOVELLA. See Dieter Meindl's comments on this term on p. 47.

Novel, novella, short story ↔ The problems involved in defining these three terms are discussed at length in Chapters 1, 2 and 3. Apart from the characteristics of prose, and fictionality, all three forms are generally restricted to works with CHARACTERS, action and a PLOT. The terms are conventionally distinguished by reference to their length, and in Chapter 3 I quote Mary Doyle Springer's proposal that a work of fiction of between 15,000 and 50,000 words be categorized as a novella. More than 50,000 words and we have a novel; fewer than 15,000 and we have a short story. Remember, however, that these are arbitrary and by no means universally accepted distinctions.

Novella ↔ See NOVEL, NOVELLA, SHORT STORY.

Obstination ↔ The reader's tendency to continue to FRAME a passage of NARRATIVE in a consistent manner (e.g. as Free Indirect Discourse) unless prompted by textual or contextual features to shift to a new FRAME.

Omniscience ↔ All-embracing, godlike knowledge. Often applied to the NARRATORS of classical realist novels for whom there are no secrets within the created world of the novel. Dorrit Cohn has, however, cited Gérard Genette's objection to the term, which is that it is absurd because the author has nothing to know because he or she 'invents' everything (Cohn, 1999, 175).

Parable ↔ A short NARRATIVE intended to convey a moral or other lesson. Best known from Christ's Biblical parables, but more widespread than is often appreciated. Many modern novelists and (especially) short-story writers have written parable-like works.

Paralepsis ↔ Presenting more information in a NARRATIVE than is strictly or logically speaking justified by the ostensible NARRATOR and his or her situation. Thus in Joseph Conrad's novel *Under Western Eyes* the narrator (the 'Teacher of Languages') claims to base his account on the written report of the CHARACTER, Razumov. Yet after Razumov has finished this report and has wrapped it up, the Teacher of Languages continues to describe Razumov's actions and experiences.

Paralipsis ↔ The omission of certain information that the NARRATOR should in 'real world' terms be aware of.

Paratext ↔ and PERITEXT See Chapter 4, p. 78.

Patronage ↔ The specific meaning of this term within the study of literature involves a particular method of financing authorship. Rather than relying upon royalties, or payments from a publisher, an author is supported in advance of publication by a patron, who is rewarded by having his or her name in the eventual book, and perhaps by having his or her person or politics supported within the book. It is generally accepted that an important element in 'the rise of the novel' was the freedom from patronage that the market (i.e. publishers' fees or royalties) gave writers.

Periodical publication ↔ Normally initial publication of a longer work in instalments in a periodical or magazine. An important source of finance for writers in the nineteenth century (periodicals paid well), the constraints of periodical publication (censorship, division into sections, writing against the clock) did have some negative effects on works and writers.

It is useful to be able to read Henry James's *The Turn of the Screw* (1898) in an edition that marks the division between the instalments of its first published version, as we can then note that James attempts to end each separate instalment at a point of increased tension or dramatic surprise (much like the old film serials for children, each episode of which typically ended with a 'cliff-hanging' finale).

Perspective and voice ↔ Gérard Genette has drawn attention to the importance of a long-neglected distinction between *who sees?* and *who speaks?* I exemplify this distinction by reference to Katherine Mansfield's 'The Voyage' on p. 122.

In Genette's terminology the distinction between *who sees?* and *who speaks?* is expressed in terms of the opposition between MOOD and VOICE (1980, 30). According to him, *mood* operates at the level of connections between STORY and narrative, while *voice* designates connections both between narrating and narrative, and narrating and story (1980, 32). Others following Genette have preferred to replace *mood* by *perspective*, as the pair 'perspective and voice' matches up more neatly with 'who sees/who speaks'. If 'who sees' = perspective and 'who speaks' = voice, then a single narrative passage may combine the voice of one character or position and the perspective of another character or position.

The matched terms perspective and voice thus provide a more fine-tuned way of investigating what was known as 'point of view' in the days prior to the emergence of modern NARRATOLOGY.

Picaresque novel ↔ A 'picaro' in Spanish is a rogue, and the picaresque novel is built on the tradition of the sixteenth-century Spanish picaresque NARRATIVE, which typically portrayed a sharp-witted rogue living off his wits while travelling through a variety of usually low-life SETTINGS. The picaro typically lives by begging or by minor theft, he is cynical in his attitude to the softer emotions, especially love, and through witty and satirical comments questions established beliefs and customs. Critics frequently relate the emergence of the picaro to the break-up of the feudal world, and his open-minded, self-interested, geographical and intellectual wandering and questing are seen by many to merge into the spirit of possessive individualism that is ushered in with the growth of capitalist social relations.

The picaresque novel is typically *episodic*, lacking a sophisticated PLOT, and psychologically complex – or developing – CHARACTERS.

Daniel Defoe's novel *Moll Flanders* is by no means a pure picaresque novel; quite apart from anything else the fact that its main character is a woman represents a significant divergence from previous picaresque novels. It is nonetheless possessed of many typical characteristics of the picaresque novel. It is constructed around a sequence of short 'episodes' none of which is longer than two or three pages, and it has little real development of character.

Part of the appeal of the picaresque lies in its concern with the ordinary and the trivial, a concern which sets the picaresque apart from the ROMANCE, and which explains the historical importance accorded the picaresque in the history of the novel's emergence and development.

See the discussion of CYBERPUNK/CYBERFICTION above for comment on picaresque elements in a recent sub-genre.

Plot ↦ See STORY AND PLOT.

Point of view ↦ See PERSPECTIVE AND VOICE.

Postmodernist novel ↦ During the last two or three decades it has become clear that 'postmodernism' has emerged as the umbrella term which is most frequently used to describe a range of formal and technical experiments that are linked to theories about reality in general and the modern world in particular. In his *Postmodernist Fiction*, Brian McHale distinguishes postmodernism from MODERNISM by differentiating between a poetics (or systematized theory of literature) dominated by ontological issues (meaning a concern with the nature of reality in general), and a poetics dominated by epistemological issues (meaning how and if we know the world or 'the real') (1987, xii). Postmodernism is seen by many to involve (among other things) the taking of certain modernist techniques to an extreme, and the more extended consideration of modernism and postmodernism in Chapter 4 (pp. 69–73) should be consulted for a fuller discussion of the term.

Post-structuralism ↦ See the discussion in Chapter 9, p. 207.

Prolepsis ↦ See ANALEPSIS AND PROLEPSIS.

Queer Theory ↦ See the discussion in Chapter 9, p. 216.

Realism ↦ See Chapter 4, p. 64.

Regional novel ↦ The regional novel involves a focus on the life of a particular, well-defined geographical region. Traditionally the region in question will be rural rather than urban (thus it would be distinctly odd to refer to Charles Dickens as a regional novelist, in spite of the fact that so many of his novels explore London life in such intimate detail). Very often a 'regional novelist' will write a number of books all involving the same territory or place – as with Thomas Hardy's 'Wessex' and William Faulkner's 'Yoknapatawpha County'. Both of these 'regions' are closely modelled on particular areas of England and the United States, in spite of their fictitious names (and, ironically, the popularity of Hardy's novels has led to the term 'Wessex' being used to denote that part of England upon which it is based).

RHETORICAL NARRATOLOGY ↔ See p. 201.

Roman à clef ↔ (French: 'novel with a key') The *roman à clef* is the sort of novel that can be 'unlocked' given the right 'key' – in other words one which refers to real people, places or EVENTS in disguised form so that once one realizes what the work is about the hidden references all become apparent. Thomas Love Peacock wrote several humorous novels in the early nineteenth century in which thinly disguised portrayals of contemporary individuals such as Shelley and Coleridge appeared.

Roman à thèse/Tendenzroman ↔ The *roman à thèse* has, as the term suggests, a particular thesis or argument underlying it. It is typically a novel concerned to encourage social reform, or the correction of a particular abuse or wrong. Central to the definition is the idea of a *dominant* and usually a simple and uncomplicated thesis. (See p. 149 for the distinction between 'thesis' and 'theme'.) Harriet Beecher Stowe's *Uncle Tom's Cabin* (1852), which is structured around an attack upon the institution of slavery in the United States, is a classic *roman à thèse*. A novel like Thomas Hardy's *Jude The Obscure* (1896) in contrast, although it undeniably involves an attack upon certain social conventions which are seen as repressive and although in a sense it clearly advocates a change in society so that women and working people have greater opportunities for self-development and for education, is too complex and involved a novel to be termed a *roman à thèse*.

Romance ↔ The medieval romance is discussed at length in Chapter 2. The modern use of the term denotes a type of formulaic prose fiction aimed at women readers and focussed on courtship and marriage seen from a woman's point of view. Although very different in many ways, there are arguably lines of continuity linking the medieval romance with its modern namesake.

Roman feuilleton ↔ This is a novel that is published in instalments in unabridged form by a daily newspaper. The method of publication is unusual today for a novel, although it is becoming more and more fashionable for certain sorts of non-fictional work to be published in abridged form in newspaper instalments. This form of publication flourished in the nineteenth century.

Roman-fleuve ↔ This term denotes a series of sequence of novels which can be read and appreciated individually but which deal with recurring characters and/or common events and which form a sequence or which complement one another. Perhaps the best-known example is Balzac's *La Comedie Humaine*, but Anthony Powell's *A Dance to the Music of Time* (1951–75) is a more recent example. The *roman-fleuve* is closely related to what is called the *saga novel* – a series of novels about a large family each of which concentrates upon different branches of the family or different events in which it is implicated. Thomas Mann's tetralogy *Joseph and his Brothers* (1933–43) is one twentieth-century example; John Galsworthy's *Forsyte Saga* (1906–35) is another.

Roman noir/gothic novel ↔ The more usual term in English is 'gothic novel'. The term denotes a type of fiction that was ushered in by Horace Walpole's *The Castle of Otranto* (1764). Walpole was much influenced by the revival of interest in the gothic that occurred in the later eighteenth century, a revival that can be seen as a precursor of aspects of Romanticism in its predilection for the wild, the uncanny and the horrific – all of which were associated by the pre-Romantics with the medieval period. The gothic novel introduced stock CHARACTERS, situations and SETTINGS that still survive in the modern horror film: gloomy medieval settings, ancient castles with secret rooms and passages ruled over by a sinister nobleman tortured by a guilty secret, and strong hints of the supernatural. The gothic novel proper flourished for a limited period, and was more or less a thing of the past by the early nineteenth century, but gothic elements can be found in a wide range of fiction during the nineteenth and even twentieth centuries. Jane Austen parodies aspects of the gothic novel in *Northanger Abbey* (begun in 1798 and published in 1816). The term 'gothic' has been applied to the works of Mervyn Peake much more recently, and present-day 'Goths' can trace aspects of their fashion and lifestyle preferences back to this sub-genre.

The work of certain recent women writers such as Angela Carter and Sylvia Plath has been claimed to contain gothic elements, and a revival of interest in the gothic has been encouraged by a feminist interest in the way in which gothic formulae can be seen both to encapsulate certain stereotypical masculine fears about women and to allow women the space to explore hidden aspects of gender formation.

Round character ↔ See CHARACTER.

Saga novel ↔ See *ROMAN–FLEUVE*.

Satirical novel ↔ Satire does not have to be either in prose or in fictional, although there is a sense in which the exaggeration upon which it typically depends necessarily involves a certain amount of fictive imagining. There is a tradition of satire which is independent of the novel and which stretches back to antiquity, and aspects of this tradition have been important influences upon the novel. Satire attacks alleged vices and stupidities – either of individuals or of whole communities or groups – and its tools are those of ridicule, exaggeration and contempt.

Jonathan Swift's satirical writings – and especially his *Gulliver's Travels* (1726) – are extremely important staging posts for the novel, although most commentators have been unwilling to allow that they themselves merit the title 'novel'. If we think of Mark Twain's *The Adventures of Huckleberry Finn* (1884) we can see how the mature novel of the nineteenth century was able to incorporate important satirical techniques from earlier writers within a much more realistic framework than Swift, for example, provides. The use of a naïve NARRATOR travelling among people whose strange ways he describes innocently while at the same time conveying his creator's biting satire of what they stand for is one element which unites Swift's and Twain's best-known works.

The satirist is by definition more concerned to draw our attention to what he or she is attacking than to create characters, situations and EVENTs that are believable in and for themselves. A novelist may, however, include satirical elements in works that do not, overall, merit the term 'satirical novel' (and indeed most novelists do). Thus E.M. Forster's *Howards End* is not usually categorized as a satirical novel, but it does include a distinctively satirical vein in its treatment of various characters. Take the following passage from the end of the first paragraph of Chapter Three. Mrs Munt is considering her responsibilities towards the two Schlegel sisters, Helen and Margaret:

> Sooner or later the girls would enter on the process known as throwing themselves away, and if they had delayed hitherto it was only that they might throw themselves more vehemently in the future. They saw too many people at Wickham Place – unshaven musicians, an actress even, German cousins (one knows what foreigners are), acquaintances picked up at continental hotels (one knows what they are too). It was interesting, and down at Swanage no one appreciated culture more than Mrs Munt; but it was dangerous, and disaster was bound to come.

The passage is clearly satirical: it attempts to diminish a set of beliefs by making it appear ridiculous. Although the passage is ostensibly related to us from the viewpoint of Forster's narrator it mimics Mrs Munt and makes her views seem absurd by pretending to adopt them (Forster makes delicate use of Free Indirect Discourse here – see p. 126).

If we compare *Howards End* with Joseph Heller's *Catch-22* (1961) we will appreciate that the latter can more properly be termed a satirical novel than the former. Heller's dominating concern is clearly to diminish war and the military in our eyes by making them appear ridiculous and vain; his major aim in the novel is, in other words, satirical.

Science fiction ↔ Some definitions link science fiction with *fantastic* literature, and the two are clearly closely related. The fantastic normally invokes the strong possibility (but not certainty) of supernatural agencies, however, while science fiction does not generally do this. Science fiction is rather character-ized by SETTINGs involving interplanetary travel and advanced technology, and is typically set in the future. In contrast to fantasy literature its settings and EVENTs are often conceivable but not actual.

Jules Verne and H.G. Wells are often granted the joint title of the father of science fiction (its most celebrated authors tend to be male), and its best-known practitioners today are Ray Bradbury, Arthur C. Clarke and Isaac Asimov.

It is possible to relate science fiction to a work such as Swift's *Gulliver's Travels*, and clearly science fiction can have a 'pastoral' element: commenting upon one society or community under the pretext of describing another, imagined one. Often abbreviated to SF, the tradition is an important source of CYBERPUNK and of various forms of electronic fiction (see Chapter 5).

Setting ↝ See p. 147.

Short story ↝ See NOVEL, NOVELLA, SHORT STORY.

Silver fork novel ↝ A now archaic term used to refer to a particular sub-genre of the novel, popular in the early years of the nineteenth century, that focussed on the lives and preoccupations of high society and that included much LOCAL COLOUR of the 'silver fork' variety. The novels of Benjamin Disraeli are sometimes so categorized. Compare the dismissive 'white telephone film.'

Skaz ↝ A MODE or technique of narration that mirrors oral NARRATIVE. The term comes from the Russian, as Russian Formalist theorists were the first to tackle the issues raised by *skaz*, but there are many non-Russian examples. For example, from a technical point of view much of Joseph Conrad's *Heart of Darkness* can be described as *skaz*, as much of what we read represents the CHARACTER Marlow's oral address to listeners. The technique allows for the depiction of such things as hesitation, tone of voice, slips of the tongue, self-correction and interaction with a depicted intradiegetic (see DIEGESIS AND MIMESIS) audience.

Story and plot ↝ A distinction comparable to that made by the Russian formalists between *fabula* (story) and *sjužet* (plot). 'Story' is used to refer to the events of a NARRATIVE in the order in which they happened (or in an order determined by cause and effect), while 'plot' is used to refer to the events of a narrative as they are ordered and presented artistically, in the work. See Chapter 6, p. 140.

Stream of consciousness ↝ The representation in words of a succession of thoughts in a CHARACTER's mind, typically when the character is alone and is allowing thought to succeed thought without external prompting. Strictly speaking stream of consciousness is the umbrella term within which INTERNAL MONOLOGUE (which requires that the words used be those that the character thinks by means of) is a subordinate category. The two terms are, however, often used as synonyms. See the discussion on p. 124.

Structuralism and STRUCTURALIST NARRATOLOGY ↝ See Chapter 9, p. 198.

Subplot ↝ The term is more commonly applied to classical drama, as in a Shakespearian tragedy for example, where it denotes a 'second and subordinate story' which accompanies or runs alongside the main STORY of the fall of a person of high estate. It is sometimes applied to fiction, although, because the novel often involves very many PLOT 'threads', it is less appropriate to this genre.

Cedric Watts has coined the term 'covert plot' to describe those subplots that are concealed and apparent only after being teased out during a second or subsequent reading.

Subscription ↝ A method of financing publication which requires prospective buyers of the work to purchase a subscription, which the writer redeems by providing subscribers with a copy of the work once it is published. Along with PATRONAGE, this is a method of financing authors which was largely replaced by publishers' fees and royalties ('the market') in the course of the eighteenth century. Like patronage, of which it can be seen to be a variant, subscription freed the author from the need to sell lots of copies of a work and it provided income while the work was being written (like an 'advance on royalties'), but it required the author to stay on good terms with the source of his or her income.

Syllepsis ↔ In traditional usage, another term for 'zeugma', or the use of a single word to modify two other words in very different ways in a single phrase, as in Pope's 'Or stain her honour, or her new brocade.' In NARRATOLOGY, a cluster or gathering (of EVENTS, circumstances, experiences and so on) ordered according to some principle other than temporal unity or sequence. Thus 'John told her all the things that had happened in his mother's house' is a syllepsis based on situational coherence.

Symbol ↔ A unit (linguistic or otherwise) which either conventionally or naturally represents something apart from itself. A white wedding dress conventionally symbolizes virginity; blood naturally symbolizes violence. See the extended discussion on p. 150.

Telling and showing ↔ A term used to distinguish two ways of providing the reader with relevant information. Telling is generally seen as the cruder technique, involving overt statement on the part of NARRATOR or CHARACTER. Showing is considered more subtle and indirect, presenting scenes of DIALOGUE, thought or action and allowing the reader to draw certain conclusions him- or herself. See also the entry for MODE above, and the discussion on p. 135.

Theme ↔ See the discussion on p. 149, and the entry for MOTIF.

Third person ↔ See FOCALIZATION.

Three-decker ↔ During the Victorian period, publication of a novel in book form (rather than in instalments in a periodical) commonly involved the production of a three-decker, that is to say a novel produced in three volumes. Such three-deckers were generally borrowed from one of the circulating libraries such as Mudie's. Publication aimed at personal sales usually followed three-decker publication, and was normally in the form of a single volume. Because circulating libraries exercised forms of censorship on authors, it is important to know if a novel was first published in this form.

Tone ↔ The sense of an author's or narrator's attitude to his or her character, situation or subject, as conveyed by the words he or she chooses. Sometimes used in a wider sense to describe the mood engendered in a reader by a particular work. See the discussion on p. 129.

Uncle Charles Principle ↔ See COLOURING.

Voice ↔ See PERSPECTIVE AND VOICE, and the discussion in Chapter 6, p. 122.

Bibliography

This bibliography also contains recommendations for further reading.

Alexander, M. (1990), *Flights from Realism: Themes and Strategies in Postmodernist British and American Fiction*, London: Edward Arnold.
If you are curious about the form that postmodernism in fiction takes, and wish to read a sensible discussion of the work of such writers as Faulkner, Beckett, Pynchon and Vonnegut, then this is a good place to start.

Anand, M.R. (1946), *Indian Fairy Tales*, Bombay: Kotub Publishers.

Andermahr, S. (2009), *Jeanette Winterson*, Houndmills: Palgrave.

Andrew, D. (1992), 'Adaptation'. First published in D. Andrew (1984), *Concepts in Film Theory*, Oxford: Oxford University Press. Reprinted in G. Mast, M. Cohen and L. Braudy (eds), (1992), *Film Theory and Criticism*, New York and Oxford: Oxford University Press, pp. 420–8.

Armitt, L. (1996), *Theorising the Fantastic*. London: Arnold.
Both an investigation into and development of theories of the literary fantastic, and a collection of useful studies of individual texts. Includes discussion of (among others) Lewis Carroll's Alice *texts, Stevenson's* The Strange Case of Dr Jekyll and Mr Hyde, *Charlotte Perkins Gilman's* The Yellow Wallpaper *and Angela Carter's* The Passion of New Eve.

Armstrong, N. (1987), *Desire and Domestic Fiction: A Political History of the Novel*, New York and Oxford: Oxford University Press.
Armstrong associates the novel with 'the rise of the domestic woman', and uses the theories of Michel Foucault to chart the development of the novel in a different way, one which sees the novel as involved in social change in more complex ways

than are covered by patterns of simple cause and effect. Includes useful discussion of Richardson's Pamela, *Jane Austen's* Emma *and the Brontës.*

Atkins, B. (2003), *More than a Game: The Computer Game as Fictional Form*, Manchester and New York: Manchester University Press.

Atwood, M. (1991), 'Weight', in *Wilderness Tips*, London: Bloomsbury, pp. 177–93.

Azim, F. (1993), *The Colonial Rise of the Novel*, London: Routledge.

Bakhtin, M.M. (1981), *The Dialogic Imagination: Four Essays.* Translated by Caryl Emerson and Michael Holquist. Austin: University of Texas Press.

Bakhtin's work has been very influential in European and North American academic circles since it started to appear in translation. This volume makes available a key collection of essays: 'Epic and Novel', 'From the Prehistory of Novelistic Discourse', 'Forms of Time and Chronotope in the Novel' and 'Discourse in the Novel'.

Bal, M. (1985), *Narratology: Introduction to the Theory of Narrative.* Translated by Christine van Boheemen. Toronto and London: University of Toronto Press.

Now available in a revised, second edn (1997; paperback 1998). This and Shlomith Rimmon-Kenan's Narrative Fiction: Contemporary Poetics *(see below) are recommended as accessible but sophisticated introductions to narrative theory.*

Banfield, A. (1982), *Unspeakable Sentences: Narration and Representation in the Language of Fiction*, London: Routledge.

An advanced and often difficult book that has been very influential in the development of debate around the topic of Free Indirect Discourse. Banfield is concerned with FID as a technique that can be used to present information that is, paradoxically, 'unspeakable'. See my comments on p. 116.

Barnes, J. (1985), *Flaubert's Parrot*, Picador edn. First published, 1984. London: Pan Books.

Beale, A. (ed.) (1961), *Selected Literary Criticism: D.H. Lawrence*, London: Mercury Books.

Beckett, S. (1957), *Murphy.* First published, 1938. New York: Grove Press.

Blewett, David (ed.) (2000), *Reconsidering the Rise of the Novel*, Special issue of *Eighteenth-century Fiction*, 12(2–3).

A collection of essays all of which attempt to engage with, respond to or counter the arguments in Ian Watt's influential The Rise of the Novel. *An essential collection for those interested in the debates around the emergence of the modern English novel.*

Booth, W.C. (1961), *The Rhetoric of Fiction*, Chicago: University of Chicago Press.

A study that really initiated the new wave of interest in narrative technique in the English-speaking world. Booth is a stimulating and accessible critic, and his book has been enormously influential. The second edition contains a useful 'Afterword'.

Booth, A. and Flanagan, M. (eds) (2002), *Reload: Rethinking Women + Cyberculture.* With an Introduction by the editors. Cambridge, MA and London: MIT Press.

Borowski, T. (1976), *This Way for the Gas, Ladies and Gentlemen*. Selected and Translated by Barbara Vedder. London: Penguin.

Boumelha, P. (1988), 'Jane Eyre, Jamaica and the Gentleman's House', *Southern Review*, 21(2): 111–22.

Bowen, E. (1949), *Encounters*. First published, 1923. London: Sidgwick & Jackson.

Bowen, E. (1976), *Introduction to The Faber Book of Modern Short Stories*. First published, 1936. Reprinted in May 1976, pp. 152–8.

Bradbury, M. (ed.) (1990), *The Novel Today: Contemporary Writers on Modern Fiction*, revised edn, Glasgow: Fontana.

A very useful collection of essays by practising novelists writing about their own, and others', fiction. Essential for any student interested in modernism and post-modernism in the novel. The 1990 edition includes a new introduction, a new piece by Italo Calvino and an interview with Milan Kundera by Ian McEwan.

Bradbury, M. (2002), *The Modern British Novel 1878–2001*, Harmondsworth: Penguin.

Brecht, B. (1977), 'Against Georg Lukács'. This consists of four pieces written by Brecht in the late 1930s. Translated by Stuart Hood, in E. Bloch, G. Lukács, B. Brecht, W. Benjamin and T. Adorno (1977), *Aesthetics and Politics*, London: New Left Books, pp. 68–85.

Brooke-Rose, C. (1981), *A Rhetoric of the Unreal: Studies in Narrative and Structure, Especially of the Fantastic*, Cambridge: Cambridge University Press.

Burden, Robert (1991), *Heart of Darkness*, The Critics Debate. Houndmills: Macmillan.

Burke, P. (1997), 'Representations of the Self from Petrarch to Descartes', in R. Porter (ed.), *Rewriting the Self: Histories from the Renaissance to the Present*, London: Routledge.

Butler, A.M. (2000), *Cyberpunk*, Harpenden: Pocket Essentials.

Butte, G. (2004), *I Know That You Know I Know: Narrating Subjects from* Moll Flanders *to* Marnie, Columbus: Ohio State University Press.

Calisher, H. (1964), *Extreme Magic: A Novella and Other Stories*, Boston: Little, Brown.

Carey, C.S. (ed.) (1912), *Letters Written by Lord Chesterfield to his Son*, volume 1. London: Wm. Reeves.

Carlier, J.C. (2000), 'Roland Barthes's Resurrection of the Author and Redemption of Biography. Translated from the French by C.T. Watts. *The Cambridge Quarterly*, 29(4): 386–93.

Chatman, S. (1990), *Story and Discourse: Narrative Structure in Fiction and Film*, Ithaca and London: Cornell University Press.

Cohen, M. and Dever, C. (eds) (2002), *The Literary Channel: The Inter-National Invention of the Novel*, Princeton and Oxford: Princeton University Press.

Cohn, D. (1999), *The Distinction of Fiction*, Baltimore and London: Johns Hopkins University Press.

Cohn argues strongly for literary fiction as a distinct category, one that must be distinguished from narrative in general. The final chapter, 'Optics and Power in the Novel', takes up a determined opposition to recent attempts to see fictional narrators in terms of Michel Foucault's extension of Jeremy Bentham's idea of the 'Panopticon'.

Conrad, J. (1971), *Heart of Darkness*. second edn (Norton Critical edn). R. Kimbrough (ed.), New York and London: W.W. Norton. (The fourth edition of the Norton edition of this text, edited by P.B. Armstrong, was published in 2006.)

Cornwell, N. (1990), *The Literary Fantastic: From Gothic to Postmodernism*, Hemel Hempstead: Harvester Wheatsheaf.

Curle, R. (ed.) (1928), *Conrad to a Friend: 150 Selected Letters from Joseph Conrad to Richard Curle*, London: Sampson Low.

Currie, G. (1990), *The Nature of Fiction*, Cambridge: Cambridge University Press.

Day, G. (1987), *From Fiction to the Novel*, London: Routledge.

Doody, M.A. (1996), *The True Story of the Novel*, New Brunswick, NJ: Rutgers University Press.

Downie, J.A. (2000), 'Mary Davy's "Probable Feign'd Stories" and Critical Shibboleths about The Rise of the Novel', in *Reconsidering the Rise of the Novel*. Special issue of *Eighteenth-Century Fiction*, 12(2–3): 309–26.

Doyle, Sir A.C. (1974), *The Memoirs of Sherlock Holmes*. First published, 1893. London: John Murray and Jonathan Cape.

Edel, L. (ed.) (1964), *The Complete Tales of Henry James*, volume 11, 1900–1903, London: Rupert Hart-Davies.

Ferguson, S. (1989), 'The Rise of the Short Story in the Hierarchy of Genres', in Lohafer and Clarey (1989, 176–92).

Fludernik, M. (1993), *The Fictions of Language and the Languages of Fiction*, London: Routledge.

Along with Ann Banfield's Unspeakable Sentences *(see above and also p. 116), on which it builds but with which it takes issue on a number of points, probably the most exhaustive and demanding study of Free Indirect Discourse available. Not recommended as an introductory text, but very rewarding for the reader prepared to grapple with its difficulties.*

Forster, E.M. (1962), *Aspects of the Novel*. First published, 1927. Harmondsworth: Penguin.

In spite of its chatty tone and of the fact that criticism of the novel has refined and expanded its repertoire of terms and concepts since 1927, this is a study that is still worth reading. Full of shrewd insights and illuminating asides on particular novels.

Fox, R. (1979), *The Novel and the People*. First published, 1937. London: Lawrence & Wishart.

Friedman, N. (1976), 'What Makes a Short Story Short?'. First published, 1958. Reprinted in May 1976, pp. 131–46.

Friedman, N. (1989), 'Recent Short Story Theories: Problems in Definition', in Lohafer and Clarey (1989, 13–31).

Frow, John (1997). *Time and Commodity Culture: Essays in Cultural Theory and Postmodernity*. Oxford: Clarendon Press.

Genette, G. (1980), *Narrative Discourse: An Essay in Method*. Translated by Jane E. Lewin. First published in French, 1972. Ithaca, NY: Cornell University Press.

Perhaps the most influential of the first wave of structuralist studies of narrative. There are more accessible introductions, and sometimes Genette's use of the linguistic paradigm (or analogy) makes for difficulties of terminology and comprehension, but this is a book rich in local insights and conceptual innovations.

Genette, G. (1997), *Paratexts: Thresholds of Interpretation* (*Literature, Culture, Theory*, 20). First published in French, 1987. Translated by Jane E. Lewin. Cambridge: Cambridge University Press.

A fascinating account of such things as titles, prefaces, forewords and so on, and their effect upon the works they penetrate and surround.

Gilbert, S.M. and Gubar, S. (1979), *The Madwoman in the Attic: The Woman Writer and the Nineteenth-century Literary Imagination*, New Haven, CT: Yale University Press.

An extremely influential account of recurrent themes and stereotypes of women as represented in nineteenth-century literature. Gilbert and Gubar devote considerable attention to prose fiction.

Gilmour, R. (1986), *The Novel in the Victorian Age*, London: Edward Arnold.

This is one of the best introductions to the Victorian English novel, intelligently blending information about the age with detailed commentary on individual novelists and novels.

Gombrich, E. (1960), *Art and Illusion*, New York: Pantheon.

Good, G. (1994), 'Notes on the Novella'. First published, 1977. In May (1994), pp. 147–64.

Goring, P., Hawthorn, J. and Mitchell, D. (2001), *Studying Literature. The Essential Companion*, London: Arnold. Second edition published 2010.

Graves, R. (1967), *The Spiritual Quixote or The Summer's Ramble of Mr. Geoffry Wildgoose. A Comic Romance*. Clarence Tracy (ed.). First published, 1773. London: Oxford University Press.

Harvey, D. (1989), *The Condition of Postmodernity*, Oxford: Blackwell.

Perhaps the most accessible introduction to ideas about the postmodern.

Hassan, I. (1985), 'The Culture of Postmodernism', *Theory Culture and Society*, 2(3): 119–31.

Hawthorn, J. (1998), 'Repetitions and Revolutions: Conrad's Use of the Pseudo-iterative in *Nostromo*', in *Joseph Conrad 1*, special Conrad issue of *La revue des lettres modernes*, Paris: Editions Minard, pp. 125–49.

Hunter, J.P. (1990), *Before Novels: The Cultural Contexts of Eighteenth-century English Fiction*, New York: W.W. Norton.

I refer repeatedly to this book in Chapter 2. It contains a wealth of detailed information about social and literary contexts within which the modern novel emerged.

Huyssen, A. (1988), *After the Great Divide: Modernism, Mass Culture and Postmodernism*, London: Macmillan.

Jackson, T.E. (2009), *The Technology of the Novel: Writing and Narrative in British Fiction*, Baltimore: The Johns Hopkins University Press.

Jakobson, R. (1971), 'On Realism in Art'. Translated by Karol Magassy, in L. Matejka and K. Pomorska (eds), *Readings in Russian Poetics: Formalist and Structuralist Views*, Cambridge, MA: MIT Press, pp. 38–46.

James, H. (1984), *Literary Criticism: Essays on Literature; American Writers; English Writers*. Selected and with Notes by Leon Edel. New York: The Library of America.

Jameson, Fredric (1981), *Postmodernism, or, The Cultural Logic of Late Capitalism*, Durham, NC: Duke University Press.

Johnson, B.S. (1973), *Aren't You Rather Young to be Writing Your Memoirs?*, in M. Bradbury (ed.) (1990), pp. 151–68. First published, 1973.

Joyce, J. (2000), *Dubliners*. First published, 1914. With an Introduction and Notes by Terence Brown. London: Penguin.

Karl, F. and Davies, L. (eds) (1986), *The Collected Letters of Joseph Conrad*, volume 2, 1898–1902, Cambridge: Cambridge University Press.

Kermode, F. (2004), 'Retripotent' (review of J. Coe, *Like a Fiery Elephant: The Story of B.S. Johnson*, and of B.S. Johnson, *Trawl, Albert Angelo* and *House Mother Normal*), *London Review of Books*, 26(15): 11–13.

Kettle, A. (1967), *An Introduction to the English Novel*, second edn, volume 1, London: Hutchinson.

Kielar, W. (1982), *Anus Mundi: Five Years in Auschwitz*. First published in Polish, 1972. Translated from the German by Susanne Flatauer. Harmondsworth: Penguin.

Kogon, E. (2006), *The Theory and Practice of Hell: The German Concentration Camps and the System behind Them*, revised edn. First published in German, 1946. Translated by Heinz Norden. New York: Farrar, Straus and Giroux.

Kundera, M. (1988), *The Art of the Novel*. Translated by Linda Asher. First published in French, 1986. London and Boston: Faber.

Lamarque, P. (1996), *Fictional Points of View*, Ithaca: Cornell University Press.

Lamarque, P. and Olsen, S.H. (1994), *Truth, Fiction, and Literature: A Philosophical Perspective*, Oxford: Clarendon Press.

Lawrence, J.C. (1976), 'A Theory of the Short Story'. First published, 1917. In May 1976, pp. 60–71.

Leech, G.N. and Short, M.H. (1981), *Style in Fiction: A Linguistic Introduction to English Fictional Prose*, London: Longman.
Those who have tried to read accounts of prose fiction by linguisticians and who have determined not to try again should relent and read this book. The authors yield nothing to literary specialists in their sensitivity to fictional texts and passages, and are able to present a conception and analysis of style which any student of the novel will find invaluable. Well provided with sensible and well-illustrated examples.

Leitch, T.M. (1989), 'The Debunking Rhythm of the American Short Story', in Lohafer and Clarey (1989, 130–47).

Levenson, Michael (1991), *Modernism and the Fate of Individuality: Character and Novelistic Form from Conrad to Woolf.* Cambridge: Cambridge University Press.

Little, T.E. (1984), *The Fantasts*, Avebury: Amersham.

Lodge, D. (1992), *The Art of Fiction*, Harmondsworth: Penguin.
A collection of short articles originally published in The Independent on Sunday, *offering both accessible and authoritative accounts of fifty different terms and concepts ranging from 'Beginning' to 'Ending' and taking in others such as suspense, stream of consciousness, defamiliarization, repetition, showing and telling, symbolism, allegory, epiphany, metafiction, aporia and the Uncanny. All are illustrated with extracts from either classic or modern texts.*

Lohafer, S. and Clarey, J.E. (eds) (1989), *Short Story Theory at a Crossroads*, Baton Rouge and London: Louisiana State University Press.
A most useful collection of extracts and articles concerned to define and discuss the short story. Updates and extends May (1976) (see below).

Lothe, J. (1989), *Conrad's Narrative Method*, Oxford: Clarendon Press.

Lothe, J. (2000), *Narrative in Fiction and Film: An Introduction*, Oxford: Oxford University Press.
A very readable and stimulating introduction to the differences between narrative in prose fiction and in film. Detailed and rewarding discussion of theoretical issues and of film adaptations of Kafka's The Trial, *James Joyce's 'The Dead', Joseph Conrad's* Heart of Darkness *(Francis Ford Coppola's* Apocalypse Now*) and Virginia Woolf's* To the Lighthouse.

Lubbock, P. (1921), *The Craft of Fiction*, London: Jonathan Cape.

Lugowski, C. (1990), *Form, Individuality and the Novel*, revised edn. Translated by John Dixon. First published in German, 1932 (revised edn 1976). Cambridge: Polity Press.

Lukács, G. (1969), *The Historical Novel.* Translated by Stanley and Hannah Mitchell. First published in Russian, 1937, and in English, 1962. Harmondsworth: Penguin.
An important book on a somewhat unfashionable topic (the historical novel is looked down upon by some recent academics, and it has often had a higher reputation in Continental Europe than in Britain and Ireland).

Luria, A.R. (1976), *Cognitive Development*, Cambridge, MA: Harvard University Press.

Mansfield, K. (1945), *Collected Stories of Katherine Mansfield*, London: Constable.

Margolies, D. (1985), *Novel and Society in Elizabethan England*, Beckenham: Croom Helm.

Marías, J. (1997), *Tomorrow in the Battle Think on Me.* Translated from the Spanish by Margaret Jull Costa. First published in Spanish, 1994 and in English, 1996. New York: New Directions.

Martin, W., with Hinrichs, D. and Baker, S. (2006), *The Art of the Short Story*, Boston and New York: Houghton Mifflin.

de Maupassant, G. (1975), *Bel-Ami*. Translated by Douglas Parmée. Harmondsworth: Penguin.

May, C.E. (ed.) (1976), *Short Story Theories*, Athens: Ohio University Press.
Along with Lohafer and Clarey's collection (see above), this provides a most useful collection of extracts and articles concerned with theories of the short story.

May, C.E. (ed.) (1994), *The New Short Story Theories*, Athens: Ohio University Press.

McGann, J.J. (1991), *The Textual Condition*, Princeton: Princeton University Press.

McHale, B. (1978), 'Free Indirect Discourse: A Survey of Recent Accounts', *Poetics and Theory of Literature*, 3: 249–87.

McHale, B. (1987), *Postmodernist Fiction*, London: Methuen.
McHale's study is extremely wide-ranging, including authors and texts from several continents, and theoretically penetrating and insightful. The author is very well versed in modern narrative theory, but he brings other theoretical perspectives to bear on his analyses.

McKeon, M. (1987), *The Origins of the English Novel 1600–1740*, Baltimore: Johns Hopkins University Press.
In common with J. Paul Hunter's study (see above), this is an indispensable inquiry into the sources of the English novel. Contains many thought-provoking arguments about such things as the relationship between the novel's linear order and 'quasi-Calvinist' view of the linear life of the hard-working middle classes.

Meek, J. (2004), 'Get a Life', *Guardian*, 3. August. Accessed on http://www.guardian.co.uk/online/story/0,3605,1274808,00.html, 30 August 2004.

Meindl, D. (2008), 'Henry James's Turn-of-the-Century Nouvelles: Centers of Consciousness and Unlived Lives', in J. Lothe, H.H. Skei and P. Winther (eds), *Less is More: Short Fiction Theory and Analysis*, Oslo: Novus Press, pp. 30–44.

Michaels, A. (1998), *Fugitive Pieces*. First published, 1996. London: Bloomsbury.

Millett, K. (1971), *Sexual Politics*. First published, 1970. London: Sphere Books.

Montfort, N. (2003), *Twisty Little Passages: An Approach to Interactive Fiction*, Cambridge, MA and London: MIT Press.

Moretti, F. (1998), *Atlas of the European Novel 1800–1900*, London and New York: Verso.
This is a book that is full of useful information about a range of important issues. Which places and geographical areas are referred to by novelists, and do they change over time? Where are books published? Which books do people have in their homes? What percentage of library books are novels – and what did nineteenth-century librarians think of this?

Newman, J. (1995), *The Ballistic Bard: Postcolonial Fictions*, London: Arnold.

Ngugi, J. (1972), *Weep Not, Child*. First published, 1964. London: Heinemann Educational.

Ngũgĩ, W.T. (1987), *Devil on the Cross*. First published in Gĩkũyũ, 1980, and in the author's English translation, 1982. London: Heinemann Educational.

Nomberg-Przytyk, S. (1985), *Auschwitz: True Tales from a Grotesque Land*. Translated by Roslyn Hirsch. Edited by D. Pfefferkorn and D.H. Hirsch. Chapel Hill and London: University of North Carolina Press.

Novak, M.E. (1991), Review of J. Paul Hunter, *Before Novels: The Cultural Contexts of Eighteenth-century English Fiction*. *Times Literary Supplement*, no. 4582, January 25, 8.

O'Connor, F. (1963), *The Lonely Voice: A Study of the Short Story*, London: Macmillan.
A quirky but insightful account of the short story, written by one of its leading practitioners.

O'Faolain, S. (1972), *The Short Story*. First published, 1948. Cork: The Mercier Press.

O'Rourke, W. (1989), 'Morphological Metaphors for the Short Story: Matters of Production, Reproduction, and Consumption', in Lohafer and Clarey (1989, 193–205).

Page, N. (1988), *Speech in the English Novel*, second edn, London: Macmillan.
A very useful account that covers such issues as methods of speech presentation, dialect and idiolect. Also contains a number of case studies, and a concluding chapter on 'Dickens and speech'.

Pearce, L. (1994), *Reading Dialogics*, London: Arnold.
For those interested in a recent application of Mikhail Bakhtin's theories of dialogism to a range of texts, this book is recommended. Pearce includes both readings of individual works (including Wuthering Heights, The Waves, Sexing the Cherry *and* Beloved*) and an extended theoretical discussion of dialogue and the dialogic.*

Phelan, J. (1996), *Narrative as Rhetoric: Technique, Audiences, Ethics, Ideology*, Columbus: Ohio State University Press.
If you want to learn about rhetorical narratology, this is the place to start.

Phelan, J. (2005), *Living to Tell about It: A Rhetoric and Ethics of Character Narration*, Ithaca and London: Cornell University Press.
A development of Phelan's 'rhetorical narratological' approach to fiction, this time focussing on the 'character narrator'. Includes chapters on Kazuo Ishiguro's The Remains of the Day *and Vladimir Nabokov's* Lolita. *Phelan is very good at showing how the ethical questions such works raise for readers cannot be separated from their rhetorical techniques and performances.*

Phelan, J. (2007), *Experiencing Fiction: Judgments, Progressions, and the Rhetorical Theory of Narrative*, Columbus: Ohio State University Press.

Price, L. (2000), *The Anthology and the Rise of the Novel: From Richardson to George Eliot*, Cambridge: Cambridge University Press.

Prince, G. (1988), *A Dictionary of Narratology*. First published, 1987. Aldershot: Scolar Press.

Propp, V. (1968), *Morphology of the Folktale*, revised edn. Translated by Laurence Scott. Austin: University of Texas Press.

Raw, L. (2006), *Adapting Henry James to the Screen: Gender, Fiction, and Film*, Lanham, Maryland: Scarecrow Press.

Rhys, J. (1969), *Good Morning, Midnight*. First published, 1939. Harmondsworth: Penguin.

Rhys, J. (1971), *After Leaving Mr Mackenzie*. First published, 1930. Harmondsworth: Penguin.

Rimmon-Kenan, S. (1983), *Narrative Fiction: Contemporary Poetics*, London: Methuen.
Still probably the best place to start for those requiring an introduction to structuralist-influenced theories of narrative. Clearly and concisely written, and very fully illustrated with examples from a range of texts. Its only competitor as an introductory text is Mieke Bal's Narratology: Introduction to the Theory of Narrative *(see above).*

Rohrberger, M. (2004), 'Origins, Development, Substance, and Design of the Short Story. How I Got Hooked on the Short Story and Where It Led Me', in P. Winther, J. Lothe and H.H. Skei (eds), *The Art of Brevity: Excursions in Short Fiction Theory and Analysis*, Columbia, SC: University of South Carolina Press, pp. 1–13.

Ryan, M.-L. (2001), *Narrative as Virtual Reality: Immersion and Activity in Literature and Electronic Media*, Baltimore and London: Johns Hopkins University Press.

de Saussure, F. (1974), *Course in General Linguistics*. revised edn. Edited by C. Bally and A. Sechehaye. Translated by Wade Buskin. London: Peter Owen.

Sedgwick, E.K. (ed.) (1997), *Novel Gazing: Queer Readings in Fiction*, Durham, NC and London: Duke University Press.
A wide-ranging selection of essays demonstrating the sorts of reading that Queer Theory (see p. 216) can generate when applied to the novel.

Seidel, M. (2000), 'The Man Who Came to Dinner: Ian Watt and the Theory of Formal Realism', in *Reconsidering the Rise of the Novel*. Special issue of *Eighteenth-century Fiction*, 12(2–3): 193–212.

Sell, R. (1983), 'Projection Characters in *David Copperfield*', *Studia Neophilologica*, 55: 19–30.

Seymour-Smith, M. (1973), *Guide to Modern World Literature*, London: Wolfe Publishing.

Seymour-Smith, M. (1980), *Novels and Novelists: A Guide to the World of Fiction*, New York: St Martin's Press.

Shaw, V. (1983), *The Short Story: A Critical Introduction*, London and New York: Longman.
A study based upon an extremely wide-ranging knowledge of the short story; full of detailed references to key writers and texts.

Skinner, J. (2001), *An Introduction to Eighteenth-century Fiction: Raising the Novel*, Houndmills: Palgrave.

A very useful study that opens with a discussion of theoretical and critical issues, the formation of a canon, and the issue of gender, and then devotes chapters to the work of a range of canonical and less well-known novelists, ending with Jane Austen.

Skvorecky, J. (1985), *The Engineer of Human Souls*. Translated by Paul Wilson. First published, 1984. London: Chatto and Windus/The Hogarth Press.

Spender, D. (1986), *Mothers of the Novel: 100 Good Women Writers before Jane Austen*, London: Pandora Press.

The title is relatively self-explanatory: this is an attempt to reclaim the work of many 'forgotten' female contributors to the development of a genre which owes an enormous debt to the female sex.

Spilka, M. (ed.) (1977), *Towards a Poetics of Fiction*, Bloomington: Indiana University Press.

This book contains essays from the journal Novel *from the period 1967–76, and includes many fine theoretical and interpretative pieces by well-known writers. Wayne C. Booth and Ian Watt comment, respectively, on their influential books* The Rhetoric of Fiction *and* The Rise of the Novel. *There are also studies of the criticism of Georg Lukács, Wayne C. Booth and F.R. Leavis, and an essay on the contributions of formalism and structuralism to the theory of fiction.*

Spoto, D. (1983), *The Dark Side of Genius: The Life of Alfred Hitchcock*, Boston: Little, Brown and Company.

Springer, M.D. (1975), *Forms of the Modern Novella*, Chicago and London: University of Chicago Press.

Stam, R. (2005), *Literature and Film: A Guide to the Theory and Practice of Film Adaptation*, Oxford: Blackwell.

Thomas, B. (1991), *The New Historicism: And Other Old-fashioned Topics*, Princeton: Princeton University Press.

Todorov, T. (1984), *Mikhail Bakhtin: The Dialogical Principle*, Minneapolis: University of Minnesota Press.

An excellent introduction to the work and ideas of a writer who has had a profound influence on our ideas about the novel.

Toker, L. (1993), *Eloquent Reticence: Withholding Information in Fictional Narrative*, Lexington: University Press of Kentucky.

A must for anyone interested in how the creative powers of readers contribute to the experience of reading novels. Toker takes a number of examples in which the reader has to 'fill in' missing or delayed information. There are excellent chapters on The Sound and the Fury, Nostromo, Bleak House, Emma, Tom Jones, A Passage to India *and* Absalom, Absalom!

Tomkins, J.M.S. (1932), *The Popular Novel in England 1770–1800*, London: Constable.

A book that has dated very little, and essential reading for those interested either in the importance to the novel of women as writers and readers or in the whole complex issue of the novel and 'the popular'. Particularly interesting on such matters as the theme of incest in early modern novels and the symbolic importance of the brother–sister relationship to early women novelists.

Toolan, M.J. (1988), *Narrative: A Critical Linguistic Introduction*, London: Routledge.

An accessible introduction to narrative theory which includes a concern not just with literary narratives but also with oral narratives and narratives in newspapers, law courts and elsewhere. Although Toolan's emphasis is a linguistic one, he is good on the ideological and political ramifications of narrative choices.

Truffaut, F. (1986), with the collaboration of H.G. Scott, *Hitchcock*, revised edn. First published, 1968. London: Paladin.

Various authors (1956), *Did It Happen? Stories*, London: Oldbourne Press.

Walsh, R. (2007), *The Rhetoric of Fictionality. Narrative Theory and the Idea of Fiction*, Columbus: The Ohio State University Press.

A difficult but original and challenging book. Walsh writes from within the new perspective of rhetorical narratology, and argues that the distinctiveness of fiction 'consists in the recognizably distinct rhetorical set invoked' by a particular use of language. Contains a fresh and iconoclastic view of the concepts of fabula and sjužet (story and plot) in discussion of literary fiction.

Warner, W.B. (1998), *Licensing Entertainment: The Elevation of Novel Reading in Britain, 1694–1750*, Berkeley: University of California Press.

Watt, I. (1963), *The Rise of the Novel*. First published, 1957. Harmondsworth: Penguin.

In spite of repeated attempts to qualify, rebuff or supersede Watt's arguments (see for example Reconsidering the Rise of the Novel, *above) this is a book that continues to require and repay attention.*

Watt, I. (1980), *Conrad in the Nineteenth Century*, London: Chatto & Windus.

Watts, C. (1984), *The Deceptive Text: An Introduction to Covert Plots*, Brighton: Harvester.

Woolf, V. (1966a), *Collected Essays*, volume 1, London: Hogarth Press.

Woolf, V. (1966b), *Collected Essays*, volume 2, London: Hogarth Press.

Woolf, V. (1967), *A Room of One's Own*. First published, 1929. London: Hogarth Press.

Woolf, L. (ed.) (1972), *A Writer's Diary: Being Extracts from the Diary of Virginia Woolf*, London: Hogarth Press.

Wyndham, F. and Melly, D. (eds) (1984), *Jean Rhys: Letters 1931–1966*, London: André Deutsch.

Zunshine, L. (2006), *Why We Read Fiction: Theory of Mind and the Novel*, Columbus: Ohio State University Press.

Index